Sergyei Mikhailovich Kravchinsky, William Westall

Russia under the Tzars

Sergyei Mikhailovich Kravchinsky, William Westall

Russia under the Tzars

ISBN/EAN: 9783743333826

Manufactured in Europe, USA, Canada, Australia, Japa

Cover: Foto ©ninafisch / pixelio.de

Manufactured and distributed by brebook publishing software (www.brebook.com)

Sergyei Mikhailovich Kravchinsky, William Westall

Russia under the Tzars

RUSSIA UNDER THE TZARS

RUSSIA

UNDER THE TZARS

BY
STEPNIAK
AUTHOR OF "UNDERGROUND RUSSIA;" FORMERLY EDITOR OF
ZEMLIA I VOLIA

RENDERED INTO ENGLISH BY WILLIAM WESTALL

AUTHORIZED EDITION

NEW YORK
CHARLES SCRIBNER'S SONS
1885

CONTENTS.

PART I.
THE PAST.

CHAPTER I.
	PAGE
THE MIR	1

CHAPTER II.
THE VETCHE 8

CHAPTER III.
A RUSSIAN REPUBLIC 15

CHAPTER IV.
SURVIVAL OF SELF-GOVERNMENT 19

CHAPTER V.
THE MAKING OF THE DESPOTISM 24

CHAPTER VI.
THE POWER OF THE CHURCH 32

CHAPTER VII.
THE RUSSIAN THEOCRACY 38

CHAPTER VIII.
THE GREAT REFORMER 44

CHAPTER IX.
EMANCIPATION 52

PART II.

DARK PLACES.

	PAGE
CHAPTER X.	
A Nocturnal Search	58
CHAPTER XI.	
The Police	65
CHAPTER XII.	
The House of Preventative Detention	78
CHAPTER XIII.	
Poor Thirty-nine	86
CHAPTER XIV.	
The Tzar's Justice	94
CHAPTER XV.	
The Question	97
CHAPTER XVI.	
Political Trials	103
CHAPTER XVII.	
Military Tribunals	111
CHAPTER XVIII.	
After Judgment	122
CHAPTER XIX.	
The Troubetzkoi Ravelin	140
CHAPTER XX.	
Siberia	161
CHAPTER XXI.	
Mutual Responsibility	166

PART I.

THE PAST.

CHAPTER I.

THE MIR.

NATIONS, like men, are judged by their appearance. The despotism which rules the Russian people is naturally regarded as the outcome and expression of the national character. It is true that of late years Russia has produced both men and women who, in patriotic zeal and devotion to freedom, have never been outdone; yet, in the seeming futility of their efforts, the public opinion of Europe sees but an additional proof of the stubborn servility of the masses, equally unable to understand any liberal aspiration and unwilling to take part in any liberal movement.

The facts cannot be gainsaid. The tillers of the soil, who form the bulk of the Russian nation, still profess devotion to an ideal Tzar—the creature of their own imagination—believe that the day is at hand when he will drive all landowners out of the country, and bestow their possessions on his faithful peasants.

But if we go beyond mere externals, if we study more deeply, and observe more closely, the character and lives of our lower orders, we shall be struck by many peculiarities altogether at variance with the received ideas as to their servility and degradation.

In a country where everything depends on the will of an autocrat, it might be expected that there would be found inferior officers of government invested with plenary powers of action within the limited spheres of activity assigned to them. But in Russia it is not so. By a strange inconsistency the peasantry of that despotic country enjoy—save for some abuses—almost as great a measure of self-government as the rural communes of Switzerland and Norway. The village assembly, composed of all adult males free from paternal authority, decides without appeal every local question. Since the emancipation (1861) the State has made several changes in the methods of rural self-government. For instance, it created a special village court consisting of ten judges elected by the assembly, whereas, in former times, the *mir*, or popular assembly, was the sole legal tribunal. Next followed an attempt on the part of the State to lay hands on the assembly, and curtail its prerogatives by augmenting the power of the *starosta* (the village Mayor), recognizing as valid only such meetings as he might convene, and making his own election contingent on the approval of the so-called mediator, a high functionary appointed jointly by the Government and the local nobility. In the original state, however, that is to say, where the administration has not been strong enough to enforce the measures it proposed, the communal autonomy has suffered no restriction.

The *mir* of Central Russia—in Southern Russia the *gromada*—is the peasant's conception of supreme authority ; it safeguards the welfare of the entire community, and is entitled to the implicit obedience of every individual of whom it is composed. It may be convened by its humblest member at any time and at every place within the limits of the village. The communal authorities must respond respectfully to the summons, and, if they fail in their duty, the assembly may dismiss them from their offices without notice, or deprive them for an indefinite period of all their authority.

The meetings of a village commune, like those of the Landesgemeinde of the primitive Swiss cantons, are held under the vault of heaven, before the *starosta's* house, before a tavern, or at any other convenient place. The thing that strikes a person who is present for the first time at one of these meetings is the utter confusion which seems to characterize its proceedings. Chairman there is none; the debates are scenes of the wildest disorder. After the convener has explained his reasons for calling the meeting, everybody rushes in to express his opinion, and for a while the debate resembles a free fight of pugilists. The right of speaking belongs to him who can command attention. If an orator pleases his audience, interrupters are promptly silenced; but if he says nothing worth hearing, nobody heeds him, and he is "shut up" by the first opponent. When the question is somewhat of a burning one, and the meeting begins to grow warm, all speak at once, and none listen. On these occasions the assembly breaks up into groups, each of which discusses the subject on its own account. Everybody shouts his arguments at the top of his voice; shrieks and objurgations, words of contumely and derision are heard on every hand, and a wild uproar goes on, from which it does not seem possible that any good can result.

But this apparent confusion is of no moment. It is a necessary means to a certain end. In our village assemblies voting is unknown; controversies are never decided by a majority of voices. Every question must be settled unanimously. Hence the general debate as well as private discussions have to be continued until a proposal is brought forward which conciliates all interests and wins the suffrage of the entire *mir*. It is, moreover, evident that to reach this consummation the debates must be thorough and the subject well threshed out; and, in order to overcome isolated opposition, it is essential for the advocates of conflicting views to be brought face to face, and compelled to fight out their differences in single combat.

The method of adjustment I have described is eminently characteristic of the Russian *mir*. The assembly does not force on the minority resolutions with which the latter is unable to agree. Everybody must make concessions for the general good and the peace and welfare of the community. The majority are too generous to take advantage of their numerical strength. The *mir* is not a master, but a loving parent, equally compassionate to all its children. It is this quality of our village self-government that explains the high sense of humanity which forms so marked a feature of our rural customs—the mutual help in field labor, the aid given to the poor, the fatherless, and the afflicted—which have elicited the warm admiration of every observer of our village life. To the same cause must be ascribed the unswerving loyalty of Russian peasants to their *mir*. "Whatever the *mir* decides is ordained of God," says a popular proverb. There are many other sayings as, for instance: "Nobody but God dare judge the *mir*;" "Who is greater than the *mir*? who can dispute with it?" "The *mir* receives no bribes;" "Where the *mir's* hand is, there my head is;" "Although last in the *mir*, a man is always one of the flock; but once separated from the *mir*, he is but an orphan;" "Every member of the *mir* is as a member of the same family."

An indispensable corollary to the integrity of the mir, and, seeing how the country is ruled, one of its most surprising peculiarities, is the full liberty of speech and debate enjoyed by our rural assemblies. Indispensable, for how could business be done and justice enforced if, instead of speaking their minds freely, members of a commune were to fear giving offence to Peter or John, and resort to subterfuge and falsehood? Rough frankness of manner and unrestrained liberty of speech being adopted as a rule and sanctioned by tradition, they are not abandoned when by chance there comes under discussion some subject outside the modest sphere of peasant life. It is a fact admitted by all observers that, while in the cities words implying "disrespect of existing institutions" are uttered even in private with bated breath and heard with trembling, the peasants in their public meetings talk as they list, criticise the very institutions which others are permitted only to admire, censure with easy impartiality the most illustrious members of the administrative oligarchy, treat boldly the burning agrarian question, and often express opinions concerning the sacred imperial presence itself which would make the hair of a wellbred townsman stand on end.

It must not, however, be supposed that this license of language bespeaks an insubordinate temper or a rebellious spirit. It is nothing more than an inveterate habit begotten of long usage. The peasants have no idea that in speaking their minds they are breaking the law. They do not understand how speech, opinion—whatever the method of its expression—can be considered a crime. There are cases on record of a *starosta* receiving revolutionary proclamations by post and, in the innocence of his heart, reading them aloud before the village assembly as something curious and suggestive. If a revolutionary propagandist happens to enter a village he is invited to meet the assembly and read or tell whatever he may think likely to edify the community. What harm could arise from so natural a proceeding? And if the fact becomes known nothing can exceed the surprise of the peasants when told by the gendarmes that they have committed a heinous offence. So great is their ignorance that they believe liberty of speech to be a right inherent in every rational being!

Such are the main features of our village self-government. Nothing can well be more striking than the contrast between the institutions which prevail among the lower orders of Russia and the institutions which regulate the lives of its upper classes. The former are essentially republican and democratic; the latter are based on imperial despotism, and organized on the strictest principles of bureaucratic control.

This contrast, so palpable and portentous, having endured for centuries, has produced, as its inevitable consequence, a phenomenon of great importance — that strongly marked tendency of the Russian people to hold themselves aloof from the State, which is one of their most significant characteristics. On the one hand, the peasant saw before him his *mir*, the embodiment of justice and brotherly love; on the other, official Russia, represented by the *tchinovniks* of the Tzar, his magistrates, gendarmes, and administrators— through all the centuries of our history the embodiment of rapacity, venality, and violence. In these circumstances it was not difficult to make a choice. "It is better," says the peasant of to-day, "to stand guilty before the *mir* than innocent before the judge." And his forefathers said, "Live and enjoy yourselves, children, while Moscow takes no notice of you."

From the very dawn of our national history the Russian peasant has shunned intercourse with the Russia of the *tchinovniks*. The two have never mingled, a fact which explains why the political evolutions of ages have made so little impression on the habits of our toiling millions. It is no exaggeration to say that the lives of the bulk of the nation and of its upper classes have flowed in two contiguous yet separate and distinct streams. The common folks live in their liliputian republics like snails in their shells. To them official Russia—the world of *tchinovniks*, soldiers and policemen—is a horde of foreign conquerors, who from time to time send their agents into the country to demand the tribute of myone and the tribute of blood—taxes for the Tzar's treasury and soldiers for his army. Yet by a startling anomaly—one of those strange contrasts of which, as a celebrated geographer has said, Russia is full—these rudimentary republics, which enjoy so large a measure of social and personal freedom, are at once the surest foundations and the strongest bulwarks of despotic power.

By what vagary of fortune or caprice of history, it may be asked, has this crying anomaly arisen? How comes it that institutions in so flagrant contradiction with the whole of our political *régime* as these peasant parliaments should flourish under the ægis of an arbitrary monarch?

The anomaly is only in appearance; we have to deal neither with an historical riddle nor the fortuitous results of incidental combinations. I lay so much stress on our system of popular self-government because I am convinced that the form which it takes and ideas whereon it is based are more in conformity with the political aspirations of the Russian people than the autocratic and centralized form of the existing system. If there be aught anomalous in our polity, aught imposed on the nation by outward and accidental causes, it is the despotism itself.

CHAPTER II.

THE VETCHE.

At the beginning of authentic history the vast country now known as Russia was divided into a number of principalities, varying in extent, having each a capital and several more or less important towns and villages. The rulers, however, were not supreme; they reigned, but they did not govern, all legislative and executive power being vested in the popular assembly. This assembly was composed of free citizens without distinction of rank or fortune, the prince being no more than a public functionary, elected by the people and obedient to their will. By traditional custom the princes were chosen among the members of the same family from generation to generation, or, rather, from a race of warriors of royal blood, all of whom claimed descent from Rurik, the supposed founder of the Russian Empire. The principle of heredity was not, however, regarded as an immutable law; the *vetche* recognized no such right, and when a native prince was not to the taste of his people, they changed him for one more to their liking. The prince was subject, not superior to his people; the subjection of the people being an idea which did not come into vogue until several centuries later. The privilege was however seldom exercised. Russian history contains but few instances of the deposition of a native prince in favor of a foreign ruler; and once only, when the people of Galitia deemed a change expedient, was a simple boyard raised to princely rank. But the custom of choosing rulers from the same family was really no restriction on the liberty of election; for the royal stock so increased and multiplied, and established so many off-shoots in different parts of the country, that suitable candidates were always forthcoming.

Some historians of the so-called Muscovite school, out of pure love for monarchic principles, have pretended to discover the germ of this form of government in the supposed laws of succession and right of birth among the princes of ancient Russia. But the more thorough and impartial researches of the new school prove that no such laws existed, that no such rights were recognized—the relations between the reigning prince and the people being in every case regulated by the *vetche*. The nearest of kin to the ruler had naturally the best opportunities of making himself favorably known; and in ancient Russia, as among all patriarchal nations, age commanded popular respect. When a prince died or was banished, the ruler generally chosen to succeed him was his eldest brother, who was probably also the head of the family, or of that branch of it which the people delighted to honor. If, however, the brother were unpopular, he would be passed over, the choice in that event falling on the son of the late prince; or, again, if the people so willed it, the uncle and the nephew might both be superseded by a prince whose kinship to the royal line was attenuated almost past recognition; for mere genealogy counted for nothing in the matter, and early Russian history affords abundant evidence that the one immutable privilege which regulated the succession was the will of the *vetche*.

The call of a prince was, however, only the first step in his election. The next proceeding was the conclusion of a convention—the *riada*—between the new ruler and the city. Both parties swore faithfully to observe the contract, and without the *riada* no prince could consider his position safe. The *riada*, in fact, was the constitutional pact. It defined the mutual obligations of the contracting parties. The conditions of the compact were subject to modifications, not only in different principalities and from time to time, but as between one prince and another. The leading conditions of the pact were nevertheless almost always identical. The highest function of the prince was that of judge. In the smaller principalities he alone filled this office, and in many of the contracts it was specially stipulated that the prince should act in person, never by deputy, the people having more confidence in the impartiality and independence of their prince than in any of his men. At a later period, when princes, influenced by other ideas, began to trespass on the popular rights, it was specified in the constitutional pacts that the prince should only act as judge when assisted by a colleague appointed by the *vetche*.

A second duty of the prince, hardly less important than the first, was to defend the country from its enemies; but the right to declare war, or to dispose of the military forces, which were composed of all citizens able to bear arms, was vested in the *vetche*. The prince, generally a man trained to arms from his youth upwards, was appointed to the command of the army only after the declaration of war, and in the more important principalities he shared the responsibilities of command with a special officer elected by the *vetche*. The prince had always in his service a more or less numerous corps of volunteers—free fighters—half of them native, and half foreign, denominated *drugina*, or "friends of the prince." And so they were—literally his friends—meeting every day in the same hall, sitting at the same table, the companions of all his amusements, his advisers in every difficulty. They were, moreover, maintained entirely at his expense, either out of the revenues granted to him by the *vetche* or his own private resources. If he desired to make war, the *vetche* was at liberty to refuse him the co-operation of the militia. In this event, he could, however, undertake it at his own risk and peril, with the help of his *drugina*, a privilege of which the princes of that age often availed themselves to their great advantage. The *drugina*, being the prince's personal companions, followed him everywhere. If he left his principality to rule over a richer and larger community, they accompanied him and shared his good fortune. On the other hand, when the citizens dismissed an unpopular ruler, the *drugina* were expelled at the same time.

Changes like these were of frequent occurrence, and there were few princes who had not occupied in the course of their lives half-a-dozen thrones (or "dinner-tables," according to the suggestive phrase then in vogue). A change of rulers was easily effected. When a prince became unpopular, the *vetche* had simply to meet and pronounce the sacramental phrase "We salute thee, O Prince!" whereupon his Highness would retire, feeling no more ill-will for his former constituents than if he were a candidate for parliamentary honors beaten at an election. If his successor did not prove a success, and the *vetche* again changed their minds and recalled him, he would resume his former position with the greatest alacrity. It sometimes came to pass that a prince was elected, dismissed and re-elected three or four times in succession by the very same city.

Thus the principalities of mediæval Russia, notwithstanding the monarchical form of their government, were in reality so many republics, and republics they are called by the best of our modern historians, Mr. Kostomaroff, although with a delicate consideration for the susceptibilities of the censorship, he avoids the use of the Latin term, substituting for it the Slav equivalent *narodopravstvo*. The princes were practically soldiers of fortune, with a following of volunteers whom the republics took into their service. A state of things not very dissimilar prevailed in the small Italian republics of the Middle Ages, the sole difference being the Russian *condot-*

tieri formed a separate caste and were all descended from the same royal stock.

Yet this difference was far from being detrimental to the democratic institutions of the period, for the most striking fact in our early history is the entire absence of any tendencies toward tyranny. Rarely, indeed, do we find a prince opposing by force the popular will. There was too much to lose thereby and too little to gain. A people half nomad, living in a country so thinly inhabited that the land had no value, could have no strong local ties. Neither did the prince's love of country count for much. As nomadic as the people themselves, he and his *drugina* cared not whither they went nor where they settled. Every prince for himself, and the *drugina* for their master, were always on the lookout for promotion; that is to say, for a larger city and better pay. It was therefore against a prince's own interest to resist the will of the *vetche*, for such a stain on his reputation would greatly impair his chances of advancement. In default of anything better, moreover, he could always find some petty principality ready to receive him; for a town governed by a simple *posadnik* always added to its distinction and independence by exchanging his rule for that of a prince. In the mean time he might look forward with confidence to something better. Princes were so often dethroned and conflicts with the *vetche* were so common that a royal adventurer with a good character who kept his eyes open had little difficulty in obtaining the promotion to which he aspired. At the worst, it was always possible for a prince of enterprise to win honor and wealth by force of arms at the expense of his less warlike kinsmen. In these conquests there was nothing tyrannical or hostile to liberty. A popular prince ran little risk of attack; for would-be aggressors knew that they would have to deal not with the *drugina* alone, but the entire military force of the country. On the other hand, when the people had no particular love for their prince it was a matter of indifference to them whether he won or lost. In the latter event they were quite ready to accept as ruler the prince who had proved himself the better man. The *vetche* elected the victor, who immediately signed the *riada*, and, after taking the usual oath, entered on his functions precisely as if he had acquired his position in the ordinary way. If he in his turn made himself unpopular, there was a simple and infallible way of getting rid of him. The *vetche* had only to offer the throne on more than usually favorable terms to some prince of military capacity, whereupon the latter would appear on the scene with his *drugina*, and, aided by the citizens, depose his rival and reign in his stead.

It was thus to the rivalry among members of the princely caste that the ancient Russian republics chiefly owed the preservation of their liberty ; and the more important cities, which by their example naturally influenced the others, could always, by very reason of their extent, and the eagerness with which their suffrages were sought, turn this rivalry to the best account.

The relations that prevailed between the prince and the *vetche* explain how, in older Russia, freedom so complete and democratic was maintained without effort and without internal strife. All other republics, either of antiquity or of the Middle Ages, were, so to speak, limited republics or constitutional democracies, the will of the people being always more or less controlled by other social forces, while our early Russian republics were absolute and unlimited democracies. The people were supreme ; every citizen had an equal voice in the government of the country, and neither the ruling prince, nor any other public functionary, had a vested interest in his place. The *vetche* could annul all or any of his decrees. Though he appointed officers to assist him in the administration, the *vetche* controlled his choice and could dismiss his nominee. They were not protected by the prince, and the *vetche* no more hesitated to punish a prince's nominee than a functionary elected by themselves. Neither the prince nor any other servant of the State was appointed for a fixed term. All held their places at the pleasure of the people. The bishops alone were nominally elected for life, but even they were sometimes summarily dismissed by the *vetche*. Thus the *vetche* was the sovereign power which regulated all the affairs of the country. There was no divided authority; the *vetche* spoke the voice and expressed the will of the people. In a word, the republics of ancient Russia were primitive states, elementary in their institutions, and purely democratic in their government.

CHAPTER III.

A RUSSIAN REPUBLIC.

If from the fragmentary notices dispersed throughout our old chronicles we endeavor to draw a living picture of these same *vetches*, the primitive and simple character of our ancient republican *régime* will be rendered more visible and striking.

On the banks of the river Volchow, and not far from Lake Ilmen, lies the famous city of Novgorod—now only a small provincial "chief-town" with some 18,000 inhabitants, but centuries ago one of the greatest of European cities, worthy, by its power and riches, of being called the Northern Venice. In the fourteenth and fifteenth centuries Novgorod was the capital of a vast republic, which included the northern half of modern Russia, stretching as far as the Ural mountains, and containing large towns and important cities. Favored by its splendid position on the great highway which united Mediæval Europe with the Levant, Novgorod the Great waxed rich and powerful on the commerce and industry of her sons, and for centuries successfully defended her liberties against the ever-growing power of the Muscovite Tzars. It was not until the sixteenth century that the resistance of the heroic republic was finally overcome. None of our old republics ever attained to the same power and splendor as Novgorod the Great, and none has left us records so rich of a glorious past. In these priceless documents we find the best material for the study of our early institutions.

On one of the squares of the now depopulated city, the stranger is shown the place where, at the stroke of the great bell which was there suspended, the sovereign people were wont to meet. Its sacred rope was free to all, every citizen being competent to summon the *vetche* for deliberation on any subject affecting the welfare of individuals or the State. The people were masters, even, as we have seen, despots, sometimes violent and hasty, but always noble and generous, like legendary Oriental kings, fathers of their country, ever accessible to the humblest of their subjects, ever ready to redress their wrongs, and prompt to punish the trespasses of the great and powerful. If none dared disturb for trivial or inadequate cause the repose of the sleeping lion, none, on the other hand, could hinder the humblest burgher from convoking the people and making complaint of any injustice committed against him; and forcing the aggressor—whosoever he might be, whether *posadnik* (lord mayor) or prince—to appear and answer to the charge.

The rules touching the convocation of the *vetche* were few and simple, its meetings being marked by an almost entire absence of formality. Supreme power was vested in the entire body of the people, and wherever and whenever they met their will was law. There are instances on record of the militia of Novgorod while encamped in the face of the enemy constituting themselves into a *vetche*, and adopting resolutions which were held as binding as if they had been passed by the assembled citizens in the great square of the capital.

But that which differentiates our ancient *vetche*, as well as our *mirs*, from all similar assemblies, is the absence of any system of voting. In every other republic, however free or democratic it might be—at Sparta and Rome, as well as at Athens and Florence—voting in one shape or another existed, and the principle that the minority should conform to the rule of the majority was the basis of all their political procedure. In the Slav nature there seems something antagonistic to this principle. I say Slav, and not Russian, because among all the peoples of that race, possessed of genuinely free institutions, we invariably find that the principle of unanimous decision is the only principle which the popular conscience is able to accept. In Poland these principles were embodied in an unalterable law, than which nothing could be more fatal and absurd. In the national Polish diets, if one man—who might be bribed by a foreign enemy—shouted his *liberum veto*, it sufficed to annul the decision of the entire assembly. In the Ruthenian republics —those of the Ukranian Cossacks on either side of the Dnieper, and in warlike Zaporogia—the principle of unanimity equally prevailed, and the system of legislation by vote was never practised. There were, however, occasions in which the more numerous, or, at any rate, the stronger party found an effective way of overcoming opposition. When some burning question arose—for instance, the choice of a military chief or higher magistrate—and none of the disputants would yield, they generally came to blows, and so soon as the physically weaker party had been sufficiently belabored, they abandoned their opposition, the desired unanimity was attained, and the candidates were elected by acclamation. These disputes were sometimes settled in a manner still more summary—with knife instead of fist. The *vetche* of old Russia, especially those of Novgorod the Great, as to which we have more complete information than any other, seem to have been also at times very turbulent. The chroniclers tell of frequent disputes, some of which ended in sanguinary struggles and loss of life. But these cases were evidently exceptional. The republic could not have existed, much less prospered and grown in power, if civil war had been chronic in its capital. As a rule, moderate counsels prevailed, and differences were pacifically settled by persuasion and mutual concession. The mildness and docility of the Slav character rendered possible the application, on a large scale, of a principle based on an undeniably generous sentiment—respect for the rights of minorities, a sentiment declared by an eminent English political writer to be the foundation of true liberty.

CHAPTER IV.

SURVIVAL OF SELF-GOVERNMENT.

We find, then, in the governing bodies of our ancient states the same striking peculiarity which distinguishes the humble assemblies of our obscure villages—the legislation by unanimous decision.

Nor, as reference to our first chapter will show, is this the only feature common to the *vetche* and the *mir*. The resemblance extends to details; their identity is almost complete, a surprising and remarkable fact when it is considered how different are the circumstances of these two institutions, and by how long an interval of time they are separated—the one perished centuries ago, the other still survives. In its methods of procedure, as well as by the primitive variety of its functions and the disorderly character of its proceedings, the obsolete *vetche* is neither more nor less than the modern commune assembly, and, though on a much larger scale, without any essential difference in its organization. If there be any difference it is certainly less than that which exists between the domestic cat and the Bengal tiger, or between the timid lizard, which hides itself at the first alarm in the nearest hole, and the ferocious saurian which haunts the rivers of the Spanish Main—in spite of their seeming dissimilarity both members of the same family.

The existence of a close kinship between the *mir* and the *vetche* is beyond doubt, and it would not be difficult to trace the noble genealogy of the descendants of our ancient system of self-government. To meet, discuss, provide for their own wants, and manage their own business are the privileges of freemen, and the *vetche* was the sole form of government which it entered the mind of the mediæval Slav to conceive. Even our "skimmers of the sea," the valiant ushconiniki of Novgorod, half warriors, half shipmen, travelling in companies like mediæval masons or modern *artels* of workmen, carried to unknown lands, together with their wares, the *vetche* and all its peculiarities. Besides the great *vetche*, whose doings are recorded in our ancient chronicles, there were the smaller *vetche* of inferior towns, and the humble assembly of the innumerable villages that were scattered over the face of the land. All these *vetche*, though differing as to size, were similarly constituted.

But in the struggle for existence, a struggle no less real in the realm of politics than the world of zoology, the greater organisms—the *vetche* of the cities—perished, like those antediluvian monsters which, notwithstanding their size, were either unable to prevail against their enemies, or survive unfavorable climatic changes. The smaller *vetche* shared the fate of their progenitors, while the village *vetche*, rendered invulnerable by their very insignificance, still live and flourish. We have thus before us a curious, if not an unique, example of historic paleontology, the conversation for centuries of an ancient institution under a political *régime* essentially different and apparently hostile.

How, it may be asked, has this anomaly come to pass? Very simply; in the same way that small fish escape through the meshes of a large net. All government is based on the idea of taxation. The body politic—the State—can no more exist without money than the human body can exist without taking nourishment. But in a wild, uncultivated country of vast extent and destitute of roads, with a population always on the move, force fails, and, except in rare cases, individual members of the community can neither be coerced nor controlled. The State may pass laws and demand taxes, but it can neither, by ordinary means, enforce obedience to the one nor payment of the other. For these reasons Russian governments have been compelled to recognize the rural communes, to confirm their privileges, treat with them as independent corporations, and allow them to manage their own affairs. The land register was kept by the communes, and not by individual proprietors; the taxes were based on the register, and paid by the village in its corporate capacity. If a villager went away and ceased therefore to contribute his quota to the common fund, the Government made no difference, always exacting the same amount until a new register was prepared, which might not be for years.

Such is the fiscal system which has been followed by the successive rulers of Russia—princes, khans, tzars, and emperors. No other system was possible. Even serfage did not interfere with rural self-government, and the great seigneurs, who owned both the land and bodies of the tillers of the soil, never attempted to restrict the autonomy of the commune. None of the political troubles which have swept over the country have affected the *mir* any more than the fierce winds which sweep over the ocean disturb the eternal calm of its lowmost depths. The *mir* can be touched only by the new methods of the present economic *régime*, a subject on which I cannot dwell in the present work.

The survival of self-government among the lower orders is a highly significant fact, proving as it does the political as well as the economic vitality of our communes, and accounting for the re-appearance of our old republican institutions every time the Russian people are free to manage their own affairs. Of this there are many instances.

In the thirteenth and fourteenth centuries, the time of the Muscovite autocracy's greatest development, tens of thousands of outlaws, fleeing from unbearable oppression, found a refuge on the steppes of Yaik (now Oural), the Don and the Dnieper. These fugitives, who called themselves Cossacks, founded a number of little military republics, identical in almost every respect with the purely Russian republics of which Novgorod was the most illustrious example. The chief difference consisted in the fact that the Cossack communities, having no princely families to supply them with rulers, elected military chiefs, who, under the titles of *ataman, hetman, koshevoi*, performed functions similar to those performed by the Rurikovetchi princes of ancient Russia. Even in our own time, whenever, as occasionally happens (for instance in 1830 at Staraia Roussa and other districts, and in 1856 in the province of Orel), a rising is temporarily successful, the insurgents never place themselves under the authority of a chief, but set up immediately a republic, *sui generis*, and supreme power is vested in a popular assembly.

Returning to our first theme, and with all the facts before us, we may affirm with full confidence that those who, judging solely by appearances, say that the Russian people have an instinctive preference for despotic government, make a great mistake. On the contrary, all their habits and tendencies, as revealed in their history, show them to possess a decided bent for freedom and strong aptitudes for self-government, wherein the vast majority of the nation are trained from childhood, and which, whenever they have the opportunity, Russian people spontaneously practise.

But what is, then, their monarchism, their devotion to the Tzar of which so much is said? The monarchism of Russian peasants is a conception which has exclusive reference to the State in its entirety, the whole body politic. If the peasants were left to themselves and free to realize their strange ideals, they would tell the White Tzar to remain on the throne, but they would send to the right about, and probably massacre, every governor, policeman, and *tchinovnik* in the land, and set up a series of democratic republics. For the peasants in their ignorance do not understand how Russia at large can govern herself; they do not see that the bureaucracy which they hate and the Tzar whom they love are essential parts of the same system, and that to destroy the former and leave the latter would be like cutting off the hands and feet, and leaving the head and trunk. This is a misconception arising from simple ignorance, a misconception which, as instruction spreads among the people, will give place to truer ideas.

Yet it was not always so. A misconception can neither endure through five centuries nor be created by imagination. In the history and social conditions of the country must be sought the causes to which the autocracy owes its being, which maintain it, and form the historic justification of its existence; for there was a time when autocracy was the popular ideal and the centre of all the aspiration of the nation.

CHAPTER V.

THE MAKING OF THE DESPOTISM.

BY what process was the ultra-democratic *régime* that prevailed in Russia during the eleventh and twelfth centuries transmuted in the course of three or four hundred years into a despotism of which it may well be affirmed, without historic exaggeration, the world has never seen the like?

To answer this question in detail it would be necessary to give a complete history of the development of the Muscovite monarchy. But so great an undertaking is beyond the scope of my present work; I must content myself with such brief sketch as will suffice to show that this unfortunate result is no fortuitous or accidental event, and that my description of our ancient liberties is in no respect overdrawn.

The organization of the central power in the oldest and most developed of our states—Novgorod the Great—was, as we have seen, of an extreme primitiveness and simplicity. Not alone may the entire controlling authority—that is to say the *vetche*—but the entire state may be likened to one of those plants which, notwithstanding their size, are composed of a single cell. The dominions of the Novgorod greatly surpassed those of the Queen of the Adriatic. They were always growing by the accretion of colonies, either conquered by arms or acquired by treaty from the wild aboriginals. Some of these colonies, waxing in wealth and population, became in their turn powerful communities. Hence the establishment of a perfect understanding—*a modus vivendi*—between them and the mother city was one of the most pressing social needs of the time, and essential to the integrity of the State.

But what did ancient Russia to meet this necessity? Nothing at all. The colonies were regarded as integral parts of the metropolis, and the colonists were free to come to the capital whenever it pleased them and join in the deliberations of the *vetche*. When matters of importance were about to be discussed they were informed betimes and invited to attend. But if the colonists came not the Assembly decided all the same, giving no more heed to their special interests than to those of any other citizens who were hindered by unavoidable causes from being present. A colony, in fact, was looked upon as being in some sort a quarter of the city. It was even denominated *pregorod*, a word which, literally rendered, signifies a ward of the capital, albeit these curious wards might be distant therefrom a month's journey. True, each colony had a *vetche* of its own which regulated all local affairs; on the other hand, general legislation was the prerogative of the metropolitan Assembly, which, as the supreme authority, the colonists were compelled in the last resort to obey. The issues of peace or war were also in the hands of the greater *vetche*. "That which the elder ordered the younger had to do," says the old chronicler. So long as they were young and struggling the colonists submitted. But so soon as they felt themselves strong enough to walk alone they dismissed the governor appointed by the metropolitan *vetche*, chose in his stead a prince with a good *drugina*, and declared themselves independent. Sometimes the separation was effected peacefully. Generally, however, the old *vetche* and the new State came to blows, and if the rebellious colony succeeded in maintaining its pretensions by force of arms, its independence was definitively acknowledged. It rose at once from the position of a ward to that of a "younger brother," and the two communities entered into an alliance, and swore eternal friendship—proceedings which of course did not in the least hinder them from falling out on the first occasion. No lessons of wisdom were drawn from these frequent scissions, and when in course of time the severed colonies founded other colonies, the process of disintegration went on as before. Thus in older Russia the interior development of the country resulted, as by the operation of a natural law, in the creation of an ever growing number of small independent states, which though republics in fact were principalities in form. The multiplication of royal families also contributed in no small degree to this outcome; for ambitious young princes, eager for power and place, were always at hand ready to encourage separation and stir up revolt.

Something like this, although due to an altogether different cause, came to pass in some other countries. The issue, however, in both cases was the same—the creation of autocracy. Like the feudal barons, these independent princes warred incessantly among themselves. Sometimes they were helped by the citizens. But when the citizens were indifferent or hostile they trusted to their own *drugina* and contingents of mercenary nomads, whom they enlisted in their service. At last the country, devastated by these eternal feuds, demanded peace at any price. The simplest and easiest, and in existing circumstances the only way of reaching this end, was the substitution of a single prince for the multitude of princelings. For it is only by long training, intellectual growth, and material development that communities become habituated to the complex and costly mechanism of representative institutions, the only means hitherto discovered whereby union and independence can be reconciled with national security and personal freedom. Old Russia, which had not even learned the alphabet of this difficult lesson, was constrained like other peoples to undergo the hard apprenticeship of despotic government. The social and political condition of the country, moreover, rendered the establishment of autocratic rule both easier and more urgent than elsewhere—more urgent because the Russia of that day had not alone to contend with internal disorders, but to make head against incessant invasion. These invasions, dangerous and vexatious at the beginning of Russian history in the tenth and eleventh centuries, became in the twelfth century, when feeble nomads were succeeded by fierce Tartars, terrible and almost fatal; and only after a struggle of five hundred years was the country finally freed from their yoke and relieved from their aggressions.

On the other hand, the social condition of Russia offered fewer obstacles to union under a single sovereign than most other countries. The ordinary process of consolidation was through conquest and the gradual annexation of neighboring states, a process which, depending as it did on the uncertain fortunes of war, was necessarily slow and difficult. Small independent states generally defended themselves vigorously and long. The powerful local aristocracy, dreading to sink into the position of a provincial nobility, threw in their lot with the princes ;. and the people, oblivious to their own interests, often joined hands with the great against those who were wrongly stigmatized as foreign enemies. The segregation of their lives gave rise to petty local differences, which, together with the ignorance natural to the age, produced in turn a crop of hatred and jealousy. It was only with the help of the industrial classes that the monarchies of Central Europe were enabled to overcome these hostile influences and complete the process of unification by the consolidation of their kingdoms.

In Russia the process of unification took a different course. If there were no burghers—no trading classes—there were, on the other hand, fewer obstacles. The agricultural population was only in part sedentary. The quantity of unoccupied land was so vast, the art of husbandry so backward, that the people were half nomad. After burning the forests, they raised in the rudest fashion such crops as they needed. When the soil was exhausted, or they wanted a change, they moved elsewhere; and this process they were continually repeating. A peasant was always willing to exchange fields with a neighbor, or even migrate to another province. The agricultural classes roamed at will over the vast Russian plains in search of a more fruitful soil or less onerous conditions. Entire villages disappeared from one place to re-appear in another. The political condition of the time, as was natural, determined the general direction of this great human flood. After the irruption of the Tartars it flowed chiefly towards the north-west, where the principalities of Vladimir, Tver and Moscow had constituted themselves into a state, and formed a settled government. But in addition to the main stream there were always minor currents flowing between provinces of the same region. This coming and going, this ebb and flow of peoples, by welding the population into a homogeneous whole, greatly facilitated the unification of the country. The peasants of Tver, Kazan, and Viatka came in time to differ in nothing from the peasants of Nijni Novgorod. Such a country as this afforded little room for the development of those peculiar prejudices and strong local ties by which populations that remain long in the same place and become rooted in the soil are invariably characterized. As for the higher or warrior class, which was at once the head and nerve force of the country, they were even more vagabond and had fewer local ties than the peasants; for the ancient *drugina*, though they received grants of land "for food," were attached to the person of the prince, and not to the soil. Yet they were always volunteers, free fighters, who had the same right to change their prince as a workman to change his master; a right which they largely used, never scrupling to abandon a chief whose star had begun to wane for one whom fortune was beginning to favor. In these circumstances an annexation was generally little more than taking possession of a territory which, by reason of the defection of its military defenders, and the migration of great part of the population to the principality of a more powerful ruler, could offer no resistance to an invader. It often befell, moreover, that a prince whose independence was endangered would anticipate his fate, and avoid the consequences of defeat in the field by proceeding to Moscow, and voluntarily surrendering his dominions to his former rival, securing, as the reward of his homage and submission, riches, honor, and the title of boyar. At the court of Moscow the families of boyar princes, all descended from once independent sovereigns, may still be counted by the dozen.

Thus, as I have observed, the method by which unification was accomplished in Russia differed from that by which it was accomplished in most other countries. It may be considered as partaking in equal measure of the gathering of nomad tribes around the standard of a valiant and successful chieftain, and the process peculiar to countries whose populations are completely sedentary. This explains at once the extreme facility with which Muscovite unification was accomplished and the origin of the despotism that followed in its wake.

While the political condition of Russia and the exigencies of a life and death struggle extending over four centuries, a struggle with enemies of an alien race and hostile religion, converted the chief of the state into a permanent military dictator—so loyally supported by his people that to oppose him was regarded as a crime—the social condition of the country lent to the despotism so terrible a conservative force that, long after its energies had begun to decline, and the causes that brought it into being, which causes, to a certain point, justified its existence, ceased to prevail, the Tzars were enabled to retain all their autocratic powers and continue their encroachments on the rights of their subjects.

The ideal Muscovite state was an army, a colossal *drugina* transformed into a military caste, and disseminated in quarters over all the vast area of the empire. Divided by immense distances, this class was divided still further by the rivalry which prevailed between one clan or section and another, and among the members of the clans themselves. It had nothing in common with feudal aristocracies, their hierarchies of nobles, and their dependent vassals. Neither did it resemble the class of Polish magnates, who maintained at their own charge thousands of poor knights trained to arms, and attached to their patron by a community of origin and interest. The country was too poor to enable the boyars to indulge in costly luxuries, and too expensive to permit the smaller nobility to flock to the palaces of wealthy potentates. The Tzar, moreover, could always recompense their services by grants of land, and confirm their allegiance by hopes of advancement. All the immense material forces of the State were thus represented by a vast horde, dependent, both individually and in mass, directly on the Tzar, and living only by his favor—a horde of whom the inferior ranks were always ready to crush at a sign any show of resistance on the part of their superiors to their master's behests.

And all this in a country where two centuries and a half of slavery had destroyed among the upper classes every sentiment of honor and dignity, and among the lower even the memory of their ancient liberties, habituating them to bow in humble submission to brute force, whereas the turbulent and irascible Russian of the olden time was always prompt to resent injustice with rebellion.

True, the same natural conditions which hindered the formation of permanent social ties prevented the central government from making its authority effectively felt over the whole extent of its wide-stretching dominions. The greater part of the nation, even the greater part of the military caste, felt only fortuitously the power of the Tzar. All the more terrible was the position of those whom he had within his grasp, for the autocracy had developed into a despotism which was distinguished less by the greatness of its power than by the boundlessness of its absolutism. What resistance could oppose to it the miserable upper class, formed as it was of boyars, men without either strength in themselves or support in the country, menials of mongrel stock, who had flocked from the four winds of heaven in search of honors and money, with nothing in common save a desire to win the favor of the Tzar, and the fear of being distanced by more fortunate or crafty rivals? Servility and sycophancy, a ready proneness to every sort of baseness and humiliation, were the sole passports to prosperity, and often the only means of saving their heads. Unlike the similar classes of other countries, the Russian nobility, instead of moderating and opposing the despotism of the Crown, were either its victims, its instruments, or its advocates. Moscow became, in some sort, a vast alembic, where, under pressure of the iron circle that enclosed them, despotism and servility were elaborated, *motu proprio*, by the reciprocal action of the ingredients of which they were composed. Having made a step in advance, and seeing all prostrate themselves at its feet, absolutism took the second step. The habits acquired by the fathers became instincts with the sons, who transmitted them augmented and intensified to their successors. The only limits to this development were the tastes and inclinations of the despots themselves. But the latter being as barbarous as the times in which they lived, and having before them the example of their still more savage Tartar predecessors, wrought havoc with every human right, as regardless of personal dignity and honor as of every other virtue which distinguishes men from brutes, until the monstrous result was reached which made the rule of the Tzars a disgrace to our common nature.

CHAPTER VI.

THE POWER OF THE CHURCH.

We shall, however, be far from understanding the strength, the character, and the durability of the Muscovite despotism if, in addition to its exterior and material influences, we do not take into account that deeper moral influence which gives governments so firm a hold over the human heart—the sanction of religion.

From the very beginning of our political life the Russian clergy have possessed great influence, for it was they, and the Christianity which they taught, that were the means of introducing the rudiments of culture among the then savage inhabitants of the land. Priests and monks were the masters and counsellors both of princes and subjects. Nevertheless, in the eleventh and twelfth centuries Greco-Slav culture began to take root in the country, and, side by side with the clerical schools, laymen, who gave themselves diligently to study, founded secular schools, even for girls, in every principal town. But successive Tartar invasions utterly destroyed these first germs of secular learning, and, according to the testimony of our historians, the Russia of the sixteenth century was far less cultured and more barbarous than the Russia of the twelfth. Even among the higher aristocracy the arts of reading and writing became rare accomplishments, and at the diet held in the reign of John IV. there were princes of the blood who were unable to sign their names.

It was the policy of the Tartars, as of most conquering

races, to respect the religion of the conquered. One of the first decrees of the Khans accorded full and entire immunity to churches, monasteries and priests. Study was confined exclusively to the sacristy and the convent, and so late as the seventeenth century the clergy alone were acquainted with letters.

If there had been nothing else, the possession of this advantage would have sufficed to confer upon churchmen an influence altogether exceptional, and their power was still further increased by their social and political position. It was to the clergy that the people, when they had incurred the displeasure of the Almighty, betook themselves for consolation. It was the clergy who encouraged them in the hour of defeat, and animated them with promises of victory in the sacred warfare against their infidel conquerors. Their two strongest passions were religious fanaticism and patriotic ardor, and of these passions the Church was at once the personification and the expression. It was the monks, again, who roused the too timorous princes to rebellion against the Tartar oppressors, and stories of saintly and fearless anchorites who themselves took up the sword to combat the enemies of Christ still live in legend and song. In a word, it was the clergy who put themselves at the head of every national movement; and when victory smiled on the Muscovite arms, it was the Church that reaped the richest reward.

And now the all-powerful clergy, who hold in their hands the ingenuous and confiding soul of the nation, have become faithful servitors of the despot and ardent supporters of absolutism.

The Russian religion was from the beginning an essentially national religion, differing in this respect from that of all other European countries, where the Church was an international institution, directed by a single chief who called himself the "King of kings," and whose members, whatever their race, held the same belief, and looked to each other for sympathy and support. For these reasons Russia has suffered less than most other countries from spiritual usurpations and ecclesiastical abuses. On the other hand, her Church has been completely subjugated by the despotic power, and made an ignoble instrument of tyranny and oppression. Theologians are pleased to say that the Tzar is not the head of the Russian Church, that she recognizes no other head than Jesus Christ. Be it so. Yet to draw from this abstract theory practical conclusions is counting without the host. As a matter of fact, in a despotic country where the *persons and bodies* of the clergy are at the mercy of a sovereign who has power of appointment and deposition, and may exile them, put them to the torture or to death at the least caprice—as the Muscovite Tzars have often done—in such a country as this the pretended independence of the Church is a delusion and a fraud. This John IV. abundantly proved. For that amiable monarch, not content with strangling the metropolitan of the Russian Church, and flogging hundreds of priests to death at Novgorod, compelled ecumenical councils to sanction practices and doctrines which the canons and the apostles condemned as abominations.

But the Tzars had rarely need to constrain the clergy to obedience by force. They had only to choose the most zealous of the mitred crowd who were always offering their services. For the education of our clergy, being based exclusively on the literature and history of the Byzantine despotism, they had and could have no other political ideal than unlimited monarchy. And when John III. took to wife Sophia Paleologus, the last scion of the imperial Greek dynasty, the Russian clergy imputed to their Tzar the heirship of the sancro-sanct eastern emperors and of all their glory and authority. The exaltation and *culte* of absolutism became thenceforth their historic mission—a mission which, in season and out of season, and among every class of the people, they have faithfully and zealously performed.

Religious propaganda is the sure, the last, and most potent of the influences which confer on the Muscovite autocracy its sacred character and its tremendous power. The circumstance arising from the hard necessities of an unfortunate political life, strengthened by social conditions which enlisted on the side of despotism every selfish instinct —ambition, cupidity, and fear—were approved, ennobled, and exalted by the supreme sanction of the Church. Obedience to the Tzar was proclaimed as the first duty and highest virtue of the Christian believer. The Tzar, on his part, almost believed himself to be an incarnation of the Divinity. Herberstein, the well-known traveller, when he visited Moscow, was greatly struck by the sacred character so implicitly imputed to the sovereign power. "If you ask a Muscovite," he said, "any question which he is unable to answer, he is almost sure to say, 'God and the Tzar only know!' And the Tzar himself, if he were asked anything—for instance, the pardon of a prisoner—would be almost sure to say: 'We shall release him if it be the will of God.'" As if he had a perfect understanding with the Deity, and their relations were of the most familiar and confidential character! God's will meant, of course, his will. According to the Russian priests, their Divine Master acted in some sort as their earthly master's obedient genii, prompt to punish every infraction, open or secret, of the orders of his terrestrial vicegerent, and ready to recompense with eternal bliss all who suffered patiently and humbly the undeserved and unjust punishments which the Tzar, by reason of human fallibility or the fault of his agents, might sometimes inflict. There is no irony in this. It is sober truth. In an extant letter written by John IV., the philosopher of this doctrine, to Prince Kourbski, he charges it against him as a sin that he escaped from the clutches of his sacred majesty, in these words: "If you are a just and God-fearing man, as you say, tell me why you have fled, instead of receiving from my hand the torture and the death which would procure you a place in heaven?" And the worst of it was that these monstrous ideas were not held by the tyrant alone; they were shared by his people. Though that ferocious brute John IV. made his reign a very orgie of cruelty, murder, and lust; though as cowardly as he was vile—seeing everywhere about him conspiracies against his life—he scourged to death thousands of his subjects, and inflicted on them tortures of which even to read makes the blood run cold; though the libidinous tyrant violated the wives and daughters of his boyars, killing all who showed the least unwillingness, and though his infamies went on for forty years without surcease, not once during his monstrous reign was protest made, not a single hand raised either to hinder or avenge these shameful outrages. Historians have not been able to discover the slightest trace of any plot against John IV. His victims might sometimes flee, but resist or conspire—never.

And yet these men were not cowards. For the most part brave warriors, celebrated for their exploits in the field, they often showed in the torture-chamber and on the scaffold high qualities of endurance and courage, and rare strength of mind. But by a perversion of their intellectual faculties, due to their training, this strength of mind served no other purpose than to overcome the natural impulse to rebellion and restrain their indignation against the Tzar, to whom abject submission was the sacred ideal which had been held before them from their earliest youth. When Prince Kepnin, after being impaled, was dying a slow death in atrocious suffering, he sang—the miserable wretch—sang hymns in honor of the Tzar, his master and murderer!

These are the services which have been rendered to the Russian nation by their Church. During all the ages of the existence of the Russian State she has been faithful to her self-imposed and degrading trust. What more natural than that at the first awakening of political conscience in the instructed classes, their first words were words of malediction against religion! What more just than now, when the first gleam of the light of culture is reaching the people, they should abandon in thousands the faith of their forefathers!

CHAPTER VII.

THE RUSSIAN THEOCRACY.

Muscovy became a veritable theocracy. True, the Tzar did not celebrate the mass, yet he united in his person all the attributes of an absolute king and of a chief of the State as irresponsible as a Tartar Khan, and as infallible as a Roman Pontiff. Nothing but the power of a dominant priesthood could have effected this wonderful transformation of the *ci-devant condottieri* chiefs, such as were once the ancestors of the imperial family, into earthly monarchs with heavenly attributes.

The reign of the latter Tzars of the Rurik dynasty was the hot youth period of the autocracy, which had only just emerged from the foam and agitation that accompanied the formation of the State. In the subsequent period, that of the Romanoff Tzars, the despotism, now fully matured, reached the last phase of its development. Sure of itself and confident in the future, it now threw off the roughness and violence that characterized the first epoch of its existence. It ceased to fear and suspect, and became as immovable, absolute, and inevitable as a law of nature.

But theocracy means stagnation. The Russian people, it should be remembered, adopted the Christianity of the Greek rite, while all other European peoples gathered round the banner of Rome. Now in the popular idea, and, above all, in that of the clergy—who are nowhere distinguished for tolerance—this was equivalent to saying that the Russians were the only nation who held the true faith of Christ. They were thus immeasurably superior to all neighboring peoples—schismatics, heretics, and unbelievers, without exception. And when in course of time Russia acquired force and splendor, not alone freeing herself from the infidel yoke, but attacking her former oppressors, and conquering one after another the Tartar tribes, religious exaltation was reinforced with patriotic pride. The Russian people were evidently God's elect, who, after having proved them in the fiery furnace of slavery, was now raising them up above all other nations. To keep His favor and deserve His blessing, what else could they do but follow the example of their forefathers, and guard intact the holy faith which had brought them so many benefits and marked them out as His chosen people?

The clergy, whose bigotry was only exceeded by their ignorance, did not content themselves with conducting public worship and attending to the strict duties of their priestly calling. Like the odor of rancid oil, they penetrated everywhere, soiling all they touched, and petrifying everything they pretended to bless. It was declared a mortal sin to change or modify any custom or practice inherited from the past. Nothing was too minute to escape their attention, and there was no single usage which they did not attempt to control. Dress, the fashion of wearing the hair, the preparation of food—trifles light as air—were gravely discussed by reverend ecclesiastics and canonized by ecumenical councils, composed of the flower of the clergy under the presidency of the metropolitan, councils which have left behind them, in a document of a hundred chapters, an ineffaceable record of human folly and their own stupidity.

Priests and people, being thus clothed in perfection from head to foot, had naturally nothing to learn from miscreant *nemzi* (mutes), as all foreigners were indiscriminately called (a word now exclusively reserved for Germans). They could only contaminate the national purity.

Thus did clerical fanaticism raise up a barrier between

Russia and the rest of Christian Europe more difficult to surmount than the great wall of China. Catholics and Protestants were regarded as being little better than heathens and Mohammedans. Contact with them was sinful. When these misbelievers visited the country on business, they had to live in separate quarters, like Jews in the Middle Ages. Their relations with the natives were limited to occasions of strict necessity, and they might not prolong their stay in the country beyond a limited time fixed beforehand. The envoys of foreign governments, who came from time to time on affairs of state, were placed under continual supervision. The access to them of unauthorized persons was barred by cordons of police, who beset their houses night and day. When they walked through the streets, people shunned them as if they had the plague, and fled in all directions—of course in obedience to orders—and ministers and others who visited the "foreign devils" in an official capacity, ran a very real risk of being charged with the dire crimes of heresy and witchcraft.

Muscovy, in truth, was sinking into a veritable Chinese torpor. The more the country indulged in self-admiration, the more it tried to preserve itself from contact with the West, the deeper it relapsed into barbarism. All the travellers who visited Russia in the seventeenth century were struck by the lowness of its culture and the backwardness of its civilization. At a time when Western Europe was covered with universities, and printing-presses were found in every city, copying with the pen was the only method of multiplying books practised by the Muscovites. In 1563 the first printing-office introduced into the country was closed by order of the clergy, who regarded it as an invention of the devil; and the compositors, John Fedoroff and Peter Mstislavez, only escaped prosecution for necromancy by flight. Arabic numerals, introduced into Europe in the twelfth century, were not used in Russia until the seventeenth.

Every industry was equally backward; and two centuries after gunpowder had come into general use, many of the soldiers of the Tzar still fought with bows and arrows—even when the national territory had become so extensive that the army required for its defence, and the consequent outlay on its maintenance, had increased threefold within a hundred years. Wars, moreover, being conducted at greater distances from the capital, were waged with greater difficulty and at much greater cost. Up to the beginning of the seventeenth century, Russia enlarged her borders towards the East. She now began to advance in the opposite direction, and came in contact with the civilized and powerful peoples of the West, against whom her army and her military equipment, however efficient against nomad Asiatic tribes, were of no avail.

Hence arose demands which the national resources of the country were inadequate to meet, and burdens were laid on the people heavier than they could bear. The reign of Tzar Alexis (father of Peter the Great), when the Muscovite Empire received its greatest accessions of territory, witnessed also, and from this very cause, a social and economic crisis of unexampled severity.

Never before had the people been so heavily taxed. Multitudes of townsfolk and peasants, unable to meet the calls of the State, abandoned their fields and their homes and fled whither they could. This rendered the lot of those who were left behind still harder to bear. They had to pay both their own taxes and those of their fugitive neighbors. Many of the unfortunates died under the tax-gatherer's stick, and hundreds of villages were deserted and their inhabitants dispersed all over the country. It was sought to combat the evil by issuing savage edicts against vagabondage; but the only effect of these measures seemed to be an increase in the number of vagabonds, and their conversion into brigands. The fugitives hid themselves in forests and desert places, and, passing the frontier in crowds, took refuge with the warlike Cossacks of the Dnieper and the Don. These turbulent settlers, who occupied the steppes once possessed by the Tartars, strengthened by so many new arrivals, renounced the passive part of refugees from oppression, and took up arms to avenge themselves on the country which had driven them forth. Then befell the terrible insurrection, led by the ferocious Cossack chief and popular hero, Stenka Rasin, who raised the whole of the south-west against the government of the Tzar, took several cities, put to the sword all the nobles and the wealthy who fell into his hands, and shook the very foundation of the Muscovite State. But when the fortunes of Russia seemed to be at their lowest ebb, the Cossack hordes were utterly routed by soldiers armed with modern weapons and instructed by German officers.

There were also popular movements arising from the same cause—the intolerable burden of taxation and the cruelty with which payment was enforced—in Novgorod, Pscov, and other parts of the country. Even in the capital the people rose several times in insurrection, and the Tzar could only pacify them by delivering for execution several of his favorite and most trusty councillors, to whom the populace, according to their wont, ascribed all their misfortunes.

It could no longer be doubted that a strain was being put on the country greater than it was able to bear. To meet the new requirements of the State and make head against the difficulties of the times, it had become necessary to infuse new life into the body politic and re-invigorate its exhausted members. These ends could be attained only in one way—by adopting the methods of European civilization, and, with the help of industry and science, increasing the productiveness of labor and developing the natural forces of the nation. The need was so evident and urgent that even the hard and superstitious obscurantism of the Muscovite

Government could no longer bar the way of progress. In the reign of Alexis, European civilization obtained a first footing at Moscow. Encouragement was offered to foreigners; a whole colony of foreign artisans settled in the capital, and a part of the army was drilled in German fashion and equipped with German weapons. This was only the beginning; it was impossible to put a limit to the advance of civilization. On the other hand, progress in a country where a slight change in the mode of dress was regarded as an enormous innovation could not be otherwise than tentative and slow, and history does not wait. Russia was so much behind other nations, that if she had wallowed in her superstitious stagnation a few generations longer she might never have recovered the lost ground. Puissant German nations were growing up at her borders; Prussia would have planted her foot firmly on the Baltic and barred for none can say how long Russia's one path to international commerce and European culture. The emergency could be met only by measures both efficacious and prompt, by the rough ways of revolution rather than by ordinary methods of reform. These measures were taken under the auspices of Tzar Peter, who has rightly been called "Great," and never was revolution more opportunely wrought.

CHAPTER VIII.

THE GREAT REFORMER.

THE career of Peter the Great is so well known in England that it is unnecessary here to recount his exploits. His work, it may be well to observe, was essentially political. Nothing could be more absurd than to represent the cruel reforming Tzar as a man of lofty sentiment, admiring civilization for itself, and desirous of introducing it into his empire for the intellectual improvement of his subjects. In order to render Russia equal to the fulfilment of her new destinies the first essential was to make her a strong state, and to this end Peter directed all his energies. Science, culture, and the arts he valued solely for their practical utility, caring for them only so far as they forwarded his political designs. The foremost of these designs was the organization of a powerful military force, well armed and disciplined, and supplied with equipments and material of war from sources exclusively Russian. The sciences that Peter protected and the schools which he founded were such as promised to give him good officers, engineers, and administrators. The industries he most favored were those which provided for the wants of his army and navy, and contributed most largely to the revenues of the State. The new culture retained this essentially material character for more than a hundred years, a period during which it enjoyed the unswerving patronage and support of the Government. It was not until near the middle of the eighteenth century, when German ideas were in some measure superseding French influence, that broader views and a more liberal and humane conception of culture began to obtain, a change which the Government regarded with the reverse of satisfaction.

But to introduce by force a new civilization—even in an exclusively material form—it was needful to enter into close relations with foreigners, break decisively with the past, and scout all the traditions and superstitions of the people, who in their repugnance to reform were supported by the strongest moral force the nation possessed—its religion. In these circumstances half-measures would have been useless. It was necessary to declare open war, not alone against popular superstitions, but against the priestly caste by whom they were encouraged and maintained. This Peter did, and though on the part of a theocratic Tzar a bold and audacious enterprise, he succeeded to the full. The old ecclesiastical organization was broken up, and the higher dignitaries of the Church who opposed reform were replaced by less stiff-necked ecclesiastics borrowed from the Orthodox Ukranian Church. But Peter's victory, though complete, was not achieved without loss. A Tzar who dragooned the Church, who foregathered with heretics, dressed German fashion, and, not content with cutting off his own beard, made his courtiers cut off theirs, could not possibly command the adoration which had been so willingly paid to his predecessors. Peter was even declared to be antichrist, and it is highly significant of the social and political condition of Russia that, while the unspeakable atrocities of John the Terrible did not provoke even a show of resistance, Peter's reforms provoked several outbreaks of open rebellion, favored by the clergy, and fomented by his more fanatical opponents, some of whom even plotted against his life. On the other hand, it is quite certain that neither Peter nor any of his aftercomers could have committed with impunity the abominations which disgraced the reigns of some of the older Muscovite Tzars. Paul I. was put to death by his own courtiers for offences far less heinous than theirs had been; and there can be no question that the conversion of tzardom into an empire has restricted the arbitrary authority of the occupant of the throne. Though still powerful he is no longer a god.

Yet so far from the chief of the State having lost any of his sovereign prerogatives, the secularization of the government—if I may be allowed to use such a term—by putting a check on merely personal caprice, has increased tenfold the real power of the crown.

The Muscovite Tzars, like Oriental despots, might oppress and maltreat individuals to the full extent of their desires; but as touching institutions they were comparatively powerless, and had only a limited influence in public affairs. It is a striking fact that when men set up a master to whom they ascribe despotic authority and more than human attributes, they often succeed in neutralizing his power by very excess of devotion. They cripple him with impalpable chains. The courtiers of old Japan succeeded in persuading the Mikado that if he moved the world would fall in pieces. So the poor man, to prevent so terrible a calamity, remained on his throne for hours together without moving a limb, dropping an eyelid, or uttering a word; and though worshipped as a demigod, he was in reality more impotent and inoffensive than the meanest of his servants. If the ingenious Japanese could have prevailed on their Mikado to prolong his repose for fifteen hours, we should have had a perfectly original example of that contradiction in terms, a powerless despotism. They did not quite succeed, however, for the Mikado evaded the difficulty by leaving his crown when he quitted his place. Yet for devices of this sort the palm of originality must be conceded to the courtiers of Japan. Nowhere else has anything at once so simple and so effective been invented. But there is found in all despotisms something not unlike it—thanks to what people call etiquette, which is no more than an expedient for checking the activity of the monarch by making him waste so much time and energy in puerile and useless ceremonial observances that he is physically unable to give sustained attention to public affairs, which, whether he likes it or not, must be left in great measure to the uncontrolled management of ministers and courtiers. It was thus at the old French court, as M. Taine has so well described, and probably even more so at the court of Moscow. The only difference was that the Bourbon kings had to give most of their time to the mere ceremonial of etiquette—receptions, levées, dressing and eating in public, and so forth; while the Muscovite Tzars were greatly occupied with religious rites, masses, prayers, visits to the monasteries, and inspection of saintly relics. Then came the regular routine of traditional observances, for in a theocratic state everything is sacred—except the lives and liberties of citizens. If the fancy took him, the Tzar might lay a town in ashes, and put the population of an entire province to the sword; but he could not, without exciting general disapprobation, neglect the least of old customs or break the unwritten laws of his court. He might behead a noble or bastinado a boyar with impunity; but it was impossible for him, without causing serious and lasting discontent, to promote a man of plebeian birth to high office. Tyrant as was John IV., he could confer only an inferior title of nobility on Adashteff, the favorite of his early years, simply because the latter happened to be the son of an inferior officer; and it was not until nearly the end of his reign that Alexis ventured to raise his father-in-law and friend, Artamon Matveeff—a simple country gentleman—to the dignity of boyar. In order to reconcile the pretensions of birth with the requirements of the public service a double administration was created. Great boyars were made ministers of state, but their functions were strictly limited to military affairs, each of them being provided with a secretary of low rank and high capacity, who did all the work and exercised all administrative power. Those were the *diaki* and *sou-diaki* of evil memory. Attached to every ministry were several of these officers, who were formed into chambers or colleges. The jealousies and conflicts that inevitably arose between these heterogeneous elements greatly impaired the efficiency of the service as an instrument of government, the boyars being much given to exchange their part of drones for that of drags, to the great detriment of the administrative machine and the injury of the country.

The secularization of the State, though it lowered the prestige of its chief as a theocratic sovereign, freed him, on the other hand, from the galling fetters of religious and governmental routine. The Tzar became master of his time, and could give the whole of it to public affairs. Master also of his people, he could make whatever appointments he thought fit. His political power was thus largely increased, and he was able to make the government really his own. The Great Reformer wanted nothing more. Making a clean sweep of antiquated and hierarchic pretensions, Peter never hesitated to pass over all his nobles, and raise to the highest posts in his service the obscurest plebeians, in whom he discerned high capacity for affairs. His administration, organized on the German model, with ramifications everywhere depending only on the chief of the state, became absolute and supreme. The entire nation—people, nobles, and clergy—Peter seized in his strong grasp, and did with them what he would. His one thought was to make Russia a powerful state. To this end he bent all his energies, and forced every interest and every class to co-operate in its accomplishment.

In old Moscow there was no standing army. The fortresses were occupied by arquebusiers, who, after finishing their term of service, returned to civil life. The army was composed chiefly of nobles, who received for their services grants of lands for life—sometimes, but very rarely, in fee simple. At the end of a war they always returned to their fields. But to place Russia on an equality with neighboring countries, and enable Peter to carry out his plans, a permanent military force was indispensable. This object he effected in a manner equally simple and effective. By a single stroke of the pen he transformed his militia, composed of men who had enlisted under conditions altogether different, into a standing army, permanently embodied. To fill up the gaps in its ranks left by war, and provide fresh food for powder, he established the conscription, under the monstrous condition that the rank and file should serve with the colors for twenty-five years. The nobles were still more unfortunate. From the age of twenty those of them who were sound in mind and body were required, when called upon, to serve the State in one capacity or other, either as soldiers, sailors, or administrators, until death—only disablement by wounds or complete decrepitude giving them the right to return to their homes. And it was not alone bodily service that Peter required from his nobles; they had to give also their intelligence, and to the end that they might give it effectively, they were ordered to be educated. All young men of noble birth were compelled to attend schools formed specially for their instruction. When they did not go voluntarily, soldiers were sent to fetch them. If they resisted they were flogged, and if their parents, too ignorant and superstitious to appreciate the advantages of culture, concealed them, they were flogged too. When the impressed scholars reached the age of twenty they were examined. Those who passed were eligible for superior appointments; those who failed were condemned never to marry, and compelled to serve in the lower ranks of the navy.

To compensate the aristocratic class for this eternal bondage to the State, or rather to enable them to support the obligations laid on them by the Tzar, the estates, which had previously been tenable only for life, were made hereditary possessions in fee simple. But as the peasants always went with the land they cultivated, they became the serfs of their noble masters, to whom their relations had hitherto been those of vassal to seigneur rather than of serf to owner.

Before the rise of the Muscovite tzardom completely free, the Russian peasantry were gradually reduced to servitude by the great, and in the middle of the sixteenth century the Government took away from them the last vestige of their ancient liberties—the right of leaving one landowner at the end of the agricultural year and taking service with another. This privilege was greatly restrained by Tzar Boris, and finally abolished a century later by Tzar Alexis. The peasants were thenceforth absolutely forbidden to leave the masters to whom they were assigned by the State. They remained, however, on the land, for to have allowed them to be removed would have been an injury to the State. But after Peter's time the seigneurs could dispose of the peasants at their pleasure, and buy and sell them as they bought and sold their cattle; and, provided the noble owner and his heirs male fufilled their duties to the State, the latter never interfered. The peasants thus became, in the fullest sense of the word, the slaves of the nobles, and from that time dates the true slavery of the Russian nation.

For all were alike held in bondage to the State. From the nobles it required their blood, their time, and their lives. The people, besides giving many of their sons to the army, supported with enforced labor the Tzar's servants and their own masters, and sustained with the taxes wrung from their toil the finances of government. Sometimes even they were constrained to give the work of their hands; as, for instance, in the construction of the second capital, which the Russian Reformer ordered to be built. Multitudes of masons, excavators, carpenters and other laborers were summoned from every part of the empire, and commanded, "under pain of confiscation of their goods and death on the scaffold," to raise on the banks of the Neva the great city which bears the name of its founder. But how many when traversing its spacious streets bestow a thought on the hundred thousand nameless serfs at the cost of whose lives St. Petersburg was built!

The reign of Peter was indeed a hard time for his subjects. Never before were a people called upon by sovereign to make such sacrifices of property and life—sacrifices, it must be confessed, in great part wasted, for though the Great Reformer's ideas were generally luminous, his methods were often injudicious. He seemed to prefer violence to moderation, even when violence was not alone adverse to his interests but fatal to his projects. But he did his work—Russia became a powerful State. His irregular hordes, of whom 85,000 had been utterly routed by 12,000 Swedes, were replaced by a standing, well-disciplined, and well-equipped army of 180,000 men. He increased the public revenues from three million roubles to fourteen millions. So great, moreover, was the vigor imparted to the natives by European culture which he introduced, that its power and wealth have continued to grow from generation to generation. Notwithstanding the incapacity of most of Peter's many successors, Russia has maintained her position as a great power; and by her acquisitions on the Baltic and her conquest of the Euxine, she has assured to the Slav race permanent independence, and the development of a national culture most conformable to their social and intellectual genius.

This was the object, and this is the merit of the military dictatorship founded by Peter the Great. It was an historic necessity, the only remedy for the lethargy of the period produced by the theocratic stagnation of the old Muscovite *régime.*

CHAPTER IX.

EMANCIPATION.

But political forms, however suitable to one age and in one set of circumstances, become, in a later age and in other circumstances, not alone superfluous but hurtful. Instead of helping they hinder, instead of promoting progress they produce reaction. It was thus with Russian autocracy.

In proportion as culture and civilization—following the impulse given by Peter—obtained foothold in the country and were accepted by the people, the element of coercion, which had been introduced into every department of public life, became less and less necessary, and finally lost altogether its right to be. In the time of the Great Reformer everything which had the least taint of "Germanism"—in other words, of European culture—had literally to be forced down people's throats. Boys were driven to school with whips, and invitations to court balls and *soirées* were accompanied by threats of confiscation in the event of disobedience. For the fathers and mothers of that age kept their daughters under lock and key in Oriental fashion, and it was an old custom, faithfully observed, to marry them to men on whom they had never set eyes. Even personal interest and desire for wealth were unable to cope with the combined forces of indolence and superstition.

Russia was rich in mines, as well of gold as of the less noble metals, hardly any of which had been explored. When it became manifest that, in this instance at least, self-interest was not a sufficient incentive to exertion, the Emperor administered a further stimulus—issued stringent decrees ordering owners of mines, under divers penalties, to turn their potential treasures to account, as well for their own benefit as for that of the State. In the event of any proprietors neglecting to obey this command, private individuals were authorized to open his mines and appropriate his minerals without either asking leave or paying a royalty.

Another generation, and all was changed. Self-interest, outgrowing superstition, no longer required the spur of Government prescription! Landowners, not content with working mines already discovered, sought eagerly fresh sources of wealth. It was no longer necessary to fine nobles who persisted in wearing the national dress, nor to cut off their beards by force, nor to drag people to balls and amusements by the hair of their heads. The influence of fashion, and love of pleasure were proving more potent than violence and threats. The masters of schools no longer frightened parents and children out of their senses, for the latter, now in their turn parents, were eager to bestow on their children that education which they had once regarded with aversion and alarm. Thus in private life coercion came to an end, for the very sufficient reason that there was nobody to coerce.

A similar result was wrought in the general functions of the State.

In the reign of Peter III. (1762), three generations after the publication of the great Peter's ukase imposing involuntary service on the aristocratic class, appeared another ukase known as the "Enfranchisement of the Nobles," whereby they were left free to serve the State or not, as they pleased, without any derogation of their rights and privileges. The reasons assigned by the Government for this measure afford a remarkable proof of the change which in less than a century had come over the social condition of Russia. In the emphatic language of the ukase it had been needful, during the reigns of Peter and his immediate successors, to constrain the nobles to render service to the State, and compel them to instruct their children; but the desire for education being now so general and so great, and the zeal of the upper classes for the public service having produced so many excellent and courageous captains and able administrators, the Emperor considered that the system of coercion had become superfluous, and ordered it to be abolished.

Though suggested mainly by a desire to please the nobility, this measure was fully justifiable on grounds of public policy. The number of men able and willing to serve the State being more than enough, it had become unnecessary, and therefore absurd, to use coercion, and neither then nor since have Russian governments had to complain of a paucity of *tchinovniks* or military officers; they have only had to "take their pick" from a host of competing candidates.

If the Government of that time had been moved solely by considerations of justice and of sound policy, the emancipation of the nobles would have been immediately followed by the emancipation of the peasants. For the latter were reduced from the condition of vassals to that of slaves solely to compensate the nobles for the obligatory service to the State imposed on them by Peter the Great. With their relief from this burden, the landowning class lost all right to the involuntary and unpaid labor of the tillers of the soil. It was perhaps an instinctive conviction of this truth on the part of the peasants that gave rise to the exaggerated hopes which culminated in the widespread and frequent servile insurrections of the period. But abstract considerations of equity have little weight in political evolutions. Serfage, no longer needed in the interest of the Government, was retained for the benefit of the aristocracy.

At last came the turn of this institution. Serfage was abolished in 1861. It would be impossible, even if it were desired, to ignore the salient causes of this great reform—on the one hand, the humane sentiments of our instructed society imbued with modern ideas; on the other, the wish to remove, once for all, the danger of violent convulsions from which, while the great mass of the people groaned in bondage, the country was never free. Both these causes were, however, in full operation fifty years before emancipation came to pass. It is therefore manifest that there must have been a third cause, a cause even more pressing than the other two, and which inclined the balance in favor of freedom.

This cause is not far to seek. Every manual of political economy tells us, and experience proves, that in every country where slavery prevails there arrives a time when it ceases to profit individuals, and becomes prejudicial to the best interests of the State. When food is dear, a slave, whose heart can never be in his work, may consume as much as he produces, and so earn little if anything for his master; and industrial development is altogether incompatible with involuntary servitude. Hence the enfranchisement of Russian serfs was not alone a question of humanity, it had become an economic necessity. During what may be called the preparatory period, from 1855 to 1860, when the Crimean War had made manifest the misery and backwardness of Russia, in comparison with other countries, the most effective arguments used by the advocates of freedom were of the economic order. And the immense industrial development which ensued in the sixteen or eighteen years (until, as we shall presently see, despotism put fresh obstacles in the way) after emancipation took place, proved to demonstration the justice of their views and the wisdom of the measure.

In this way, and as a direct consequence of the growth of enlightenment and the internal development of the country, the last economic burden laid on the people by political coercion was removed. All the functions of the national life were now performed without Government interference, simply by the spontaneous operations of ordinary causes and the promptings of individual needs. The knout was no longer required to drive peasants to the fields and craftsmen to the workshop. Public life became tranquil. The country ceased to be a volcano in a state of ebullition, because for the implacable hatred felt by the slave for his master was substituted the relatively mild antagonism between employer and employed.

This being the case, what need was there for an autocracy —a military dictatorship? What need for the Central Government to retain its absolute authority and unlimited power if it had only to perform simple and peaceful administrative duties as they are performed in neighboring countries? It is a grotesque anomaly. The autocracy has lost its political *raison d'être*—its right to be. It has become useless, and consequently, insupportable and tyrannical. The instructed classes were the first to perceive this. It was they who felt so strongly the shame and injustice of keeping the people in bondage, and who wrought so ardently for their emancipation. How, then, could they help being moved to indignation by the virtual slavery imposed by the autocracy on themselves and the country at large?

It was only in the nature of things that concurrently with the movement of 1860 in favor of freeing the serfs, there should be a general movement among all the instructed classes of Russian society in favor of liberalism and all that it signifies. But the autocracy remained immovable. Owing to the peculiar condition of the country the Government had at its disposal an immense force, and it resolved to resist to the utmost.

There are two causes which render an open struggle against the Russian absolutism extremely difficult. The first is that which, during the whole of our unhappy past, has served so well the turn of despotism—the vast size of the country, the immensity of distances, and the poverty of great centres of population—conditions that make the common concerted action of considerable masses materially impossible. The second cause (less important because less permanent, though it promises to disappear within a measurable time and is for the present of great gravity) arises from the want of moral union among the different classes of the nation. Russia has no *bourgeoisie*, in the proper sense of the word, none like that which made the French Revolution of 1789, and provided the people with leaders and guides. Our instructed and liberal class is composed for the most part of *ci-devant* nobles and small landowners, to whom the people have not yet forgiven the wrongs they suffered at the hands of their forefathers.

Thus the Government, which keeps its forces terribly concentrated, has before it an enemy scattered and crushed, materially and morally disunited. The strategic position of the Government is therefore cruelly strong. It makes the most of its advantages, runs counter to the best interests of the nation, and while oppressing the still ignorant masses, wages against the instructed class a war without mercy and without truce. For twenty-five years has this contest continued, ever extending, ever developing fresh phases, and becoming ever more cruel and desperate.

In the following pages I propose to make clear the true nature of the struggle which is now going on, and the phase which it has reached. That done we shall endeavor to present its probable result.

PART II.

DARK PLACES.

CHAPTER X.

A NOCTURNAL SEARCH.

At St. Petersburg on a night in the year 1875. The clocks have just gone two; the town is asleep, and a deep silence reigns in the capital of the Tzar. The wide and empty streets, dimly lighted with flickering gas lamps, straight and erect like a line of soldiers, look as if they, too, were taking their repose after the fatigues and excitement of the day. The innumerable little carriages, with their diminutive horses, which form so striking a feature of the great city, converting their now deserted thoroughfares into an ever-flowing stream of wheels, horseflesh, and human heads, have vanished from the scene, and the few drivers that still remain on the stands, vainly hoping for fares, are fast asleep on their own droshkies. The *dvorniks* (porters) of great houses, having neither visitors to receive nor suspects to watch, sleep in their niche the sleep of the just, while the hollow ring of his footsteps on the granite flagstone reminds the solitary wayfarer of the lateness of the hour. At the corner of Liteinaia Street and the Basseinaia, a *gorodovvi* or city sergeant stands on guard. Having to keep order in his beat, he is supposed to be wide awake, and as he leans against a wall with his hat pressed low on his head, it would puzzle the sharpest of inspectors to know whether all his senses are steeped in oblivion, or he has merely shut his eyes the better to meditate on the world's wickedness, and the most effectual methods of defeating the wiles of pertubators of the peace. The good man may indulge without compunction in these solitary musings. The soothing influence of the night has appeased for a while the passions, the greed and the struggles of the human ant hill around him. St. Petersburg sleeps its first sleep and all is quiet.

But what is that strange company which emerges noiselessly and mysteriously from the great house near the suspension bridge over the dark and deep canal? One by one they come until some fifteen are assembled in the street, whereupon, in obedience to a whispered order, they "fall in" and glide swiftly through the deserted streets. Half of them are clad like common folk, the others are in uniform. Had the civilians marched in the centre, there could be no doubt as to the character of the *cortége*, but the men in mufti go in front and lead the way, the military bringing up the rear. As this strange company pass towards the Liteniaia, the tramping of their feet and the rattle of their arms seem to affright all who hear them. The slumbering gorodovvi rouses himself with a sudden start, pushes back his hat, stands bolt upright, and gives the military salute to the leader of the company, which, however, the latter does not deign to return. The droshky driver, wakening up, rubs his eyes and glances in fear at the portentous apparition. The belated passenger, when he sees it, turns hastily into a by-street, and there waits until the procession has gone past; then, coming from his hiding place, he follows the group with his gaze, wondering whither they are bound, and perchance regretting that their destined victim, less fortunate than himself, will be unable to keep out of their way.

For these men are intent on no errand of kindness or mercy. They are servants of the State, guardians and representatives of public order, on their way to vindicate the authority of the law and perform an act in its defence.

Let us follow them.

After traversing several wards, they turn into a little street on the right, and call a halt, whereupon three of their number draw aside and literally and figuratively put their heads together. Then they separate, and the owners of the heads give whispered directions to the others, pointing the while to a large house hard by. It is against this building, which contains many dwellings, and looms through the darkness like a great grey giant—the windows all closed like the eyes of a man who sleeps in security, fearing no evil—that the attack is to be made. The force divides, one slipping round the street corner to take the giant in the rear, while the other goes boldly to the front, and wakens the slumbering dvornik. The man, jumping up in sudden alarm, mutters some incoherent words, but is speedily silenced by one of the men in civil dress. Then, without question or hesitation, he lets these peremptory visitors, who may be robbers in disguise, into the house of which he is the appointed guardian, lights a lantern, and, hatless and half-clad as he is, his long beard streaming in the wind, leads the way. With catlike steps, procurator, policemen, and spies mount the staircase, the gendarmes raising their sabres and treading softly, while the civilians exchange remarks in lowered voices. They might be taken for a band of brigands, led by a man whom they had forced to be their accomplice.

"It is here," says the dvornik at length, pointing to a door.

On this the leader makes a sign to his men "to hurry up," and the next moment they are all assembled before the door. After assuring himself by a rapid glance that every man is in his place, the chief whispers something in the dvornik's ear, and asks him sternly "if he understands."

The dvornik nods his head, goes to the door and gives a strong pull at the bell. This he rings a second time, and a few minutes later the sound of footsteps is heard inside.

"Who is there?" asks a woman's voice.

"It is I, Nicolas Ivanoff. I have a telegram for the master."

On this the key is heard turning in the lock, the doors open, and the crowd of *sbirris*, pushing back the half-dressed servant, swarm into the dwelling.

The vindicators of order are now in possession of the fortress. Their next proceeding is to secure the garrison. Everybody being asleep, they can only do this by going into bedrooms, heedless of the screams and protests of frightened women and the cries of suddenly awakened children.

The first surprise over, the father of the family demands of the one who seems to be the leader, who he is, and the meaning of the intrusion.

"I am the *pristav*," is the answer, "and this gentleman is the procurator. We are come to make a search."

"I have not the pleasure of knowing you. You have a warrant, I suppose?"

"Of course. Otherwise I should not be here."

"Would you be good enough to show it me?"

"It would be useless. Besides, I have not brought it with I left it in my office. But there can be no mistake. You are surely Mr. N——. Your daughter lives with you. She is in that bedroom. We want nothing more. It is on her account we are here."

"But you will at least send your men out of the rooms. My wife and daughter cannot dress in their presence."

"They will have to do so, though," says the police officer, with a grim smile. "Do you think I am going to leave them unwatched? They might conceal or destroy something that could be used as evidence against them."

The father, after a further remonstrance, finding himself

altogether powerless to hinder the threatened outrage, asks that his protest may be recorded in the protocol.

"Certainly, if you wish it," says the officer, with a contemptuous gesture. "But what difference will that make?"

The mother and her young daughter are then made to rise from their beds and dress before the men who have taken possession of their room. If the commander of a search party in these circumstances withdraws his men for a few minutes from the room, it is an act of pure courtesy and complaisance on his part. The law and his superiors allow him to do as he thinks fit.

At length all the members of the household are up and clothed. Every adult is then given in charge to a policeman —one to each. Another officer is told off to watch over the children and prevent them from communicating with their elders, and the search begins. First the chambers are overhauled, bedclothes turned topsy-turvy, drawers opened, their contents tumbled on the floor, and everything minutely examined. The next proceeding is to search the attic rooms, for not a hole or corner of the dwelling is overlooked. Books, papers, and private letters—especially the last—are eagerly sought and carefully inspected. Nothing is sacred to Russian police agents. The young lady who has incurred their suspicion and given them all this trouble, watches their doings unmoved, as it would seem, in full assurance that the search will lead to no compromising revelation. But unfortunately for her this confidence proves to be premature. A policeman opens the drawer of a little cabinet in which she keeps her own particular letters, and as he fumbles amongst them she perceives a bit of paper whose existence she had forgotten. The sight of this morsel of manuscript moves her to the quick; she becomes painfully agitated; for though there is nothing in it to hurt her, it contains a name and an address which may be the means of delivering another to imprisonment and exile;

and the fault will be hers! After a cursory glance at the paper, the officer lays it aside and goes on with his inspection of her letters, a proceeding which suggests to the poor girl a desperate expedient. With a single bound she is at the cabinet, and, seizing the paper, puts it into her mouth. But the very next moment two brutal hands are at her throat. With a cry of indignation the father rushes forward to protect his child. In vain! before he can reach her he is pushed back, forced into a chair, and held there fast, while three of the ruffians deal with the young girl. One holds her hands, another grasps her throat, and a third, forcibly opening her mouth, thrusts into it his dirty fingers to get out the paper which she is trying to swallow. Writhing, panting, and desperate, she does her utmost to accomplish her purpose; but the odds against her are too great. After a short struggle the *zerbere* lays on the table a piece of white pulp, streaked with blood, and as the men loose their hold, their victim falls fainting on the floor.

"The insolent conduct," as it is called, of Miss N—— will be fully set forth in the official depositions.*

Whether the address which Miss N—— desired to destroy be deciphered or not w'll now make very little difference to her personally. The mere attempt will be taken as proof of conscious guilt and punishment meted out to her accordingly.

The search is now conducted with greater zeal than ever. Many of the letters are read at once, others are taken to be read at leisure. Everything in the house is necessarily, in these circumstances, at the mercy of the police—plate, jewelry, cash, all pass through their hands—and it is an open secret that the victims of a search often lose both liberty and

---

* The scene above described is no imaginary one. It happened thus to Miss Varvara Battushkoff, daughter of General Nicholas Battushkoff. The police, in trying to force a piece of paper from her mouth, broke one of her teeth, and many more young girls have been similarly maltreated.

money, or money's worth. Yet complaints are rarely made, and for very good reason. Even if the thief could be identified, a most improbable contingency, restitution would almost certainly be refused, and the man who attacks the police makes for himself a host of implacable enemies, who are sure sooner or later to have their revenge.

The search goes on until daylight. Every corner has been examined; even the chair cushions have been ripped open, and the flooring of the young lady's bedroom taken up, on the chance of finding beneath it some forbidden books or compromising papers. For, as all English readers may not be aware, the possession of literature which the State deems pernicious is in Russia a penal offence.

The business is now over and the tragic moment has arrived. The young lady is sternly bidden to say farewell to her kindred. No tears are shed, they are too proud, too indignant to show such weakness in the presence of the enemy. Yet in the outwardly calm countenances of the parents, as they fold their child in their arms, may be read a very agony of apprehension and sorrow. What will become of her? Will they let her out alive? Shall they ever see their darling again? It may be with her as with others... With a desperate effort the mother keeps down a rising sob—her heart is torn with anguish—she kisses her child again, perhaps for the last time; the prisoner, too much overcome to speak, tears herself away and hastens to the door.

Five minutes later is heard the rolling of the wheels which convey the lost one to the dungeons of the Tzar; and a darkness, as of night, has descended on these three lives, it may be for years, it may be forever. One is that of a young creature now doomed to unknown sufferings, but yesterday full of energy and life; two others are those of parents long past their prime, whose secret tears and silent grief are all the more bitter and intense that they have neither the martyr's courage nor the hero's hope.

CHAPTER XI.

THE POLICE.

THE kind of search I have described, known in continental countries as a "perquisition" (albeit in most of them no domiciliary visit can be made in the night), but for which the English language has no equivalent, because no English-speaking people have the thing, though it may be regarded as the ordinary and normal Russian method, is not the only one, being modified according to circumstances and the caprice of those by whom it is conducted.

From time immemorial Russian police searches have been made by night—deeds of this sort loving darkness rather than light; but it would be wrong to infer therefrom that Russian families enjoy absolute immunity from these unwelcome visitations during the day. The police often make searches during the day, because it is the time when they are least expected, when people are the least prepared to receive and, possibly, to deceive them. They like to take their victims by surprise, and they know that a man whom they want generally leaves his friend's house towards midnight and repairs to some undiscoverable hiding-place. A secret meeting will adjourn rather than continue its deliberations until a late and, therefore, a dangerous hour. As the police, by appearing unexpectedly, may make a rich prize, they do not restrict their visits to any particular time. On the other hand, there are good reasons why they should make them mostly at night. In the first place, nocturnal searches cause less scandal than daylight visits. All that the neighbors know next morning is that somebody has disappeared.

At one or two o'clock A.M., moreover, the police are pretty sure to find people at home and to take them more or less by surprise. Hence the watches of the night, when, in other countries, the sanctity of the home enjoys the special protection of the law, is of all others the time when the subjects of the Tzar enjoy the least security and are exposed to the gravest perils. During the periods of "white terror," which generally follow on great attempts or detected plots, when searches by the hundred are made right and left, there is hardly a family belonging to the educated classes who, on retiring to rest, do not tremble at the thought that before morning they may be roused from their sleep by the despot's emissaries. At one of these periods (after the Solovieff attempt), the ordinary gaols being so crowded with prisoners seriously compromised that there was no room for the many persons who were merely suspected, without a shadow of evidence, the latter had to be confined in the common room of Litovsky Castle. They lived together and were very gay, as in Russia is always the case when many friends meet unexpectedly in prison. Before going to bed, as one who was there has told me, they would say to each other, "Ah, we shall sleep soundly to-night, for here we are in safety"—a grim pleasantry of which none but those who have lived "under the Tzars" can understand the full significance.

Deceiving people by a falsehood or a stratagem in order to make them open a door without mistrust is a common proceeding of the Russian police. When (on December 16, 1878) they wanted to arrest Doubrovkin, an officer quartered at Starai-Russa, a town not far from St. Petersburg, they caused the chief of his battalion to say that he had an important communication to make to him on the business of the regiment. The police of Odessa, desiring on one occasion to make an arrest, raised a cry of fire at the door of their victim, who, rushing out in all haste, only half clad, fell into their hands and was carried off without ceremony.

But when searches are so frequent that everybody expects them, the police, as a rule, reserve their artifices for special cases. For as an engineer may be hoist with his own petard, so may an artifice be turned against its contrivers. That of the telegram brought by a dvornik in the dead of night is becoming somewhat stale, and when an alarm of fire, or of any other calamity is given, you scent a still greater danger and forthwith burn your papers and otherwise prepare yourself for an imminent police visitation.

Your arrangements completed, you open the door and play the part of an ingenuous innocent. The police cannot well punish you for not making haste to receive an apocryphal despatch, or to escape from an imaginary fire. Knowing this, they mostly prefer to knock loud enough to awaken the dead, crying at the same time, " The police ! the police ! open the door or we will break it in."

Nor is the threat a vain one. The Russian police make no scruple about housebreaking, an art in which they are as accomplished as professional burglars. They sometimes begin in this way—when they can do so without making a noise. At the seizure of the clandestine printing-office of the *Tcherny Peredel* (on January, 1880) the gendarmes, either by lifting the doors from the hinges, as the official report said, or by using skeleton keys, as ran the rumor, took the inmates by surprise and arrested them all as they lay in bed.

Violence and brutality were always in Russia the concomitants of domiciliary searches and arrests, and with the increase of severity in the treatment of political criminals generally, the violence has become greater and the brutality more ruthless.

What causes, it may be asked, are held sufficient to justify the defenders of order in making these nocturnal visitations and troubling so cruelly the repose of peaceful citizens ? The question is one which occurs naturally to an Englishman, but if put to a Russian he would merely shrug his shoulders, and smile at the simplicity of the observation. "Could anything be more absurd!" he would probably exclaim; for in Russia it is a question of the zeal of the police, never of the rights of the subject. Russia is in a condition of internal warfare, and the police, being the right arm of one of the belligerent parties, does not protect, it fights. Wherever the enemy is they must be ready to attack him; any place where he is supposed to be they must beset. An officer of police who hesitates to make a search without sufficient cause, or an arrest without a warrant, would be looked upon as not worth his salt, an idler who wanted to receive fat pay without giving anything in return. A member of the force who desires to win promotion or even to keep his place cannot afford to be scrupulous. He must be as keen, as vigilant, and as ready as a sleuth-hound on the quest. At the least sign, or the merest suspicion of a scent, he must join in the chase and seize the quarry, where he can. And come what may, let the sign be ever so deceptive, the chase ever so fatal, he is always encouraged by the thought that he will merit the approbation of his superiors. For never yet has it happened for an officer of police to be punished for making a search on insufficient grounds. I doubt if for this cause a reprimand has ever been given, and it is quite certain that the men who have the fewest scruples are the most rapidly advanced.

Here are a few instances—by no means extreme—of the methods of our Russian police, taken almost at random from the great mass of materials at my disposal:

On a fine day in May, 1879, a small army composed of infantry, Cossacks, and gendarmes set out from the town of Koupiansk, province of Karkoff, drums beating, music playing, drum-major at their head, and muskets at the trail, as if they were marching to meet an invader. But the force being under the command of the procurator it was evident that the enemies they were about to encounter were either actual rebels or suspected Nihilists. The first object of attack was Mr. Boguslavsky, a large landowner. The garden and grounds were surrounded by a cordon of soldiers, while the procurator Metchnikoff, at the head of a posse of policemen and gendarmes, beset the house, which naturally surrendered at discretion. After turning everything upside down in their usual fashion, they examined the garden with equal care, dragged the fishpond, and left no corner of the premises unvisited. But their search was fruitless, and they had to go away as empty-handed as they came. Nevertheless Mr. Boguslavsky was placed under domiciliary arrest, and a guard left in possession of his house.

The detachment next paid a visit to Mr. Balavinsky, justice of the peace for the district of Senkoff, whom they treated in like manner, but, as before, the police discovered not a shred of evidence to justify their suspicions. Were searched also the houses and grounds of Mr. Voronez and Mr. Dihokovsky, rich landowners who had filled public offices, with the same result. Nothing was found. Nevertheless Mr. Voronez was taken away to prison, and, after being kept for some time in custody, exiled to a remote province in the north, that of Olonez. What he had done to merit this punishment he never knew. It was said at the time that there had been some rumors to his disadvantage among the peasants.

At length the procurator withdrew his men and took his departure, leaving the representatives of the Koupiansk nobility in a state of utter bewilderment as to the cause of the sudden and unwelcome visit they had received, and the annoyance to which they had been exposed. Nor had they yet done with this zealous official. A few months later he paid them still another visit, proceeded precisely in the same way as before with precisely the same result. But as it was deemed necessary to show some wool for all this cry several innocent persons were arrested and exiled by administrative order; for, on the principle that guilt should not be imputed until it is proved, we have a right to assume that the very fact of these unfortunates being neither brought to trial nor accused of specific offence implies their innocence.

With Mr. Kotchalovsky, justice of the peace for the district of Ekaterinoslav, the procurator was more fortunate. The police found in his house the manuscript copy of a speech delivered by a workman called Peter Alexeeff, at the "Trial of the Fifty." For this crime the judge was exiled to Archangelesk, in the extreme north of Russia.

Until it was revealed by the indiscretion of one of his clerks, the cause of the procurator's excessive zeal remained a mystery. In 1874, that is to say five years previously, Mr. Leo Dmokovsky, one of the early apostles of revolution, was sentenced to eight years' hard labor for having printed, in a clandestine printing-office, two socialist pamphlets. But a part only of his type and plant were taken, the rest he had either destroyed or hidden safely away. Now, as it happened, this gentleman was also a Koupiansk landowner and akin to several of the neighboring gentry. So Mr. Procurator Metchnikoff, turning things over "in what he was pleased to call his mind," came to the conclusion that the missing type was concealed in some country house of the district. Hence this military pomp and parade, all these portentous visits, house searchings, fish-pond draggings, and the rest, proceedings which both surprised and amused the peasants and other inhabitants of the neighborhood.

According to another version—in a country where the press is fettered rumor naturally takes the place of news—the procurator had some old scores to settle with the nobility of Koupiansk, and took this means of "serving them out," the affair of the lost type being merely a pretext.

An equally characteristic incident came to pass in August of the same year in the government of Tchernigoff. Mr. F——, doctor of the district of Borzensky, a public functionary in the service of Zemstvo, received a visit from Madame B——, wife of a magistrate of Kieff, a lady of rank and a *persona grata* in the *salons* of the governor of the province. She was accompanied by a maid and a man-servant. Immediately on Madame B——'s arrival her host as in duty bound notified the fact to the local *ouriadnik*, a sort of rural constable, at the same time showing him her papers—a passport granted by her husband, the magistrate, and a certificate signed by the president of the judges of Kieff. The doctor mentioned that there were two persons in the lady's suite, but that their papers had been inadvertently left behind at Kieff, whither he proposed to telegraph for them. This, however, as Madame B—— was staying in the neighborhood only a few days, and the doctor could personally vouch for her respectability, the *ouriadnik* declared to be unnecessary. Judge then of her surprise when, three days afterwards, the *pristav* (chief of police) called at the house and wanted to see her. Thinking that the man had made a mistake, that it was her host he wanted to see, she sent word by her maid that Doctor F—— was not at home. But this only led to a repetition of the demand, the *pristav* insisting that it was Madame B—— he wanted to see, and see her he would. So she went to him in no very good humor, and asked what he meant by thus importuning her. But instead of apologizing, he stigmatized her as a "suspect," and put her under domiciliary arrest. He also arrested her two servants, and led them off to the prison of Borzna.

The true and only motive for this proceeding was the desire of Kovalevsky (the *pristav*) to distinguish himself, and emulate the example of his comrade, Pristav Malakoff, whose zeal in making arrests had been rewarded by the approbation of his superiors, rapid advancement, and better pay. The reason assigned for the arrest of Madame B—— and her servants as set forth in the official report sent to the chief of the Kieff police by the *pristav* of Borza, was that a woman had arrived there without papers, who, according to current rumor, kept a milliner's shop in the Krechtchatik (one of the principal streets of Kieff) the better to conceal her participation in revolutionary plots; and milliners and shopmen being, as was well known, Nihilists in disguise, Madame B——'s pretended maid and man-servant, as well as their *soi-disant* mistress, were placed under arrest. A few days later, when the passports had been verified, the lady's identity established beyond doubt, and everything found in order, they were all released "without a stain on their characters;" but they received no amends for their unwarrantable detention, nor the *pristav* any reprimand for his sharp practice.

Mr. Henri Farino, member of a highly respectable French firm, being at Klinzy, a manufacturing town in the province of Moscow, for a purely business purpose, happened to meet at the house of his host, a notary of the name of Szelovsky, the chief of the local police, to whom he was presented in due form. For some unexplained reason the latter gentleman before leaving asked his host for the Frenchman's passport. The document granted by the republic, and visé at St. Petersburg, as also by the Governor of Moscow, was found to be unimpeachably correct. Nevertheless Mr. Farino's luggage was overhauled, his person searched, his money taken, his letters and other papers carried off to be searched, and himself placed under arrest. But the intercession of Mr. Subzelovsky, and of Professor Isaeff of the Jaroslav Lyceum, procured his provisional release, and a few days later the French Consul obtained from the central authorities an order for the restoration of his countryman's effects, and his full discharge.

With such instances as these volumes might be filled. It will be observed that in every case which I have adduced, the initiative was taken by the police. The cases in which the police are set in movement by the denunciation of private enemies and amateur informers, are, if possible, still more numerous and revolting. Creatures, the vilest and most abject, the very offscourings of society, who would not be believed on their oaths, have it in their power, by secret accusations and pretended revelations, either to gratify spite begotten of envy, or avenge imaginary wrongs on the objects of their hate. No denunciation, by whomsoever made, remains innocuous. A cook whom you have dismissed, or a thieving man-servant whom you have threatened to prosecute, has only to say you are a Socialist, and the nocturnal search follows as a matter of course. Is there a competitor who annoys you, a former friend to whom you want to do an ill turn?—you have only to denounce him to the police. When the Government, in a lucid interval, instituted the so-called Committee of Revision, they were shocked by the number of false denunciations that came to light; yet which, despite their fraudulent character, had been most disastrous for their victims. It was said at the time that the minister would prosecute these perjurers and false witnesses. But the times changed. The reaction set in, and under the *régime* of Count Tolstoi, every hope of reform was abandoned, every good resolution forgotten, and the crowd of spies and denouncers were allowed to resume their dirty work.

Informers are not even obliged to give their names. An anonymous denunciation has just the same effect as a duly signed charge. It sets the police to work. The domiciliary visit and the midnight search follow as a matter of course. Subsequent proceedings depend on the discovery of compromising documents, or of facts which the leader of the search party may deem suspicious.

The police are respecters neither of numbers nor persons. There is a house in Cavalregarde Street, St. Petersburg, not far from the Tavreda Gardens, which occupies nearly a whole quarter. It is a building of five stories, contains scores of small dwellings, and is probably inhabited by at least a thousand persons. Many of the inmates are medical students, attached to the Nicolas Hospital hard by. The heads of the police heard a vague rumor that, somewhere in this rabbit warren dangerous people were in hiding, and, possibly, subversive plots being hatched. A nocturnal visitation was promptly organized. At dead of night the vast building, big as a cotton factory, was beset with a battalion of infantry and an equal force of policemen. The latter, broken up into detachments of threes and fours, swarmed into the corridors, the staircases and the stair-landings. They made incursions right and left; a dozen inmates were summoned "to open to the police" at the same time. The alarm spread like wildfire; in a few minutes everybody in the house was awake and afoot, and lights gleamed in all the windows. But a sentinel posted at every door kept the inmates prisoners until their turn should come. The dwellings were searched in batches of twelve at a time, by as many different search parties, and the inquisition went on until every part of the building had been thoroughly overhauled. Nothing whatever was found; but the police, not liking to go away empty-handed, carried off several captives, all of whom were released a few days afterwards.

This is far from being a solitary case. After great "attempts," above all, after the first and the last, it was seriously proposed to search every dwelling in St. Petersburg. This, of course, could not be done—the thing was physically impossible—but several streets were actually overhauled from house to house, and from end to end. One block of buildings at a time was surrounded by a regiment of soldiers who arrested and detained every one who tried to enter in or go out. While this went on outside, the police were at work inside. When they had done, they went to the next block, and repeated the operation until the whole street had been gone through.

These marchings of soldiers at dead of night, this breaking like burglars into the dwellings of peaceful citizens, rifling their rooms and terrifying their children, seems to have been conceived in the very wantonness of despotism. The system was equally scandalous and absurd. The searches were useless; the searchers found nothing, for their visits being expected—sometimes mysteriously announced beforehand—measures were always taken to render them abortive. Sudeikin understood this. After his advent to power they were discontinued, for one reason, perhaps, because since that time there has been no great "attempt." Yet none the less is the fact of the system having existed, and been so rigorously practised, highly characteristic of the methods of Russian government, and the views of those who rule on the important principle known as "inviolability of the domicile." Judged by the infallible test of their actions, they deem the sanctity of a man's home, the quiet of his house, to be utterly unworthy of respect. Police on the quest are no more expected to give heed to the trouble and harm they may inflict on peaceful citizens than the hunter, hot in chase, is expected to give heed to the grass on which he tramples, or the brambles which he thrusts aside.

Another extraordinary incident of the system of search, as practised in Russia, is that, as the right of domiciliary visitation belongs to sundry functionaries, who act independently of each other, several descents—two, three, and even four—are sometimes made on the same house in the same day. This, though hardly credible, is strictly true. In the spring of 1881, there was staying at Clarens, on the shores of Lake Leman, a Russian lady, the widow of Councillor R——. She was then about forty years old, and had four children. During the panic that followed the 13th of March, this lady received seven police visits within the space of twenty-four hours. Seven times in one day and night did she hear the terrible summons, "Open to the police;" seven times was her house ransacked, and herself compelled to undergo a cruel ordeal.

"This was more than I could stand," she said. "I have four children; so I left St. Petersburg and came here."

It may be thought that this lady was deeply and notoriously compromised, or, that at any rate, the police had strong ground for suspecting her of complicity to some revolutionary enterprise. Not the least in the world. In that case she would have been promptly arrested. She was innocence itself, and so void of offence that when she wanted a passport for Switzerland, the police made no difficulty about complying with her request. The seven searches were made at random, "by pure misunderstanding," as was afterwards explained. Misunderstandings of this sort are frequent in Russia. It has befallen only too many to be arrested by mistake, exiled by a misunderstanding, and kept several years in prison under a misapprehension. All this has happened. I shall say more thereupon in a future chapter. It is a fact well known to every Russian; and when the police limit themselves to making unwelcome visits, and searching our houses by night, we consider ourselves fortunate in being let off so easily.

The position of Russian subjects with reference to the inviolability of their domiciles, is aptly described in a scene by our great satirist.

"Do you know what it would be necessary to do, to satisfy everybody?" asked Glousnov of his friend.

"It would be necessary to have two keys for every house. One I should take for myself, the other I should give to the police, so that they might come in whenever they chose to satisfy themselves as to my innocence. Would it not be equally advantageous for both sides?"

The friend sees the matter in precisely the same light; the proposed arrangement, he thinks, would be a great advantage for everybody concerned. But he gravely reminds

Glousnov, that in most houses there are a strong box and a plate chest, that his project might possibly expose him to the suspicion of desiring to tempt the guardians of order to "lay hands on the sacred vessels." That would be serious!

CHAPTER XII.

THE HOUSE OF PREVENTATIVE DETENTION.

But let us return to our heroine, whom we left on her way to prison under the escort of a brace of gendarmes.

From the corner of the vehicle in which she is ensconced she can see over the closed blinds into the street, where, early as it is, people are beginning to move about. The poor girl seems quiet and resigned, but her eye dwells on every object she passes as if she might never see it again, and despite her outward composure her brain is working with feverish activity. In half an hour, perhaps in a few minutes, the prison doors will be closed upon her. She will have to undergo an examination. That is certain. But of what will she be accused—what can the police have against her? And as the carriage rattles over the stony pavement, her eyes still fixed on external objects, she turns her mental gaze inward and examines herself before the tribunal of her own conscience. She is only eighteen years old, and has lived at St. Petersburg—where she came to pursue her studies—but a few months. Not a long time, yet long enough for her to have committed several high crimes and misdemeanors, poor child! First of all she is on terms of close friendship with a certain X, once a student, now an ardent and successful revolutionary propagandist among the peasantry. He was the companion of her childhood. When they were in the country he sometimes wrote to her, and it was one of his letters which she had tried to destroy. At St. Petersburg they met as occasion served, and through his introduction she had made several new acquaintances of like views with himself. One was Miss Z——, to whom she was indebted for many acts of thoughtful kindness, and to whom she rendered several in return. Once, when the former anticipated a visitation from the police, she took into her charge a packet of forbidden books. Another time she took a pamphlet to a fellow student, and, last of all, she had allowed Miss Z—— to use her address for the former's correspondence. Serious offences all of them, and if the police knew everything she would be utterly lost! But they could not know everything. Impossible! Yet something they must know —or suspect. How much, and what? That was the question.

Here our captive's reverie is interrupted by the sudden stoppage of the carriage, and looking through the window she sees a fine four-storied building in a style of architecture at once elegant and severe. It is the palace of the new inquisition—the House of Preventative Detention. How well she knows the hypocritical building with its long ranges of high and beautifully arched windows, hiding, like the serried squares of soldiers at an execution, the horrors going on within! How often had she stopped before the double-faced building, thinking with a mingled sense of admiration and sorrow of the unfortunates who languished behind those pretty semi-rustic walls! Who could have thought that in so short a time their fate would be hers! She alights, and with a grave, preoccupied face approaches a tall, majestic gateway, like that of some beautiful temple, just high enough to admit the car of the condemned, who are prepared for their last journey in the prison yard. A wicket in the massive brown door silently opens, and the sentinel, a great giant of a man who handles his big musket as easily as if it were a bamboo cane, gives no more heed than the stone posts that border the footpath. Then there is a rattle of bolts behind her; the wicket closes. Who can tell when it will open again—for her?

They take her to the office; they put down her name, age, and description. Then a voice cries from below:

"Receive number (let us say) thirty-nine!"

"Ready!" answers a voice from above.

Number Thirty-nine, escorted by a warder, mounts the staircase. On one of the landings she is delivered to another warder, who conducts her to cell thirty-nine.

This cell is thenceforth the captive's world. A little box, but new, clean and neatly arranged, four paces wide and five long. A truckle-bed, a little table fastened to the wall, a little stool, a gas-pipe and a water-pipe. She examines all these objects with curiosity and a sense of pleasant surprise. After all, the devil is not so black as he is painted. She has hardly finished her examination when she is startled by strange noises—mysterious rappings coming, as it would seem, from the inside of the wall. Placing her ear to it she listens intently. The knocks, though weak, are distinct. They do not come regularly and mechanically, but with a rhythm and cadence, as if they were inspired by an intelligence, and were meant to convey some hidden or spiritual meaning. What could be the import of the mysterious sounds? Ah, she understands! She has heard say that the inmates of prisons sometimes communicate with each other by means of little knocks—after the manner of a telegraphic alphabet. These rappings must come from a neighbor—some companion in misfortune who wishes to speak to her. So in token of thanks and sympathy she gives back a few answering knocks. The next moment, to her utter surprise, there are rappings all round her. From the opposite wall comes a series of sharp loud knocks as if the knocker were boiling over with impatience or anger. There was then another fellow sufferer in need of sympathy! As she raises her hand to reply there comes a sound from below as rhythmic, yet more sonorous than the others. The medium in this case is the water-pipe, and then, as if it had been an echo, comes a similar call from above. The little box is filled with these little sounds, as if crickets were at work, or as if the mysterious beings believed in by spiritualists were rapping messages from the invisible world.

The captive's first feeling was one of fear. Were there, then, prisoners above her, prisoners below her, prisoners on every side of her in this sinister abode? Was she but a solitary unit in a swarm of unfortunates? Then came a sense of annoyance, of keen regret, that it had never occurred to her to learn this prison alphabet. Her inability to understand the rappings which continued to resound in her cell made her ashamed of herself—almost desperate. What could they mean? What were her unseen neighbors saying? Not knowing the interpretation she could answer nothing. One by one the knocks ceased, and the same profound silence as before reigned around her. But a few moments later one of the knockers began afresh. Perhaps he pitied the new comer's ignorance, and was offering to instruct her. This time the knocks are lighter and more distinct, as if to enable her the better to count them, and are not, as previously, so interrupted by pauses. As she listens, strenuously trying to make out what they can mean, she has a happy thought. It is that each knock may correspond with a letter of the alphabet according to the order in which it is given. In that case the reading of the rappings will be an easy task. She will wait for the first pause, and when the knocks recommence link them with letters of the alphabet—one for the first letter, two for the second, and so on. The pause comes. It is followed by more knocks. Listening eagerly, and counting with rapt attention, she makes out a letter, then another then a third. The three form a word. Then two more words are spelled out. "Who are you?" asks her neighbor.

"How shall she answer?" In the same manner of course. So she telegraphs her name, and a few other phrases are exchanged. Her obliging neighbor next teaches her the code, equally simple and convenient, by means of which, after a little practice, conversation becomes easy and rapid.

It is through this acoustic language that hundreds of intelligent and sensitive beings, though invisible to each other, and forever divided, exchange ideas and commune together. Deprived by the implacable cruelty of their fellow men of human society, condemned to live and suffer in a silence as of death, it is to the walls that shut them in—dumb witnesses of their solitude—that they communicate their musings and tell their griefs. And the stones and the iron, more compassionate than men, transmit their thoughts to others equally unfortunate. When detected, the rappers are severely punished for these infractions of the rule which condemns them to unbroken silence. Yet the walls, kind, faithful friends—accomplices who never betray—are always there inviting them again to beguile their solitude and disburden their griefs by converse with their unseen companions.

But it is not possible to punish every violator of the rule of silence; the black dungeon would not hold them all, and the offenders are so numerous that the authorities are compelled to wink at the offence. There is no prison of the Tzar in which communication by knockings does not prevail, and it is more prevalent in the House of Preventative Detention than in any other.

Number Thirty-nine is quickly familiarized with the strange and original life of her prison-house, and forms fast friendships with people whose existence is revealed to her only by the rhythmic rappings on the wall. But community in suffering and similarity of disposition take the place of less abstract relations, and ties are sometimes formed in captivity which last a lifetime. It is said that love laughs at locksmiths; he laughs also at gaolers, and people have been known to fall in love through the medium of prison walls. Number Thirty-nine is an apt scholar, and shares to the full in the sentiments, the ideas, and the enthusiasm of the new world, which the Tzar's police have discovered for her. Never before has the young girl lived so full a life. Occupied almost exclusively with her studies, she has felt hitherto for the cause of liberty but a silent sympathy, accompanied by ideas more or less vague. Now she understands everything. She has heard of the sufferings and sounded the souls of the prisoners around her. She sees how devoted they are, how faithful and ardent; and now, full of the zeal of proselytism, she rejoices in the thought that she also is strong to suffer and to do.

Yet she is sad withal, for the life histories of her invisible brothers and sisters have been unfolded to her, and they are dark with suffering and sorrow. They belong to every order, from the merely suspected to undoubted rebels and notorious propagandists.

Number Forty, her next-door neighbor, is seriously compromised. He was taken in *flagrante delicto*, disguised as a peasant, provided with a false passport, and carrying on an active revolutionary propaganda. He was a rich landowner and magistrate, and will certainly be condemned to a long term of penal servitude. Sixty-eight can hope for no milder punishment. A young woman of high culture and noble birth, she finished her studies at the University of Zurich; then, returning to Russia, she took a place as factory-girl in a Moscow cotton mill. Arrested on suspicion of being a revolutionary emissary, several contraband pamphlets were found in her box, and a workman was frightened by the police into confessing that he had heard her read one of them aloud to some of his comrades. No very heinous offence, it may be thought, yet quite enough to ensure conviction and, probably, a long term of penal servitude. These, however, are among the more fortunate. They know the fate in store for them, an advantage denied to many of their companions. Nineteen, in the cell below, for instance, is accused of nothing in particular. The pamphlet seized by the police was really too frivolous to make its possession an offence. But on the pretext that he was a friend of Number Forty they have kept him in prison two years and a half. The charge against Sixty-three is equally trivial. He once made a visit to the estate of a propagandist, since convicted. But not one of the peasants with whom he was confronted could testify anything against him. Yet the procurator was "persuaded in his own mind" of Sixty-three's guilt, and this is the latter's third year in prison.* Though quite a young man, confinement has seriously impaired his health. Number Twenty-one, on the upper story, is even worse. He suffers from phthisis, and the deadly disease is making rapid progress. He was on friendly terms with a celebrated propagandist, and attended several private Socialist meetings, where politics formed the subject of discussion. For two years he has been in daily expectation of release. But when he leaves his narrow cell it will be for the still narrower confines of the tomb, that last and sure refuge of the oppressed.† All night through she hears the stricken man's hollow cough, and her heart is full of pity and sorrow.

But her neighbor of the right gave her yet keener pain, even more than pain—horror and dismay. This neighbor was one of her own sex; and so rapid and strange—incoherent even—were her rappings, that it was some time before Thirty-nine could understand them.

"Distrust Forty," she said, "he is a spy. So is Twenty-one. They are put there expressly to surprise our secrets. They come into my cell when I am asleep at nights. They put a pipe into my ear, and pump up all my thoughts to show them to the procurator."

The woman was mad. The charge against her was preach-

---

* A fact. This is precisely the case of Nicolas Morozoff (arrested 1873 at Tver).

† Equally a fact. The victim in this case was Voinoiasezky.

ing the gospel of Socialism. Like Sixty-three she got work in a cotton mill and played the part of a factory-girl. A few days later, and before she had time to commit any breach of the law, she was arrested. But the fact of her disguise was regarded as proof of her guilt. Eighteen months' solitary confinement turned her brain, but they still kept her in seclusion. And from all parts of the vast prison-house the rhythmic rappings on the wall brought equally heart-rending stories of suffering and sorrow.

CHAPTER XIII.

POOR THIRTY-NINE.

AND the examination? And the interrogation? Why have I forgotten the main point, and relegated the secondary to the first place? my readers will probably ask.

Because in Russia juridic procedure is not the main point. It is secondary and accessory. The chief point is to secure the prisoner, to keep him in "durance vile." As for trying him, examining the proofs against him, determining his innocence or his guilt, these are things about which there is no hurry—they can wait.

Here is a case in point, perfectly authentic and susceptible of fullest proof, which affords an excellent example of Russian judicial methods. In 1874 Mr. Ponomareff, a student in the Saratov Seminary, was taken into custody on a charge of belonging to a secret society. Among the papers of one of the leaders of the movement, P. Voinaralski, had been found a ticket on which was written Ponomareff's name. This was held to be a sufficient justification of his arrest. At the interrogatory the latter denied all knowledge of the former, saying that he had not the least idea how Voinaralski became acquainted with his name. Persisting in this denial he was accused of obstinacy, urged to confess, and still proving recalcitrant, sent to prison and advised to "reflect." As he reflected there three years, it cannot be said that the authorities did not give him ample time to consider both sides of the question. Similar instances of obstinacy are far from rare among political prisoners. But the richest part of the affair—the point of the story—did not come to pass until 1877, when Ponomareff, at length placed on his trial, retained Mr. Stassoff, a well-known St. Petersburg advocate, for his defence. The advocate, naturally enough, asked to see the *pièce de conviction*, the ticket on which his client's name was affirmed to be written. The ticket was produced accordingly, when lo and behold! the name was not the name of Ponomareff at all. Owing to a slight similarity in the spelling of their cognomens the police had mistaken him for somebody else, and arrested the wrong man! So lax is the administration of the law, so cynically indifferent are the dispensers of the Tzar's justice to the rights of the Tzar's subjects, that it took three years —the time allowed Ponomareff for reflection—to rectify an error that in any other country would have been rectified within twenty-four hours.

But let us take up the thread of our story.

The very day of her arrest Thirty-nine was taken before the procurator, from whom she learnt that the visits she had occasionally made to X. were known to the police; and his letters, which the latter had seized, showed that their relations were of a somewhat friendly character. The suspicions already conceived—suspicions which had suggested the nocturnal search—were confirmed by the attempt of Thirty-nine to destroy her friend's letter. Than this, she found to her great relief, nothing more was known. All the same, she was roundly accused of belonging to the secret society directed by X., a society having for its object "the overthrow of the existing order, subversion of property, religion, and the family," and so forth. These charges she naturally denied. She was accused of other offences, and many searching questions were put touching her supposed connection with the revolutionary movement. All were answered in the negative.

"Very well," said the procurator at length, "you will

have to reflect. Take Number Thirty-nine back to her cell, warder."

Thirty-nine went back to her cell, rejoicing that she had come so well out of the ordeal, and that the police had so little against her. Her spirits rose, and she was full of hope as to the future.

She was allowed to reflect at her ease; she could not complain that the even tenor of her thoughts was disturbed by too many distractions. A whole week passed, a second, a third. An entire month elapsed, and still nothing was said about another examination. The month multiplied by three, by four, by six. Half a year went by without any break in the monotony of her life, a life passed within the four walls of her little box, from which she emerged but once a day for a few minutes' lonely walk in another box, differing from the first only in being open to the sky—a compartment of the court divided into squares, each enclosed within high walls for the use of prisoners kept in solitary confinement. No wonder the poor girl began to be somewhat weary with the insupportable sameness of her existence; and wondered, not without anxiety, what would be the end.

But towards the end of the seventh month, when she has almost abandoned hope, she is called before the procurator to undergo still another questioning. Surely they will let her go now!

At any rate, they did not keep her long in suspense. The examination was brief and sharp.

"Have you reflected?"

"Yes, I have reflected."

"Have you anything to add to your previous depositions?"

"Nothing."

"Indeed! Go back to your cell, then. I will make you rot there."

"I will make you rot there." This is the stereotyped expression; an expression which few political prisoners have not repeatedly heard.

Thirty-nine does not this time return to her cell with a light heart and a beaming countenance, as she had done after her first interrogatory. She feels crushed and confused, weighed down by a strange, almost agonizing sense of apprehension and despair, which at first she is unable either to define to herself or to understand. What can it be? whence came it? Ah, that snake of a procurator! And then she remembers the words with which he had dismissed her to her cell. He would let her rot there! And there were proofs all around her that he did not threaten in vain.

The maniac in number thirty-eight is knocking furiously at the wall.

"Wretched traitress, you have been to denounce me. Here is a man with a sack of hungry rats that he is bringing to devour me. Coward, coward, that you are!"

The poor lunatic is in one of her paroxysms.

A horrible fear takes possession of the prisoner's mind.

"Dreadful! dreadful!" she cries; "shall I one day become like her?"

The months go and come, as if time and memory were not; the seasons follow in their unvarying round. It was autumn when she lost her liberty, then another autumn came and went, and now a third is passing away—yet freedom returns not; it seems as far off as ever. Poor Thirty-nine still languishes in her cell, so wofully changed by confinement and solitude that even her own mother would hardly know her.

At the end of her second year of prison the captive underwent a terrible crisis. Her wretched life within the four walls of the diminutive cell, the frightful sameness—no change, no occupation, no society, no anything—became utterly intolerable. The yearning for air, movement, liberty, grew intense, almost to mania. On waking in a morning she felt that unless she was released that very day, she would die. And she had nothing before her but prison—always prison!

She bombarded the procurator with letters, entreating him to order her into exile, to send her to Siberian mines, to sentence her to penal servitude. She would go anywhere or do anything to escape from her living tomb.

The procurator came several times to her cell.

"Have you anything to add to your depositions?" was his invariable question on these occasions. "No." "Very well, I must still leave you to your reflections."

She begged her mother to try to get her enlarged on bail, pending her trial. But her parents could in no way help her. All their applications received the same response: "Your daughter is obstinately impenitent. Advise her to think better of it. We can do nothing for you."

She fell into utter despair. Dark ideas of suicide began to haunt her brain. More than once she thought she was going mad. From these calamities her physical weakness, by lessening the intensity of her life and numbing her susceptibility to suffering, alone saved her. (This is why in Russian prisons the young and vigorous succumb the soonest. The feeble and delicate have a better chance.)

Want of air and exercise, and insufficient and unsuitable food, have produced their natural effect on that young and undeveloped organism. The bloom of health has long since vanished from those cheeks, once so fresh and fair. Her complexion has assumed that yellow-green tint peculiar to sickly plants and to the young who linger long in captivity. But she is not thin; on the contrary, her face is swollen and puffy, the result of softening of the tissues, produced by seclusion and inaction. All her movements are slow, indolent, and automatic. She looks six years older. She can remain half an hour in the same position, with her eyes fixed on the same object, as if she were buried in deep thought. But she is not, for her brain has become as flabby as her muscles. At first she read greedily all the books which the prison authorities allowed her mother to bring her. Now, however, she finds concentration of thought so difficult that she cannot read two consecutive pages without extreme fatigue. She passes the greater part of her time in a state of torpor, in heavy drowsiness, moral and physical. She has no desire to talk or lay plans. What can it profit to talk to the air, to speak of the future when you are without hope ? The early friends of her imprisonment, the kindly and responsive walls to whom she had once imparted her innermost thoughts, are almost abandoned. She rarely goes near them. And the walls themselves, with the delicacy of true friendship, understand her silence and respect her sorrow and despair. From time to time they speak softly words of consolation. But receiving no answer they desist, lest they should annoy her with what, in her hopeless condition, might seem like mocking phrases. Yet they ceased not to think of her and to watch over her with loving care.

"It is not well with Thirty-nine," said one wall to another.

From wall to wall, from stone to stone, the evil tidings run, and the entire building vibrates sadly in response—

"Something must be done for poor Thirty-nine."

The voice of the stones at last finds expression in human voices. The prisoners beg the warders to send a doctor to Thirty-nine.

The prayer is heard and the doctor comes, accompanied by a policeman. Thirty-nine is examined. It is quite an ordinary case—prison anemia. The lungs are severely affected ! the nervous system is thoroughly deranged. In a word, she is suffering from prison sickness.

This physician was young at his business as a jail doctor. He had some humanitarian ideas, and his heart was open to pity. But he was so accustomed to the sight of suffering that he could contemplate it unmoved. To show over-much compassion for a political prisoner, moreover, might expose him to the suspicion of being a secret sympathizer with the disaffected.

"There is nothing serious the matter," said the man of physic.

The stones learnt the verdict in mournful silence. Oh, how terrible are the sufferings, how unutterable the sorrows, these walls have witnessed! But they can still feel, and when the doom is pronounced they sigh: "Poor Thirty-nine! What will become of poor Thirty-nine?"

Yes, what will become of poor Thirty-nine? Oh, there are many alternatives for her, all equally possible. If by some shock her vital energy should be awakened and the acute crisis return, she may strangle herself with a pocket handkerchief or a piece of linen, like Kroutikoff; or poison herself, like Stransky; cut her throat with a pair of scissors, like Zapolsky, or, in default of other means, with a bit of broken glass, as Leontovitch did at Moscow, and Bogomoloff in the Preventative prison of St. Petersburg. She may go mad, like Betia Kamenskaia, who was kept in prison long after her lunacy had declared itself, and only released when her condition was utterly desperate, to poison herself shortly afterwards in a fit of suicidal mania. If she continues to fade she will die of phthisis, like Lvoff, Trutkovsky, Lermontoff, and dozens of others. Relenting too late, her custodians may release her provisionally, but only to let her die outside the prison, as they did with Ustugeaninoff, Tchernischeff, Nokoff, Mahaeff, and many others, all of whom fell victims to phthisis a few days after they were provisionally enlarged. If, however, by reason of abnormal strength of character, vigor of constitution, or other exceptional circumstances, she should survive until the day of trial, her judges, out of consideration for her tender age and long imprisonment, may let her end her days in Siberia!

All these eventualities are equally possible for Thirty-nine. Which will come to pass none can tell. The fates must decide. For as I propose in this book to say nothing doubtful or uncertain, I will hazard no conjectures as to the issue. So let us drop the curtain and say farewell to Number Thirty-nine.

CHAPTER XIV.

THE TZAR'S JUSTICE.

As I have just observed it is impossible to foretell categorically the fate in store for any individual prisoner of the Tzar. Yet, by making a calculation of probabilities, according to the rules admitted by statistical science and based on indisputable facts, we may form a fairly accurate idea of what is likely to befall any of these unfortunates in whom we may happen to take an interest.

In the trial of the 193—one of the principal trials of the period in question—the imperial procurator Gelechovskij said, in his requisition, that of the entire number there were no more than twenty who deserved punishment. Nevertheless, of the 193 accused persons no fewer than seventy-three committed suicide and went mad during the four years that the examination lasted. Hence, almost four times as many as the public prosecutor himself deemed worthy of punishment were either killed by inches or visited with a doom more terrible than death.

The 193, moreover, did not include all on whom the police laid hands and brought before the tribunal. The arrests and imprisonments in connection with the trial were at least seven times greater, reaching a total of 1400, of whom, however, 700 were set free after a few weeks' or a few months' detention. The other 700 were kept under lock and key for periods varying from one year to four years, and appeared at the trial either as principals or witnesses, the latter being of course the more numerous. The senate, by whom the 193 were tried, pronounced two different sets of sentences—the one nominal, and of extreme severity, the other milder, real, and intending, in the form of a recommendation to mercy, to be laid before the Tzar and by him sanctioned and confirmed. One was sentenced to penal servitude, 24 were sentenced to exile in Siberia, 15 to simple exile, and 153 were acquitted. I call the latter the real sentences, because recommendations to mercy, above all, when coming from an exceptional tribunal composed of high magistrates, are, as a rule, never refused by the Emperor. But, less merciful than his own judges, Alexander declined to act on their recommendation, and ordered the sentences, passed by the senate in the belief that they would not be enforced, to be carried out in all their rigor. These sentences—thirteen of the 193 only being sentenced to penal servitude—amounted in the aggregate to seventy years' penal servitude, the heaviest penalty—inflicted in one case alone—being ten years' penal servitude.*

Now if we reckon, on the other hand, but two years of preliminary detention for each of the 700 persons originally implicated in the prosecution—and this is decidedly below the mark—we get a total of 1400 years—fourteen centuries of a punishment far more fatal to its victims than the penal servitude of Siberia.

Thus the pains inflicted by the police were twenty times greater, for the same offence, than the penalties imposed by the tribunal, albeit the latter went to the utmost limit allowed by the draconian code of Russia. In other words, to obtain evidence for the conviction of one man, the same punishment meted out to him was inflicted on nineteen innocent persons. This, without taking into account the

---

* Exclusive of the 700 who were released in the course of the first year, and taking no account either of the twenty sentences of police supervision inflicted by the tribunal, or of the sentences to exile afterwards inflicted by the police.

seventy-three unfortunates that died during the examination, and whose deaths in at least seventy instances were directly traceable to the effects of their preventative detention, passed, be it remembered, in the solitary, soul-destroying confinement which either maddens or kills. That these seventy-three persons were nearly every one virtually murdered is proved by the fact that, according to a calculation based on the mean mortality of St. Petersburg, and taking into consideration their ages, only two or three of them ought to have died during the period in question.

Such are the methods of the Russian Inquisition.

CHAPTER XV.

THE QUESTION.

THE system described in the foregoing chapter may be called the slow and quiet system. The "impenitent" are left to rot peaceably in their cells, in the expectation that these fruits of official zeal, which are still green, will after a period of rotting become more pervious to the inquisitors' pincers, and admit of the extraction of their hidden grains.

Yet, despite its evident advantages, this system has one great drawback. It requires time and patience. So long as Nihilists did not go from words to acts, and limited their proceedings to a peaceful propaganda, there was no need for hurry. The agitation was not feared. From time to time suspected propagandists were caught here and there, and, after putting them in prison, their captors awaited with folded arms in the generally vain hope of revelations which might enable them to get up a monster indictment for conspiracy.

But when the revolutionists, weary of merely passive resistance, took up arms and gave back blow for blow, the authorities could temporize no longer. With a view to guard against the terrible reprisals which the police had reason to believe were being prepared by the Nihilists outside, the police deemed it imperative to obtain from the prisoners the fullest information in the shortest possible time. In these circumstances, the slow process of letting prisoners rot until one or other might think fit to reveal did not answer. To obtain prompt results it was needful to intensify their sufferings. From this necessity the police did not shrink. The rigors of preventative detention were augmented. With cruel craft they struck first at the most sensitive point. The isolation of the prisoners was made absolute and complete. Every indulgence was withdrawn; it became the isolation of the tomb. The House of Detention, with its comparatively mild discipline, was reserved for prisoners the least compromised. Serious cases were relegated to that vast and gloomy fortress, where the police can work their will on their victims, unchecked and unseen. In towns so fortunate as not to possess a sufficiency of suitable dungeons, temporary lock-ups were improvised. Political prisoners were hindered from communicating with each other by placing common gaol birds in the intervening cells. Their places were sometimes taken by gendarmes and spies, who, knowing the language of the walls, acted as eavesdroppers, and even as *agents provocateurs*. No means were spared to break the spirits of impenitent suspects and render their lives intolerable. They could neither write nor receive letters, were forbidden to see their friends, and deprived of pens, paper, and books, a deprivation which to an intellectually active man is alone dire torture. On the other hand, signs of yielding were warmly encouraged, and on the pusillanimous who made depositions favors were showered with lavish hands.

The cruelties inflicted on the obstinate—and most of the prisoners were obstinate—gave rise to a frightful struggle, the so-called strike by famine. Having no other means of asserting their rights against their relentless oppressors, the prisoners refused to eat. In some instances they went without food seven, eight, and even ten days, until they were on the verge of death, when the police, afraid of losing their victims altogether, would promise concessions, such as the privilege of reading and writing, taking their daily walk in common, and the rest—promises, however, which were often shamelessly broken. Olga Lioubatovich had to refuse food for seven consecutive days before she could obtain a needle and thread wherewith to vary the monotony of her life with some womanly work. There is not a prison in which the hunger-strikes have not taken place three or four times.

But the method of examination is that into which the most subtle refinements have been introduced. Beforetime the resources of the inquisitors were limited to somewhat remote threats—Siberian exile, hard labor in dismal mines, solitary confinement, indefinite preliminary detention—penalties severe enough, in all conscience, yet, as was thought, not sufficiently striking in their effect on the imagination. Now it is very different. The Tzar's procurator can hold before the eyes of his prisoner the spectre of the gallows. He tries to compel confessions by threats of death, which are much more terrifying than threats of transportation and penal servitude. The horror of capital punishment for puerile offences lends peculiar efficacy to this method of extorting admissions.

"You know that I can hang you," Strelnikoff was in the habit of saying to his victims. "The military tribunal will do whatever I direct."

The prisoner knew it only too well.

"Very well, then," would continue the public prosecutor, "confess, or in a week you will be hanged like a dog."

Falsehood and perfidy were likewise resorted to without scruple.

"So you won't peach. Very well; you are determined to sacrifice yourself in order to save men who have admitted their guilt and betrayed you into the bargain. Read this."

Whereupon the inquisitor would show the prisoner a counterfeit deposition—counterfeit from beginning to end, with bogus signatures and forged evidence—containing all the things which Strelnikoff wanted the prisoner to confess.

He practised at times other and, if possible, still more cruel devices. After letting a young husband catch a glimpse of his wife, also a prisoner, pale, worn, and sick, he would say—

"You have only to cease your useless denials, and both of you shall be set at liberty."

There were occasions on which this Torquemada of despotism would blend cruelty, deception, and lying in a cynical and ingenious combination.

"I do not want to harm you. I am a father myself. I have a young daughter like you," he said to Miss P——, in Kieff, in 1881. "I am touched by your youth. Let me save you from certain death."

The young girl still refused to confess.

On this Strelnikoff had her father led in, an old grey-haired man, devotedly attached to his daughter, and described to him in highly colored language the peril of her position, and the terrible charges that hung over her head.

"She will die, die ignominiously in the flower of her youth," he exclaimed. "Nothing but confession and sincere repentance can save her. But I am powerless to move her. You try. Beg of her, implore her—on your knees, if necessary."

And the poor old man, distracted with terror, sinks weeping before his child, and beseeches her not to bring his grey hairs with sorrow to the grave; and the child, shutting her eyes that she may not behold the terrible sight, tries to flee.

Though tragical enough for the victims, this was a pure comedy contrived by Strelnikoff, who had not in his possession a shred of evidence against Miss P——; a stratagem to draw from her damaging admissions.

A man who is not very clever, especially a young man, may easily fall into one of these perfidiously laid traps, and let a word or a detail more than he intended inadvertently escape him. So soon as the mistake is perceived, it becomes a cause of burning remorse. It may be a mere bagatelle, a nothing. But that matters not; the overwrought imagination, with its monstrous exaggerations and fantastic apprehensions of possible consequences, makes everything tend to the worst. The mind of the unhappy prisoner is haunted by the fear that he has ruined his friends and betrayed his cause. We must read the autobiography of Khudiakoff, a pure-minded and honest man, who behaved with the greatest firmness in the Karakosoff trial, if we would understand the hell that such an apprehension as this may create for a sensitive and conscientious nature. Nothing can compare with suffering so horrible, self-torture so intense—suffering, moreover, which, on account of the complete isolation of the prisoner, may last for months. In the deadly loneliness to which he is doomed there is no kindly soul to offer him a word of consolation, no thoughtful friend to point out the insignificance of the mistake which he has committed.

It may, without exaggeration, be affirmed that the ravages wrought of late years among Russian political prisoners are due even more to their infamous method of juridic procedure than to the cruel system of preventative detention, the brutality of jailers, or the privations to which their victims are exposed.

Strelnikoff is the general type of the modern inquisitor, albeit the type necessarily varies according to the predominance of one or other of the characteristics of which it is composed. Paniutin, once aide-de-camp to Mouravieff the hangman, afterwards the right hand of Todleben, hangman of the Souths, is the type of the ferocious inquisitor. The leading features of his methods were violence and brutality. "I may have to hang five hundred and exile five thousand, but I will purge the city." These were his very words.

The celebrated Soudeikin—who was so well known that I need say no more about him—is the refined inquisitor of the

Judas type, the type most prevalent at St. Petersburg, and whom the highest dignitaries are not ashamed to take sometimes as their model.

For instance, the Dictator Loris Melikoff presented himself in person to prisoners condemned to death, the day after trial, and under threat of confirming the sentence, and with the rope almost literally in his hands, demanded names and betrayals. Yet the General had in his possession commutations of their sentences signed by the Emperor.

I will not bewilder and shock my readers with further description of the different species of this family of reptiles. I shall only observe in conclusion that the judicial code of Russia, repeating the codes of neighboring countries, runs thus: "The object of preliminary detention is to prevent the accused from evading examination and judgment." Another paragraph of the same code interdicts the use of "threats, cajoleries, promises, and all other like means for prevailing on the accused to give evidence." And it is further laid down that in the event of the examining judge having recourse to such means the depositions shall be null and void.

This, as will be seen, is the very antithesis of the practice with regard to political prosecutions. Here the system of the inquisition is in full force. The Government having decided that avowals and revelations are necessary for its own protection, stops at nothing to obtain them. In its eagerness for useful information, it neither heeds the sufferings of the innocent nor respects the laws itself has ordained. The examination designed for the furtherance of justice has become a system of moral torture and physical pain; and preventative detention an expedient for rendering it impossible for suspected persons to escape these new substitutes for the thumbscrew and the rack.

CHAPTER XVI.

POLITICAL TRIALS.

"BUT we must finish, my dear sir. We cannot let a preliminary examination last ten years. It will become a scandal. Foreign papers are beginning to make a noise about it. The Emperor is dissatisfied. Do the best you can, but in any case see that your requisition is ready at the latest in two months."

These words were addressed by the minister to the public procurator at an early stage of the revolutionary movement.

A little later a general—satrap of his district—spoke as follows:

"The Court is quite furious about the last attempt of these cursed Nihilists. We must let them see that we mean to have an eye for an eye. Fudge a trial for two weeks hence. We must strike the iron while it is hot."

And the procurator, fired by ambition and a wish to be well thought of in high quarters, did "get up" a trial. The merit of a public prosecutor, it may be well to explain, is always estimated by the magnitude of his prosecutions and the complexity of the plots which he discovers and exposes. It seldom happens, however, that in cases of supposed conspiracy the procurator can obtain sufficient evidence to convict justly those whom he suspects and has decided to arraign. But that matters little. He treats conjectures as certainties, suspicions as evidence, personal friendships as proofs of affiliation, visits of courtesy as proofs of complicity in the supposed plot. In a word, the trial is "fudged up." It is sometimes not unlike a game of cross purposes and crooked answers. People who have never met in their lives before are accused of belonging to the same secret society, the offence of one person is attributed to another; a man is charged with instigating an act which he did his best to prevent. But these are trifling errors, unworthy of serious attention. The indictment was drawn at haphazard and by fits and starts. The main point is that a sufficient number of persons, supposed to be implicated in the same diabolical conspiracy, having been got together they can be tried in common.

And the tribunal before which they are brought, what is it, how does it work? English readers of a judicial turn of mind may be desirous of knowing how a court for the trial of political offences is composed in Russia. I will try to satisfy them, but before doing so I must observe that it is merely a question of curiosity, and that the subject possesses no more than an academic interest. In a country like Russia, where the authorities can do absolutely what they please with a man, after as well as before judgment, the way in which trials are conducted becomes a matter of secondary importance. If the history of Russian political tribunals be really worthy of attention, it is as showing the character of the Government, as an illustration of its pusillanimity, of its lack of confidence in its own functionaries, and, still more, of the contemptuous disregard which, at the slightest awakening of its suspicious timidity, it displays for the miserable thing that in Russia bears the name of law.

The Nechaeff case (September, 1871), the first after the promulgation of the new judicial regulations, was the only one tried—not by a jury, that the Government could not think of, but by the regular courts, before magistrates of the Crown performing judicial functions under ordinary conditions. It was, moreover, the only political trial as to which the privileges allowed by the law of publicity were not more restrained than is usual. The court-house was open to the public as in other trials, and the papers were permitted to publish reports of the proceedings, under the general conditions imposed by the censorship of the press.

This unfortunate case was not of the class which appeals to the sympathy either of society or of youth. The tribunal did not err on the side of leniency, but it acquitted those of the accused against whom there was really no evidence, and it treated them with too much consideration, allowed them too much liberty in the conduct of their defence. Moreover the president, in addressing, after the verdict, the prisoners whose guilt had not been proven, reminded these reprobates that, being acquitted, they were now in the same position as all other honest citizens. Mr. Katkoff, albeit he was then far from being all that he has since become, protested that this was the prostitution of justice and the perversion of power. The Minister of Justice, Count Pahlen, was beside himself with rage, and a few months later (1872) appeared a "law" withdrawing political cases from the jurisdiction of the ordinary tribunals and placing at the same time considerable restrictions on reports of political trials. It was ordained that political cases should henceforth be judged by special tribunals, created for the purpose, under the designation of Particular Senatorial Chambers. A number of senators, named by the Emperor, *ad hoc*, formed the nucleus. That the constitution of the new court might not be too bureaucratic, there were added to it so-called representatives of the three orders—nobility, third estate, and peasants. These representatives were chosen by the Government for each trial from among the marshals of the nobility, the mayors of towns, and the *starschina* (managers) of rural communes throughout the empire. On the first trial which took place after the introduction of the new law, there sat with the three senators the marshal of the nobility of Tchernigoff, the mayor of Odessa, and the *starschina* of Gatschino. Thus, in order to find three representatives to whom he could commit this delicate charge, the lynx-eyed Minister was constrained to search the entire region between the Euxine and the Baltic. The upshot showed that Count Pahlen had not labored in vain. He made a choice which did credit to his discernment. The so-called representatives of the three orders represented, in reality, nothing but the Minister's wishes. Their docility was admirable. The representative of the peasantry distinguished himself by a zeal which might be called excessive. When the witnesses had been heard and the pleadings were finished, the six judges retired to their consulting-room, Mr. Peters, the president, requested this gentleman, as the junior member of the hierarchic order, to say what sentence, in his opinion, should be passed on the delinquents.

In every instance the worthy man gave the same answer :

"Hulks. Give them all the hulks." On this the president suggested that, as the accused were not all equally guilty, it would not be right to visit every one of them with the same punishment.

But the *starschina* of Gatschino was quite impervious to such fine drawn distinctions.

"Give them all penal servitude, your Excellency," repeated the improvised judge, "all of them. Have I not sworn to decide impartially ?" *

The minister, it must be admitted, could not have made a better choice. Even he, the exacting Count Pahlen, was satisfied ; so much so, indeed, that he relegated the next trial to the same representatives, except, I believe, to him of the nobility, for whom somebody still more pliable was substituted. But it is an incontestable fact that the *starschina* of Gatschino and the mayor of Odessa retained their positions and continued to exercise their judicial functions for a considerable time.

---

* This is authentic.

With a tribunal of this sort there could be neither difficulty nor apprehension of difficulty. It not alone conformed to positive injunctions, but listened with bated breath to the veriest whisper from above. All depended on the Minister's good pleasure. When the reactionary current was in full force the sentences were of an atrocious severity. When it slackened somewhat, and the alarm at Court abated, the tribunal became more indulgent. I can, however, recall but one instance of the latter mood having any practical result; and even Mr. Peters and his worthy colleagues made, to use an expressive colloquialism, "a bad shot."

The incident came to pass shortly after the return of Alexander II. from the Turkish war. According to common report his Majesty had seen so many proofs of devotion on the part of young Nihilists, some of whom acted as nurses in the hospitals, others, fresh from the medical schools, as assistant surgeons, that he was deeply moved. He had, it was said, completely changed his views concerning the youthful enthusiasts who had been described to him by his courtiers as monsters of iniquity. The judges were therefore all for indulgence. But it was precisely at this time that the memorable trial of the 193 took place, and, anticipating, as they thought, their master's wishes, the dispensers of imperial justice gave him the opportunity of exercising the prerogative of mercy in the way I have already mentioned. Unfortunately, however, an accident altogether unforeseen marred the finely calculated scheme of the courtly tribunal. On the very day after the declaration of the verdict, Trepoff, who, during six months had remained unpunished for his shameful treatment of Bogoliuboff, whom he had flogged for not doffing his hat—met with his deserts. Vera Zassoulich's pistol-shot not alone startled Europe, but changed in an instant, and to an extent almost incomprehensible, all the Emperor's ideas about young Nihilism, and converted his good intentions into bitterest anger. Instead of a gracious smile Pahlen received a terrible reprimand, which he transmitted in due course to the dismayed senators, and their recommendations to mercy, as the reader is aware, were contemptuously disregarded.

On another occasion—the trial of the fifty (March, 1877)—it was the Government itself that did not stand to their guns. The sentences in this case were neither under nor over the limit fixed by the law for the crime of propagandism—from five to nine years' penal servitude. Among the prisoners most hardly dealt with were several young girls from eighteen to twenty years old, belonging to the best families of Russia. For these ladies wide-spread sympathy was felt, even among their enemies. Most of them had studied science in Swiss universities, and they might have had a brilliant career as physicians, but fired with revolutionary ideas, they returned to their native country, there to take part in the movement. But a seemingly insurmountable obstacle hindered the accomplishment of their wishes—the deep distrust felt by the lately enfranchised people for all who belonged, really or apparently, to the same class as their former masters. Then in their burning enthusiasm these young girls resolved to renounce all the refinements of life and take upon their delicate shoulders the very same burdens which were crushing women trained to hard work. They became common mill hands, wrought fifteen hours a day in Moscow cotton factories, endured cold, hunger, and dirt, and submitted uncomplainingly to all the hardships of a sordid lot, in order that they might preach the new gospel as sisters and friends, not as superiors.

There was something profoundly touching, something that recalled the times of primitive Christianity, in this apostolate. The public present at the trial, among whom were several high dignitaries and ladies of the court, were deeply impressed, and the authorities deemed it expedient to commute the ferocious sentences passed on these young girls (whose worst offence was reading a few Socialist pamphlets to their fellow-workers), to perpetual exile in Siberia. This indulgence was not, however, extended to their companions of the other sex. Danovitch, Dgebodari, Prince Zizianov, Peter Alekseeff, whose offences were precisely the same, were compelled to undergo penal servitude in all its rigor and in its cruellest form.

Except in these two cases the tribunal and the Government have had the courage of their convictions. On no other occasion have they shown "the quality of mercy." Every act of propagandism is punished by penal servitude. And this propagandism, it should be remembered, resembles only very remotely that which is known by the same name in other countries. It does not mean the vast and sustained activity of a German, a French, or an English political movement. The conditions of Russian life do not admit of open agitation. The propaganda has to be conducted secretly in private houses and informal meetings. In the great majority of cases, moreover, the propagandist, unless he be a man of extraordinary ability, follows his arduous calling only a very short time before he falls into the hands of the police. As was proved at their trial, Dolgtshinzi printed but two pamphlets, and to neither of them were brought home more than two or three cases of propagandism. The only act proved against Gamoff was giving a couple of pamphlets to two factory operatives, an act for which he was awarded the terrible sentence of eight years' penal servitude. Those convicted in the trial of the fifty were not more fortunate. Sophia Bardina, though one of the most deeply implicated, was found guilty of nothing more serious than reading, on two or three occasions, revolutionary pamphlets to an audience of factory folks, yet for this trifling offence, the tribunal condemned her to nine years' penal servitude—afterwards commuted by special favor of the Tzar to lifelong exile in Siberia.

Prosecutions of single individuals, when there can be no question of conspiracy or the organization of a secret society, and the charge is therefore limited to simple propagandism, almost always result in sentences equally severe. In September, 1877, Marie Boutovskaia, accused of giving one book to a workman, was awarded seven years' hard labor. Malinovsky, a working man, convicted of propagandism, was sentenced by the tribunal to ten years' penal servitude. Diakoff and Siriakoff, who, though tried together, had no accomplices, received the same punishment for a like offence.

Thus the utterance of a few words in favor of social or political reform is visited with precisely the same punishment—ten years' penal servitude—as that which the comparatively mild criminal code of Russia awards for premeditated murder (unaccompanied by aggravating circumstances), and for highway robbery with violence, provided violence does not result in death.

CHAPTER XVII.

MILITARY TRIBUNALS.

SUCH was the way in which political trials were conducted in Russia during the propagandist period, corresponding with the first five or six years of the revolutionary movement.

When the attacks on Government servants began, which marked the opening of the Terrorist period, the Government promptly repealed the existing law and abolished that strange judicial machine, the famous Senatorial Chamber. Why this was done, why the worthy gentlemen who composed the tribunal were deemed unworthy of confidence, it is not easy to guess. It was so docile and obedient, so well in hand, and its high-sounding designation, the character imputed to it of "representing the three orders," were all in its favor. People at a distance might easily take this simulacrum of a court of justice for a genuine tribunal, and deem it worthy of its pretentious title. It is true that after the disappearance of the Senatorial Chamber the Government was no longer satisfied with sentences of penal servitude. Resolved to answer the red terror with the white, it demanded the gallows, always the gallows. But why not have required this from Mr. Peters? The spirited senator would certainly not have refused, and the honest *starschina* would doubtless have cried, "Give the mall the rope," as he formerly cried, "Give them all penal servitude." And the courtly and cultured Mr. Novoselski, the mayor of Odessa, would probably have answered that he was too well bred to differ from his Excellency. If the highly improbable contingency of these gentlemen professing scruples of conscience, or showing some sense of humanity, had come to pass, the Government could easily have replaced them with instruments who would stop at nothing. It is really impossible to suggest any plausible reason for the withdrawal of political cases from the competence of the civil courts, unless it was the hope that Nihilists would be terrified by the formidable spectacle of courts-martial, a hope, however, which could only have been realized if the Nihilists had reposed some confidence in the previous tribunal. But the fact being altogether the reverse, the conclusion was self-evident.

But the point is of little importance. Whatever may have been the motives of the Government, the fact remains that after August 9, 1878, a certain category of political offenders, and after April 5, 1879—when Russia was divided into six satrapies under military dictators—political offenders of every sort were tried exclusively by officers of the army, the only class in the country whom the authorities considered competent to exercise judicial functions.* The part of Minister of Justice was taken by generals and other military dignitaries in high command.

But he is no good captain who, having to operate against an enemy, follows in the track of common routine. A good captain possesses the faculty of adaptability; he knows how to conform to local conditions and the varying phases of a campaign. Nothing is more natural than that our valiant generals, transformed into satraps, and being called upon to combat Nihilism, should act on the same principle of sound military tactics. The present political jurisdiction lacks the uniformity of the time of Pahlen, who, like a true German, had a passion for method, regularity, and rule. The composition of the courts varies according to the taste, the

---

* Only two trials out of sixty-one—that of the tzaricides, on 13th March, and of Solovieff—were judged by the High Court, another special tribunal.

caprice, and the ideas of the different generals by whom they are ordered. The normal military tribunal is composed of officers of various grades, divided into two categories. The president and two acolytes are permanent members of the court. The others are selected for each session from among officers of the line. The governors-general sometimes let the court remain unchanged. Sometimes they vary its *personnel* by replacing a portion of the members with other officers named *ad hoc*. Prisoners are allowed counsel, only the latter must be military officers who are candidates for juridic functions, and officially subordinate to the procurator as to their own chief. At Kieff prisoners cannot be defended by civil advocates independent of the administration—although the law permits it—and at St. Petersburg, in the prosecution of the fourteen, permission was given to the accused to retain regular counsel. But the latter were not allowed access to the depositions until two hours before the trial ; and all the members of the court-martial were named *ad hoc* by the Government.

On certain occasions, when a general desires to strike the imaginations of friends and foes alike by some act of extraordinary vigor, he goes straight, and with soldierlike promptitude, to his point, equally regardless of legal subtleties and judicial precedents. Thus Mlodezki, who attempted the life of Loris Melikoff, was judged, condemned, and executed on the same day. The tribunal hardly took the trouble to ask a question. Kaltourin and Gelvakoff, who killed General Strelnikoff (of whom I have spoken in a former chapter), a favorite of the Tzar, received the same measure. Roused at dead of night, the two men were taken to a private house, where they found several officers, nominees of General Gourko. These, they were told, were their judges. Fifteen minutes later Kaltourin and Gelvakoff heard their doom, and on the following day both were hanged.

Yet, though differing somewhat in their form and their

methods of procedure, these courts are alike in one essential point—passive obedience to the orders of their superiors. The old judges obeyed the Ministers as *tchinovniks* are in duty bound to do ; the men render military obedience to their commander, and the latter would be very much surprised if they did not. It is an incontestable fact that the sentences are prescribed beforehand. Hence they vary, not according to the degree of a prisoner's guilt, but according to the ideas of the governor-general of the province where the trial takes place. We know, for instance, beyond doubt that the sentences proposed to be passed on the accused in the case of Drobiasgin, Maidanski, and others (December, 1879) did not exceed deportation to Siberia, and a term or two of penal servitude. This, in ordinary circumstances, would have been quite sufficient to satisfy even the exigences of Russian justice, for the most seriously compromised of the prisoners had nothing worse against him than a doubtful and problematic charge of complicity in an attempt (that did not end fatally) on the life of a spy, and for which, at a later period, the principal got fourteen years' penal servitude.* But a few days before the trial Hartmann's attempt took place (December 19, 1879).

Seized by a panic, the Government resolved to make a salutary example.

General Todleben (or, probably, Paniutin) gave orders that sentence of death should be passed on the prisoners. Seeing, however, that the crime laid to their charge was neither capital nor very clearly proved, the execution of these orders, if any show of legality whatever had to be observed, was not very easy. But the tribunal was equal to

---

* Leo Deutch, secretly surrendered to Russia by the Grand Duchy of Baden, on the condition that he should be tried as an ordinary criminal by a civil tribunal. The promise was not kept, Deutch being tried by court-martial, which, however, in consideration of the exceptional circumstances of the case, did not pass on him an extra-legal sentence.

the occasion. In the expedient known as "accumulative sentences," it found a way out of the difficulty. In its judgment, which may be read in all the papers of the time, there is set down opposite the name of each prisoner crimes, any one of which would, in ordinary circumstances, have been more than adequately punished by a few years' transportation to Siberia. Then these sentences were added together, and the sum of the whole was—death! This judgment, and the tribunal's expositions of its reasons for passing the sentences in question, formed one of the most curious episodes in the annals of Russian jurisprudence.

The case of Lisogub (August, 1879) is still more extraordinary, for he neither belonged to the terrorist party nor committed any overt act whatever, either as principal or accomplice. He was a rich proprietor, whose worst offence was aiding with money the revolutionary cause. Drigo, his steward and confidant, betrayed him, and received as recompense for his treason his benefactor's considerable property. The Government, however, hoping to turn the informer's services to further account, did not expose him. Drigo neither appeared as a witness against Lisogub, nor was his evidence mentioned in the indictment. The facts were privately communicated to the judges before the trial by Paniutin, who told them, at the same time, that Lisogub must die. The order was obeyed, the capital sentence duly passed, and on the 10th of August, 1879, Lisogub was hanged.

Some five years ago—to be exact, on February 23, 1880—there took place at Kieff, under the rule of General Tchertkov, the trial of a young pupil of the gymnasium, named Rosovski. While searching his room the police found a proclamation of the Executive Committee.

"Does this belong to you?" asked one of the searchers.

"Yes, it belongs to me."

"Who gave it to you?"

"That I cannot say. I am not a spy," was the answer.

In ordinary times he would have been sent to Siberia by administrative order (without trial); possibly, as he was a minor (nineteen years old), he might have got off with a term of exile in one of the northern provinces. But, on the fifth of the same month, an attempt had been made to blow up the Winter Palace. General Tchertkov was in the same truculent mood as General Todleben. An example was needed, and young Rosovski paid with his life the penalty of other men's deeds. His sentence was death, and he died on the scaffold (5th March, 1880).

At Kharkoff General Loris Melikoff showed every disposition to emulate the patriotic example of his colleagues. Yet, although it rained political trials in other places, hardly any had taken place in his government. From April 5, 1879, when the six satrapies were created, there had been but one prosecution at Kharkoff, and even then the two principal prisoners were not Nihilists. The case, however, was a very remarkable one. Two ordinary escaped convicts, got up as gendarmes, presented themselves at the Kharkoff prison, provided with forged warrants in the name of the general of gendarmes, Kovalinski, for the delivery to them of a political prisoner called Fomin, who, as they pretended, was wanted by the examining magistrate, their idea being, of course, to effect his escape. All the papers were in order, and General Kovalinski's signature was so well imitated, that on the first blush he acknowledged it as being veritably his own. But the attempt was foiled by the treachery of a *tchinovnik*, from whom the conspirators had bought the blank warrant forms, and the counterfeit gendarmes fell into the hands of the police. But the contrivers of the enterprise were warned betimes, and got safely away. Only one of the supposed accomplices was arrested—a student named Efremoff, in whose room the plotters had met. He had, however, no idea of what they were about, had never been present at their meetings, and denied all knowledge of their doings. This was likely enough, nothing being more common than for Russian students to place their rooms at the disposal of a friend. It is, moreover, in the highest degree probable that, in order not to expose their host to danger, the conspirators would refrain from taking him into their confidence. Before leaving his apartment they were careful to burn the paper on which they had practised the imitation of General Kovalinski's signature. But they made a fatal omission. It did not occur to them to scatter the charred remnants with the poker; they were left in the grate in a heap, and when the police came, and, after their wont, examined everything, they were able to decipher, on a piece of paper not completely carbonized, the general's name. They showed it to Efremoff, who, suspecting nothing, had the imprudence to read the name aloud at the very moment the fatal fragment fell asunder. This was the sole proof of Efremoff's alleged culpability, and of his complicity in the attempt to liberate Fomin. But a victim being needed, he was condemned to death, and Loris Melikoff confirmed the sentence. It was not, however, carried into effect, for Efremoff sued for the pardon which all the others had hitherto disdainfully refused to demand, and, in consideration of his submission, his sentence was commuted to twenty years' hard labor.

These examples abundantly prove that the military tribunals charged with the trial of political prisoners are merely judicial purveyors for the hangman; their duty is strictly limited to providing victims for the scaffold and the hulks. The orders they receive they slavishly obey. Their function is to put into the shape of articles and paragraphs of the law the decrees of the administration, and give to their proceedings the sanction of a seeming legality. In the case of Kovalsky (August 2, 1878),* the first who was condemned

---

* Although Kovalsky's trial took place before the law of August 9th, he was judged (by special order) by a court-martial.

to death, the judges, deeply moved by the speech of the advocate, Bardovski, had a moment's hesitation, asked each other how they should act, and finally resolved to demand further instruction from St. Petersburg. A dispatch was sent accordingly, and, pending the arrival of the answer—some three hours—the court reserved its decision. The answer was a decided negative, the preceding order being strictly confirmed. After this there could be no further hesitation; the death sentence was duly passed, and Kovalsky duly shot.

Did not Strelnikoff boast that the tribunals would do everything he desired? Yet, until these later times, there remained a sort of check which, though in nowise acting as a restraint on the arbitrary proceedings of the Government, imposed on its agents in ordinary cases a certain measure of decorum. This was the publicity of trials; not, however, the publicity to which other European countries are accustomed, for in Russian official methods there is nearly always something equivocal, and concessions made with one hand are generally more than half taken back with the other. In order to prevent manifestations in favor of the prisoners, the audiences were sorted with particular care. Only those provided with special tickets, signed by the president of the tribunal, were allowed to be present at a trial. A certain number were given to representatives of the press, and the liberalism of the presiding judge was gauged by his generosity in this regard. But without risking instant suppression, the papers might not publish their own report of the proceedings, however guarded or insignificant it might be. They had to wait until the official text, revised, purged, and retouched by the Minister and the police, was placed at their disposal. They could not print anything not contained therein, and the mutilated report had to be strictly followed.*

Access to the courts being allowed to representatives of

---

* This rule gave rise to a curious custom. The official *Monitor*, having kept the press waiting an undue time for the details of a trial

the national press, it could not well be refused to correspondents of foreign journals, who were always both more importunate and indiscreet than their Russian *confrères*. Their telegrams, it is true, could be intercepted, and their letters seized as they passed through the post-office—sometimes; for the writers had learnt the trick of sending them by ways unknown to the police, and somehow or other the communications generally reached their destinations and appeared in print. The efforts put forth by the Government to check publicity at home and hinder the publication of unpleasant facts abroad showed how much it fretted under these practically impotent restraints on their proceedings.

Since the trial of the tzaricides (Sophia Perovskaia, Geliaboff, and others), this last remaining check—if such it could be considered—has been removed. All subsequent political trials have been conducted with closed doors. Nobody unconnected with the proceedings is permitted to be present. To this rule no exception is allowed, even in favor of the *tchinovniks* of the Tzar; for albeit these gentlemen are not likely to have revolutionary sympathies, they might conceivably hear something that would sap their loyalty or corrupt their morals. At the last trial, that of the fourteen (October, 1884), the interdict was extended to the nearest kindred of the accused. The public on that occasion was represented by the Minister of War and Marine and five superior *employés* of superhuman fidelity. So well kept was the secret, moreover, that, according to the correspondent of

---

in which the public took great interest. the ingenious idea occurred to a paper—if I mistake not, the *St. Petersburg Messenger*—an idea afterwards acted upon by all its contemporaries, of printing, so to speak, the outside of the trial. For several consecutive days it amused its readers with graphic descriptions of the demeanor of the prisoners, their faces, the play of their features, the impression they made on the public, and a mass of other insignificant details, without letting fall a single word about the thing essential, the indictment, the evidence, and the pleadings, until the official report, having undergone the ordeal of the constabulary, was allowed to be published.

the *Times*, the inhabitants of the neighboring houses had no suspicion that a political trial was going on in the courthouse.

This, then, is our present position.

For political offences there is in Russia neither justice nor mercy. There never has been. Ordinary breaches of the law may be tried by a jury, but only once has the Russian Government tried the experiment of appealing to the representatives of the public conscience in the matter of political offences. That was the case of Vere Zassoulitch. On this occasion, as is well known, the authorities burnt their fingers, and it is unlikely that the experiment will ever be repeated. The courts have always been the organs of the executive; they differ only in form from the police, the gendarmery, and other branches of the administration. All are organized on the same arbitrary principles. The judgment, with its pomp and circumstance, is simply a dress parade, a sort of homage paid by Russian despotism to modern civilization.

And now the Government, out of mere hysterical nervousness, has little by little stripped its tribunals of every attribute which gave them the outward show of courts of justice. The present tribunals are the police, the gendarmes, the administration in all their nakedness. I do not say that this is barbarous, or despotic, or infamous. It is simply stupid. The Russian Government may be likened to a shopkeeper who, after exposing in his window goods of seemingly fair quality, gradually replaces them with articles whose rottenness is visible to all beholders, the quality of which nobody blessed with eyes and a nose can fail to detect. I ask pardon for this unsavory comparison, but there is really no other that fits in with the facts. The conduct of the Tzar's Government in this regard can only discredit it in the opinion of Europe without making the least impression on its enemies. For once it is decided to put a fowl in the pot, it must be a matter of supreme indifference to the victim with what sauce it will be eaten.

So far as revolutionists are concerned, the question of political jurisdiction is of the least possible moment, and among Russians generally, it excites little if any attention. I have dealt with the subject because I am writing for readers to whom it is naturally of great interest. In European countries where the courts of justice are the supreme if not the sole power whereby, in the last instance, the relations between the whole body of citizens represented by the State and each individual citizen are regulated, the right constitution of the tribunals and the full development of every needful guarantee for the equity of their judgments is a matter of the highest importance. In Russia, on the other hand, where the police can set at naught the decision of a judge, the constitution of the courts may interest you as a political tribune, in that it affords you a means of expressing openly your ideas; but in itself, as a true court of justice—a body competent to pronounce on your fate—you cannot discuss the subject seriously. What matters it though you receive a light sentence, if on its expiration the police gives you another far more severe? What does it profit you to be discharged "without a stain on your character" if the police arrest you in the very precincts of the court, put you a second time in prison, and send you to Siberia! What, again, is the advantage of having your sentence of twenty years' penal servitude commuted to one of five, if the administration puts you in a dungeon so horrible and noisome that, unless you are superhumanly robust, you have not the remotest chance of outliving even the shorter term?

If we would learn how the Government treats its enemies, it is not to the tribunals that we must address ourselves; we must know how they are dealt with after the verdict and after the judgment.

CHAPTER XVIII.

AFTER JUDGMENT.

LET us suppose that a prisoner is condemned to the hulks for as many years as it may please the reader to give him—for truly this is a point of slightest importance, a mere matter of detail. The sentence is read with all the circumstance prescribed by the law, and the work of the court is done. Yet it is precisely at this point, when his fate is seemingly decided, that for the prisoner and those he loves arises the burning question: What will the Government do with him?

But how! And the sentence? Does Russian despotism go the length of changing at once the punishment ordered by the judges and inflicting penalties which they never contemplated? Not yet. For that there will be ample time later on. Meanwhile, the sentence is respected. But in Russia, as every one well knows, there are hulks and hulks, gaols and gaols. It makes all the difference in the world between being sent to Schlüsselburg and a Central Prison, to the ravelin of Troubetzkoi and the bagnios of Siberia.

Hence, all who take an interest in our prisoner's fate—his kinsfolk and his friends—move heaven and earth to obtain for him the unspeakable favor of being sent to Siberia. The father and mother—above all, the mother, as being the most likely to succeed in this momentous enterprise—are generally the first to make the attempt. If they are poor their son's comrades subscribe among themselves a sufficient sum to defray the parent's expenses to St. Petersburg. If, besides being poor, they are ignorant and without friends in bureaucratic spheres, they are instructed and advised—

directed to appeal to some functionary whose heart is believed to be not altogether hardened, and who may, perchance, listen to their prayers and use his influence on behalf of their child. They are directed, too, to address themselves to certain tender-hearted women who, behind the scenes, have great influence in high quarters which they are often disposed to exercise in favor of an unfortunate prisoner.

Next to a mother, a wife is the intercessor whose mission of mercy is the most likely to be crowned with success. When there is no wife—and political prisoners being mostly young, are generally unmarried—the part of intercessor is taken by a sweetheart. Sweethearts are never wanting. If a prisoner has neither father nor mother, neither sister nor brother, nor one still dearer to visit him, to think of him, and intercede for him, his friends at once provide him with a *fiancée*. There are few young girls who, in such circumstances, would refuse to play the painful and dangerous part of sweetheart—dangerous, because acceptance of the position implies a degree of sympathy with revolutionists and their ideas which may bring upon them the undesired attention of the police, with all its consequences. If the prisoner be not too seriously compromised, the lower administration, which in these cases is the arbiter, is good-naturedly blind to the now common artifice, and grants the improvised sweetheart the privilege of seeing her supposed lover, lets her take him books and, perhaps, an occasional bottle of wine. It is she also who, either alone or in company with the mother, undertakes the onerous and anxious duty of soliciting a commutation of his sentence or his transfer to more desirable quarters.

To attain this end every possible effort is made, every influence called into play. Mother, sister, wife, or sweetheart, and friends, all set to work and beseech, importune, and torment in turn procurator, police, and gendarmery, and every person in authority whom they are suffered to approach. Refused in one quarter they try in another; and for days, perhaps for weeks, alternate between the pleasures of hope and the agonies of despair. At last they can breathe a sigh of thankfulness and relief; their object is accomplished, their prayer granted—it has been decided to send the prisoner, on whose behalf so many efforts have been made, to the bagnios of Siberia, to the land of cold and misery, of brutal taskmasters and cruel punishments, of hard labor in mines, where men's hands and feet are burnt by the frozen fetters that bind them. And father and mother, sweetheart and friends, are content withal; they congratulate each other on their success, and say that their beloved prisoner was born under a lucky star!

I shall have some observations to offer further on as to the delights which await the Benjamins of fortune who are sent to the frozen north. Let us, in the meantime, accompany the unlucky ones who are consigned to one or other of the two central prisons situate a short distance from Kharkoff, in our beautiful South, in that Ukraine which has been justly called the Russian Italy. The first of these prisons is in the district of Borisoglebsk, the other in the district of Novo-Belgorod, near the village of Petcheneghi. I shall confine my remarks to the latter, for there exist authentic documents which describe in full detail the manner of life of its inmates. These documents are two invaluable memoirs, written by two prisoners who underwent, or saw with their own eyes, all the things they have set down. One of the memoirs deals with the time before 1878, the other takes up the narrative at the point where it was abandoned by his predecessor, and brings it down to 1880. Both are of undoubted authenticity. They were written secretly, day by day, in the semi-darkness of the writers' cells, and smuggled out of the prison by one of those underground ways which, despite the vigilance of gaolers and policemen, are always to be found in the country of the Tzars. The first memoir, entitled "Buried Alive," and completed and sent away in July, 1878, was forthwith printed in the clandestine printing-office of the *Zemlia e Volia*. The second, which bore the title of "Funeral Oration on Alexander II.," left the gaol of Novo-Belgorod about the middle of 1880. It was copied and re-copied and circulated in manuscript in every important town of the empire, and a few months ago the *Messenger* of the *Narodnaia Volia* published the memoir *in extenso*.

The Central Prison is a large group of buildings, hard by the village of Petcheneghi, inclosed within a high wall, which completely isolates them from the rest of the living world. The uniformity of this wall is broken by a great gateway, the only one which gives access to this dark abode of sorrow and suffering. On a large board above the gateway are inscribed the words: "CENTRAL PRISON OF NOVO-BELGOROD." In the middle of the inclosure, and about fifty paces from the outward walls (to render escape by undermining more difficult) rises a vast building—the central body of the gaol. Turning the corner of this edifice the curious visitor, or newly arrived prisoner, sees at the end of the court, and over against its either angle, two single-storied houses which, though large, are much smaller than the principal building. Each has a gateway; on the pediment of one is carved the inscription, "RIGHT CELLS;" and on that of the other, "LEFT CELLS."

These two houses are reserved for State prisoners.

Unlike the fortress of St. Peter and St. Paul, the inmates of the Central Prison do not consist exclusively of political convicts. It is a penitentiary for the reception of common law-breakers of the worst type—confirmed malefactors—whom the Government does not send to Siberia for fear they should escape. The whole of the great central building is occupied by convicts of this class, who form three-fourths of the whole. Only by comparing the lot and treatment of these two categories of prisoners can the tender care, the kind thoughtfulness of the Government for political offenders be properly appreciated.

The common criminals live and work together; minds and hands are alike occupied; they have the solace of congenial society, and, beyond the loss of liberty, have little to complain about. But their political *confrères* are doomed to complete isolation. Each man lives a lonesome life in his little cell. Even outside he is still solitary, for in order that prisoners may see as little of each other as possible, they are made to take their walks at different times and in three different yards. Attempts to exchange words with fellow-captives, casually encountered, are strictly forbidden and severely punished. No exclamation may be uttered, no voice raised in this tomb of the living.

Nevertheless, some half-dozen common malefactors are confined in as many cells of the thirty which the two houses contain. They are, of course, the greatest scoundrels of the entire collection—parricides under sentence of hard labor for life,* professional brigands, and wretches who have murdered whole families. Yet even these monsters of crime are treated more humanely than the politicals. They are free all the day long, are allowed to work in the society of their companions, and only shut up in their cells during the night. They are neither tutored, watched, nor hindered from communicating with their fellows. Heinous as are their crimes, their yoke is easy and their burden light.

When in July, 1878, the political prisoners of Novo-Belgorod, reduced to the extremity of despair, adopted the terrible expedient of refraining from food, and began the longest and bitterest "famine strike," recorded in the mournful

---

* Capital punishment for other than political offences has not prevailed in Russia for more than a century, being abolished by the Empress Elizabeth in 1753.

annals of Russian prisons, the ultimatum they presented to the governor contained but these demands :—That they might work together in the prison workshops, that they might receive food from without, and be allowed to read any books approved by the official censorship—not merely such as the governor in his caprice thought fit to select. In other words, they desired no more than to be placed on the same footing as murderers, fire-raisers, and highway robbers; for the latter enjoyed all the privileges in question except that of reading, which, as they were utterly illiterate, they could not well have turned to account.

Yet the director of the prison, and the governor-general of the province (Prince Krapotkin, cousin of Peter Krapotkin, the prisoner of Clairvaux), let them endure the pangs of hunger for eight days (from the 3d to the 10th of July inclusive) before acceding to these reasonable requests. It was only when the strikers were so weak that they could not rise from their beds, and every hour brought them within measurable distance of death, that, to prevent a catastrophe which would have horrified all Russia, Krapotkin yielded and promised that what they demanded should be done. But this, in the issue, proved to be a deliberate lie—a subterfuge to induce them to eat. The promise made to the ear was broken to the hope; the privileges granted to robbers and murderers were still withheld from the prisoners of state. They remained as before pariahs among outcasts.

And what, it may be asked, were the crimes of these men? Their guilt was surely great; to deserve punishment so severe, treatment so cruel, they must have been inveterate offenders—Terrorists of the deepest dye. Not at all. In a subsequent chapter I shall describe the lot of the Terrorists who were not deemed sufficiently guilty to be dealt with by the hangman. In the Central Prison were only propagandists, peaceful workers of the early dawn, the flower of the noble generation of 1870, the first that was bred and grew up in a Russia free from the stain of slavery; generation which from the sorrowful past, pusillanimous and decrepit, inherited but a great yearning and pity for a suffering people, oppressed during centuries, and which brought to the fatherland an amount of eager devotion, a beautiful ardor, unmatched probably in any other age or country. First among these prisoners of liberty was Hypolitus Myshkin (hero of the trial of the 193), a Government stenographist and owner of a printing-office, which he devoted to the production of revolutionary literature. When brought up for trial Myshkin proved himself to be an orator of rare power. The president was utterly confounded by his apt replies and ready wit; the vast audience, one half of whom were State functionaries, hung spell-bound on his lips, transformed for a moment by the magic of his eloquence into admirers and friends. His speech (November 15, 1877) was an event. On the day before, almost unknown, Myshkin, by this single achievement, became famous throughout the land. His name still lives. In the sanctuary of hundreds of solitary students, and of many a young enthusiastic girl, the portrait most often seen beside the likeness of Sophia Perovskaia is that of the intrepid young orator, with his high and noble forehead, his intellectual beauty, his large dark eyes, and his defiant bearing.

In striking contrast with Myshkin was his companion-in-arms Plotnikoff, a quiet, modest young fellow, once a student. He had not distinguished himself by any striking achievement; his political life did not last, so to speak, more than a week. Member of the Propagandist Society of the Dolgoushinzi, of which I have already spoken, he got into trouble through giving a few pamphlets to some peasants in the province of Moscow. But after his arrest his high courage and martyr-like zeal won him a lofty place even among the men of his circle, all of whom showed Russia a splendid example of hardihood and resolution.

"As for Plotnikoff," said the public prosecutor, in the bureaucratic language of his requisition, "albeit he has acknowledged all the crimes laid to his charge, he has not done so in any spirit of contrition, but out of pure perversity of mind ; a perversity amounting to fanaticism, and excluding all hope of repentance." Better eulogy than this could hardly be made on a man devoted to a great idea.

Plotnikoff's comrade and friend, Leon Dmokhovsky, the oldest member of the Dolgoushinzi circle, was a rich landowner of the province of Kharkoff, a man of science with a heart of gold. Everywhere—in the society of his young companions as well as in the Central Prison and the hulks, where they sent him to perish—this man was a faithful friend, a wise counsellor, and, in case of need, a just arbiter for all with whom he was brought into contact, and who required his help. His offence was printing clandestinely, with his own hands, two socialist pamphlets—his sentence eight years' penal servitude.

Then there were the two sons of Kaukaze Djebadori, and their adopted brother, Zdanovitch, son of an exiled Polish father and a Circassian mother; all three revolutionary missionaries among the workmen of Moscow and St. Petersburg, and all three as full of fire and spirit as the warriors of their noble country. They were sentenced to nine years' hard labor.

Next on the roll of martyrs come Bocharoff and Cherniavsky, two young men, one of whom was condemned to ten and the other to fifteen years' penal servitude for taking part in the peaceful demonstration in Kazan Square.

Peter Alexeeff, another victim, was a peasant whose bold sonorous words at his trial startled the judges, and resounded in the hearts of his companions like a battle-call. Convicted of spreading subversive ideas among his fellow-workmen, Alexeeff was sentenced to ten years' penal servitude.

Donezky, Gerasimoff, Alexandroff, Elezky, Papin, Mouravsky—their shadows, too, pass before us in this abode of gloom. All are there. All this intelligence, all this boundless love for the unfortunate, all their striving to raise the lot of the lowly, all are buried in that granite tomb, doomed to languish and decay.

But there are dwellers in that sinister prison-house whom I have still to mention. I have said nothing of the director and chief—its right arm and moving spirit—the man Grizelevski. He displayed his peculiar talents and gained his reputation in Poland, where he was the colleague and collaborateur of Mouravieff, the hangman. He has shed the blood of Poles; he now sucks the blood of Russians. It is curious to note, by way of parenthesis, the strong predilection shown by the Government for the butchers of Poland. Paniutin, Grizelevski, Kopnin (Grizelevski's destined successor), and a crowd of gaolers in Siberia, won their spurs in Poland.

Promoted by special favor of Prince Krapotkin to the lucrative and honorable post of chief of the great prison of Novo-Belgorod, Grizelevski has shown that he fully understands what is expected of him. By petty vexations without number, contrived with no other end than to torment the prisoners, and by a boundless brutality, he renders their lives a perfect hell.

Proofs and instances of his tyrannies are only too abundant.

One evening in February, 1878, Plotnikoff was walking sadly to and fro in his little cell, reciting in a low voice some verses of his favorite poet, when the door burst suddenly open, and the director appeared on the threshold.

"How dare you recite verses!" he exclaimed with a furious gesture. "Know you not that absolute silence must reign here? I will have you put in irons."

"I have already finished my probation term,* and accord-

---

* A preliminary period lasting several years, during which the prisoner is treated with the greatest severity.

ing to the law I can no longer be put in irons," answered the prisoner, courteously, "and the less so that I am ill : you can ask the doctor."

"Ah ! you want to discuss," cried Cerberus; "very well ! I will teach you the law. Bring the irons at once."

The irons were brought, the young man seized, hustled about, dragged to the office and manacled.

Another incident of the same kind (the victim in this instance being Alexandroff) befell in the month of June, 1877. Towards nightfall the song of some peasants returning from their work was heard in the distance. The song found an echo in the aching heart of the prisoner. For a moment he forgets himself and commits a dire offence—he sings. Informed of this extraordinary fact, the all-powerful master hurries in person to the scene of the crime. The criminal has long been silent, and is lying on his bed—*i. e.*, on a piece of felt without covering or pillow. He gets up.

"Who allowed you to sing ? Answer ! Ah, you forget who and where you are ! Well, I will remind you."

Before the prisoner, taken aback by this unexpected address, had time to answer a single word, the director gave him a blow on the face, accompanying the cowardly deed with a volley of oaths.

On another occasion Grizelevsky flew at Gerasimoff, formerly a student.

"What," he shouted, "you have dared to be rude to a gaoler ?"

"I said nothing rude, sir," answered Gerasimoff, quietly.

"But you treated him as an equal, and he is your immediate superior, whom you are bound to venerate and respect. Do you hear ? Venerate and respect. You are always to remember that you are not a man, but a convict, that you are not free, but in gaol. You have no right to expect being treated with deference. If a stick is set up before you, and you are told to bow down to it, you must do so without a word. Do not forget what I have told you, for if another time you allow yourself to be impertinent to your warder, I will skin you from head to foot with rods. Do you understand? From head to foot!"

And for what offence had the poor prisoner incurred these brutal threats and vile insults? Because he, the convict, had not yet learnt to treat his warder, a common illiterate soldier, with sufficient veneration, and because in answer to the latter's question, "What do you want?" answered, "Bring* me some water," instead of, "Would you have the goodness to bring me some water?"

It might be supposed that walking being a pleasure and not a duty, the prisoners would be free to walk or not as they might think fit. But when the same Gerasimoff, being rather late, and exasperated by the brutal calls of the gaoler, refused to go out, the director, on being informed of this act of insubordination, gave him the following paternal advice: "Why do you not obey the gaoler? If you are shut up—you must remain; ordered to go out—you must go; if told to walk—you must walk. That is all you have to do, and if you disobey, I'll have you flogged."

I will not tire my readers by multiplying these descriptions. I will only beg them to stop one moment at this last cell. The inmate is an old man, and if he were not without beard and moustache and his head half shaven (as stupid and barbarous a practice as that of mutilating the face), it would be seen that his hair is grey. His hands are in gyves, he is dressed in a grey jacket, and sits near the table, absorbed in melancholy thought. And then from behind a rough voice bids him "Good-day." He rises, and slightly bowing his head, answers "Good-day, sir."

---

* Speaking to him in the 2d per. sing. *Tutoiement* of prisoners by gaolers is universal, but the prisoner must never so address any of the officials, not even common warders.

Could there be anything more polite and modest? And yet this quiet answer infuriates the foul-mouthed director.

"How dare you answer me thus, beast that you are?" he cries. "Do you forget that I am your superior?"

And this because, according to the military rule, soldiers are not allowed to answer their superior officers as men do among themselves. They have to say, "I hope you are well," adding the title of the officer. For this infraction of the rules Elczki (it is he of whom I speak) was thrown into the punishment cell. Has the English reader any idea what punishment cells in the Central Prisons are like? They are cages at the back of the *cabinets d'aisance*, and so dark and so narrow that they look, without exaggeration, like coffins—coffins, moreover, that for a man of middle height would be far too small. Prisoners cannot stand upright in them, and after a few days in this fetid hole even a strong man is seized with giddiness, is unable to stand, and seems to have passed through a serious illness.

Even when they are innocent of offence, Grizelevsky does not leave his victims in peace. Either out of pure malice, or without any motive whatever, he is always annoying and tormenting them. One day, when he was visiting the cells, he found on a prisoner's table a French exercise book he himself had permitted the man to have.

"What!" he said with a cynical laugh, "you are learning French, are you? To prepare for a journey to Switzerland, I suppose?"

And he took the book away with him, thus robbing the wretched captive of a priceless solace, and depriving him of an occupation which, by exercising his mind, helped him to support the heavy burden of his solitude. If you had asked the creature why he did this—why he so harshly withdrew a favor which he had only just granted, he would have been unable to answer you, except that he so acted because it pleased him. It was a sudden caprice; he wanted to show the prisoner his power. When he is in a particularly bad humor, or things have gone wrong at home, he orders the sick to be deprived of their beds (sick prisoners are allowed a mattress, a counterpane, and a pillow), leaving them only the felt rug, which is the normal sleeping accommodation of the political prisoners of Belgorod.

But, it may be urged, these are merely tyrannical eccentricities of a brutal and ignorant soldier, demoralized by despotic power and left without control. The superior administrators cannot possibly know of these doings; if they did, they would surely put a stop to them.

Let us go a step higher, then.

The person immediately above the director is the governor of the province. For some slight infraction of the rules the director ordered a political prisoner, affected with consumption, and who had finished his "probation time," to be put in irons. Exasperated by this cruelty, several of his companions had the audacity to inform the director that they would complain to the governor of his brutal and unjust conduct, giving all the facts, etc. The director could not stop a letter to his superior, but he could punish the prisoners for writing it. So he deprived them of books, forbade several to go out for exercise, and shortened the exercise time for others. Finally, he had the sky-lights in the cell-doors, used for purposes of ventilation, closed and nailed down. When Seriakow, who was ill, said he could not breathe, the director expressed the wish that he might choke as quickly as possible.

But most interesting of all was the decision of the governor. While admitting that the director had *no right to* put a prisoner who had served his probation time in irons, he nevertheless ordered him, together with *all the other prisoners* who had signed the petition, to be manacled, on the ground that they had insulted the director by their complaint; and gave them each, further, from one to three days in the black-hole!

Let us go another step higher.

In the summer of 1877, the Minister of Justice visited the prison of Belgorod in person. He entered the cell of Plotnikoff, who was almost dying, and who told him, if the horrible conditions of actual prison *régime* were not changed, all the prisoners would ere long pass from this provisional to an eternal tomb. On this, Count Pahlen, with the deliberation and German accent peculiar to him, pronounced these ferocious words: "So much the better! Suffer! You have done Russia much harm."

At this epoch, be it remembered, the Russian Socialists had done nothing more than distribute Socialist pamphlets! For no Terrorist, properly speaking, was ever sent to the Central Prison. The last group of political convicts for which Novo-Belgorod opened its doors, were the condemned of the Kovalsky trial — Svitych, Vitashevsky, and two others.*

With the setting in of the Terrorist period, the position of the prisoners of Novo-Belgorod became more and more intolerable. The Government looked on them as hostages, and after every blow struck by the Terrorists, discharged on their devoted heads all the vials of its impotent rage.

---

* To be quite exact, I should say that these men cannot fairly be described as propagandists; on the other hand, they were certainly not Terrorists. Though more than the one, they were less than the other. They came to the front during the short interval between the end of the propagandist and the beginning of the terrorist periods. Before deciding to punish, by attacks on the agents of authority, deeds such as those I have been describing, and preventing the infliction of further cruelties on their friends, the revolutionary party resolved to take the defensive, and resist the police whenever the latter sought to arrest them. This was the time when defence of the domicile by force of arms was proclaimed as a duty. The offence of Svitych and Vitashevsky was taking part in one of these acts of resistance.

"You shall pay dearly for this," said, on each occasion, the director.

When Mezenzoff was killed, all their books were taken away; when Krapotkin was killed, they were put in irons; and when somebody else was killed, all the prisoners' parents were exiled from the province of Kharkoff, and forbidden to return to their homes. After the first attempt on the Emperor's life some of these unfortunates were even sent to Siberia.

Another piece of petty torture by which the prisoners were vicariously punished, was closing the ventilating orifices in their cells. In the end nearly all were closed, and they could hardly breathe. It seemed as if the director wanted to suffocate them.

In short, the system adopted in the Central Prison is substantially the same as that practised in the House of Preventative Detention. The same isolation, the same denial of opportunity for active exercise, the same deprivation of useful work, mental and physical, followed by the same results—loss of health, phthisis, scurvy, and general bodily decay; with this difference, that prisoners awaiting their trial may cherish hopes of acquittal, and when brought up for judgment can expose the hardships they have endured, and stigmatize as they desire those by whom they were inflicted. But the others have no such consolation; hope for them is no more; protest they cannot, and complaint serves only to intensify their sufferings. Altogether at the mercy of their gaolers, they are continually vexed with brutalities and overwhelmed with insults. At the capital, moreover, prisoners under preventative detention can communicate secretly with their friends outside, and are cheered by the expectation of meeting their enemies face to face, as warriors are cheered when they look forward to the day of battle. The others have none of these advantages; cut off from human fellowship, and oppressed with the deadly monotony of their sombre existence, infirm in health and weakened in mind, they have nothing to look forward to but a life of suffering and death before the expiration of their sentence.

I have already called attention to the effects on the health of prisoners of the system of solitary confinement, as practised in the House of Detention. At Novo-Belgorod, where the conditions are much less favorable, the consequences are naturally far more deplorable. Phthisis and typhoid fever are always among them. If a half or three-quarters of them still survive, their survival is in no wise due to the care or tenderness of their custodians, who have left nothing undone to shorten their days, but to the fine climate and salubrious air with which nature has blessed the Ukraine, the land of their captivity. Nevertheless, of the twenty young men in the prime of life—their ages ranging from twenty-three to thirty—six have gone to their long home since their incarceration in the Central Prison some four years ago. Five died within the prison walls; the sixth (Dmokhovsky) succumbed while being conveyed to the bagnios of Siberia. But the most terrible scourge endured by the victims of solitary confinement, a scourge against which favorable climatic conditions are of no avail, is insanity. At the time when the second of our chroniclers completed his memoir he says that in the right-hand cells, one of which he occupied, there were five madmen among fourteen inmates —more than a third. He gives their names—Plotnikoff, Donezky, Botcharoff, Bogoluboff, and Sokolovsky. The two first were melancholy mad; the three others raving lunatics, who filled the little cellular prison with fierce howlings and wild cries, heartrending sobs and maniacal laughter. Words cannot picture, the imagination is powerless to conceive, the horror of life in that bedlam for those who, though still of sound mind, are continually haunted by the fear that their stricken companions' fate will soon be theirs, and see ever before them the shadow of their coming doom. All their efforts—and, as may be supposed, they were urgent and persistent—to obtain the removal of the unfortunates to an asylum were for a long time fruitless, and never entirely succeeded. Botcharoff, one of the more violent lunatics, remained months in his cell raving mad before they took him away, and it was only after long importuning, both on the part of the doctor and the prisoners, that the director allowed him to be transferred—but not to an asylum, only to the neighboring central prison of Borisoglebsk, where he shortly afterwards died. As for Gamoff, they took not the least trouble about him, and he died mad in his cell. Plotnikoff, it is true, was removed to an asylum, but only when his state had become so desperate that it was evident he had not long to live, and he survived his removal only a few weeks.

And this is not the worst. The way in which these poor lunatics are treated by the officers of the prison is barbarous beyond belief. An access of madness is punished as if it were an act of wilful insubordination. They are kicked and cuffed without mercy, and, when they persist in making a noise, thrown violently down on the floor of their cells and compelled to lie there. This within the hearing of the other prisoners, who are rendered still more wretched by the spectacle of so much suffering and cruelty, and the consciousness of their inability either to prevent the one or avenge the other.

The insane receive no indulgence in matters of discipline. They are compelled to observe the same rules as the sane, and undergo the same penalties for neglect or disobedience. Boguloboff, condemned, for the part he took in the demonstration in Kazan Place, to fifteen years' hard labor (the same who was flogged by order of General Trepoff, and avenged by the pistol of Vera Zassoulitch), had a fixed idea that everybody about him was in a conspiracy to take his life. Yet he was compelled to be shaved just as the others were. When the barber came to perform his offices the poor wretch screamed with terror and resisted with the fury of despair. But it was of no use. The warders throttled and pinioned him, and he was shaved whether he would or no.

When in April, 1879, a general, deputed by the new governor of the province, made an official visit to the Central Prison, asked the prisoners the stereotyped question, "Have you anything to say to me—any request to make?" one of the Circassians, Prince Zizianoff, made this answer:

"Yes, General. I ask a favor which you may easily grant. I ask to be condemned to death. Living here—which means slowly dying—is more than I can bear. I beseech you to put me out of my misery. I beg of you to let me die."

This answer, which I translate literally, is a full summing up, a complete picture. Comment were useless.

So we leave the Central Prison, with its horrors and sufferings, its martyred prisoners and tyrant gaolers; and I invite the reader to accompany me to another region and other scenes. But I warn him to brace up his nerves, for the tale I am about to unfold is still more terrible than that to which he has just listened.

CHAPTER XIX.

THE TROUBETZKOI RAVELIN.

On the banks of the Neva, over against the Imperial Palace, stands the Russian Bastile—the Fortress of Peter and Paul. An immense building, wide and flat, surmounted by a meagre, tapering, attenuated spire like the end of a gigantic syringe. As it is situate between the two quarters of the town, the public may, during the day, pass through the fortress, entering by a narrow defile of sombre and tortuous vaults, occupied by sentinels, with the images of saints, holding burning tapers, in the niches. But at sunset all is closed, and when night broods over the capital, and thousands of lights illumine the quays of the swift-flowing Neva, the fortress alone remains in darkness, like a huge black maw ever open to swallow up all that is noblest and best in the unhappy city and country which it curses with its presence. No living sound comes to break the grim silence that hangs over this place of desolation. And yet the lugubrious edifice has a voice that vibrates far beyond this vast tomb of unknown martyrs, buried by night in the ditches, far beyond the *oubliettes*, where lie those whose turn is to come next. Every quarter of an hour the prison clock repeats a tedious irritating air, always the same—a psalm in praise of the Tzar.

Here, indeed, is the altar of despotism. From its very foundations the Fortress of Peter and Paul has been the principal political prison of the empire. But there is a wide difference in the character and position of the unfortunates who have been its involuntary tenants. In past centuries the chief sojourners were court-conspirators on their way to Siberia or the scaffold. One of the first was the unhappy Prince Alexis, son of Peter the Great, presumptive heir to the crown. They still show you the cell where the poor wretch, after being put to the torture, was strangled by his father's order. Then came generals, senators, princes, and princesses; among others the celebrated Tarakanova, drowned during the floods that inundated the subterranean cells of the fortress. Since the definitive establishment of the present dynasty, at the end of the last century, palace conspiracies and *coups d'état* have ceased. The fortress remained empty till 1825, when it received the *élite* of the Russian nobility and army—the Decembrists, who had not sought to overthrow one man in order to put themselves in his place, but to destroy the principle of autocracy itself.

Two generations passed—and again the picture is changed. Discontent with the present *régime* has deepened and spread among all classes. It is no longer the army, but the flower of the Russian people that is rising against despotism; it is no longer an isolated attack, but an implacable war, without truce or intermission, between the Russian nation and its Government. The fortress is crowded with prisoners. During the last twenty years hundreds have passed through it, and are being followed by more hundreds, without pause or let.

But until lately the fortress was a "preventive" rather than a penitentiary prison; those accused of political crimes were kept here pending their trial, after which they were usually sent to the bagnios of Siberia. There has, nevertheless, been here at all times a certain number of prisoners—and these the most wretched and rigorously guarded—sent without any formality of trial, simply on a personal order of the Tzar, and kept in prison for years together, often for life.

In the ravelin of Alexis there is, or was in 1883, a mysterious prisoner, a woman dying of consumption, of whom no one—neither gaolers nor political prisoners—knows the crime or even the name, and who in the prison registers is merely designated by the number of the cell she occupies.

In the not very remote past, before the bureaucracy had succeeded in destroying all individuality, even in the despotism itself, the number of prisoners in the last-named category was much greater than at present. The fortress, with its flinty dungeons, was always ready to swallow up all who might make themselves disagreeable to the master of the hour. For Russia, being a Christian country, there were scruples about adopting the rough Oriental expedient of sewing up objectionable persons in canvas bags and casting them into the sea. In the course of ages, and under a despotic *régime*, this use of Peter and Paul naturally became more frequent and regular, and its advantages better understood. The point never lost sight of was the necessity of seeing that those who were buried alive in its gloomy recesses, depositaries of dark and shameful secrets, both of the masters and their acolytes, should never have the chance of revealing them to living soul. Hence the practice of covering a man's identity with a number as with an iron mask, and concealing his name, origin, and antecedents, a practice, however, of ancient date. Those of our historians who are allowed to search the archives of the secret police often find orders for the incarceration and detention of persons whose names the director of the fortress is forbidden, at his peril, to demand, or to ask any questions concerning them. The warders who took one of these men his food went in fear, and hastened away as quickly as possible, lest a chance word spoken by the mysterious prisoner might bring him into the torture chamber of the suspicious secret chancellery.

No wonder that there has always been an abundance of strange stories and fantastic rumors about this awesome prison-house, and that the popular imagination, taking hold of them, has added legend to legend. One arose out of the revolt of the Decembrists, which, as the people believed, was favored by the Tzar's eldest brother, the Grand Duke Constantine, heir-presumptive to the throne, and to whom the country swore allegiance before it became known that he had secretly abdicated in favor of Nicolas. The rising created the myth of the Grand Duke being shut up in the fortress, a gray, decrepit old man, with a long white beard reaching to his knees, whose one thought and desire was to redeem the peasants from slavery. Years after the real Constantine, who led a savage and brutal life, had joined his ancestors, the legend still lived in the popular imagination.

But the spirit of the age, and the crowds who now fill the fortress, are not propitious for the creation of phantoms, and myth and legend are evolved no more. The reality is enough. On the other hand, the habits and ideas formed during a century and a half have been transmitted from one generation of gaolers to another, all animated by the same spirit. In the officers of the fortress the Government possesses an incomparable staff of warders, as well fitted for their duties as the mutes of some Grand Signior's seraglio.

The fortress differs from most other gaols, in that everything about it—*personnel*, organization, and description—are strictly military. There are no civil and salaried warders, as in the Preventative and Central Prisons. All the duties are performed by soldiers and gendarmes, over whose heads is ever hanging the Damocles sword of the military code. The charge over prisoners, whom it is desired to keep strictly in solitary confinement, is confided to gaolers carefully selected from among their fellows by a system of supervision and mutual espionage. This is the more easily done as the fortress, like all similar constructions built on the design of Vauban, is divided into bastions, curtains, and ravelins, every one of which forms a totally distinct prison, with its own director and staff of warders, who are never changed, live quite by themselves, and seldom come in contact with any officers of the prison not belonging to their own section.

The fortress, moreover, differs from other prisons in the details of its organization, the strictness of its supervision, and the severity of its discipline. Thus, whilst in most other gaols it is considered sufficient to prevent prisoners from communicating with each other, in the fortress they are not allowed to communicate even with the warders. The latter are forbidden to answer any question put to them by a prisoner, however trivial or innocent it may be. A friendly greeting, an observation on the weather, an inquiry about the hour, it is all the same—no answer. In silence they come to your wicket, in silence they hand in your bread, in silence they depart. At the time fixed for the daily walk they open in silence your cell door, and in silence lead you to the yard set apart for exercise. Silently they watch you take your "solitary constitutional," and when it is finished, reconduct you to your cell without having once opened their mouths. "They," because there are always two, the warders of the fortress being absolutely forbidden to enter a prisoner's cell, or even go near a prisoner, under any pretext whatever, except in pairs. The advantages of this regulation are self-evident; it acts as a check, as well on prisoners as on officers, and facilitates that system of mutual espionage among the members of its staff which is one of the most characteristic features of the Russian Bastile.

The vast size of the building and its peculiar construction enable the Government to do here what they have vainly attempted to do elsewhere—completely isolate the prisoners among themselves. In the House of Preventative Detention the numerous iron pipes which run through every part of the building, permit the inmates, even when separated by a considerable interval, to exchange messages ; while in the Central Prison the cells are so small and the walls so thin that it is impossible to prevent the prisoners from talking by raps and, when they accidentally meet, by spoken words. In the fortress it is altogether different. The walls of the casements, laid in concrete and built of brick, are of a thickness that renders audible rappings, and consequently communications, almost impossible. To make them altogether so it was at one time (1877-8) proposed to deaden the sounds by coating the walls with felt. But as the adoption of this expedient, besides being expensive, would have made the cells drier and warmer, and the prisoners more comfortable, it was renounced in favor of a plan which possessed neither of these drawbacks. Prisoners were put only in every alternate cell, the intervening cells being either left empty or occupied by gendarmes. This entailed some reduction in the number of their inmates ; but the fortress is very large, and those who remained were better cloistered. As to prisoners whom it was desired to isolate absolutely, special arrangements were made.

To give an idea how complete these arrangements are, how well the great State prison of the Tzar keeps its secrets, a single example will suffice. Netchaef, surrendered by Switzerland, and condemned as an ordinary law-breaker to twenty years at the hulks, instead of being sent thither, was sent to the fortress (1872), and so closely guarded and immured that for seven years none of his friends knew what had become of him ; albeit during this period incessant inquiries were made by many who were interested in his fate, and hundreds of prisoners entered and left the fortress. Not until 1880 was the place of his reclusion discovered, through the intermediation of Shiraeff, a prisoner in the Alexis ravelin, who had secret relations with the outer world, and to whom Netchaef, who was also confined in the ravelin, had contrived to send a message by a friendly gaoler.

As may be supposed, the treatment of prisoners incarcerated in this Russian Bastile does not err on the side of leniency, nor did it become more humane during the last Terrorist period, which was precisely the time when its dark and lonesome cells received the greatest number of inmates. If in the Central Prison, thousands of miles from the scene of action, the propagandists were made to "pay dearly" for every Terrorist attempt, it may be taken for granted that those of them who were in bonds at St. Petersburg would not fare better at the hands of their enemies. As a matter of fact, they fared worse. They were the victims of every sort of insult and violence, the commission of which was regarded as proof of loyalty and official zeal, and their complaints—if they had dared to make any—would either have passed unheeded or been answered by an insulting laugh or a cynical sneer.

But there is always a lowest depth, and in the place of torment which the fortress in these later days has become, a dungeon-house—human slaughter-house, rather—has recently been contrived, the horrors of which surpass anything that Englishmen can imagine. This is the Troubetzkoi ravelin. It is not a preventative prison where suspected people await judgment, but a penitential gaol where convicts condemned for life or very long terms are confined and punished—a sort of bagnio to which are consigned those for whom the bagnios of Siberia or the cells of the Central Prisons are not considered sufficiently severe. Hither, too, are sent the Terrorists, whom their great numbers hindered from being hanged. Converted to its present purpose towards the end of 1881, or about the beginning of 1882, this dungeon within a dungeon has from the first been placed under the most rigorous supervision, and strict precautions taken to prevent knowledge of what goes on in its dark interior from coming to light. Three letters from prisoners have nevertheless passed the barriers, and reached the hands for which they were destined. They tell a tale which has thrilled educated Russia with pity and indignation, and reveal horrors to match which in Western Europe we must go back centuries. Two of these letters were written in haste and very briefly; they are little more than heartrending cries of suffering and despair. The third and most important is long and full of detail. It was printed forthwith in the clandestine press of the *Narodnaia Volia* under the title of, "Torture at the Bagnio of St. Petersburg in 1883." Though he had contrived to get a pen and some paper, the writer was compelled to write with his own blood, which (in the absence of a knife) he obtained by biting his flesh. This is a common device in Russian prisons, and we often receive letters written not alone metaphorically, but literally, with their author's blood. It was this blood-written letter that so deeply moved the lettered public of St. Petersburg, and from which some extracts appeared in the columns of the *Times* in June, 1884. To this very blood-written letter (which I have had in my hands), supplemented by information given by the two other letters, I am indebted for the following particulars.

Prisoners are generally transferred to the Troubetzkoi ravelin a few weeks after their conviction. You are told one fine morning, at a time perhaps when you are in daily expectation of being sent to Siberia, that you must change your cell. You are ordered to don a regular convict suit, the principal garment of which is a gray coat, ornamented with a yellow ace. Preceded by one gendarme and followed by another, you are then led through a maze of passages, corridors and vaults, until a door, which seems to open into the wall, is reached. Here your conductors stop, the door is opened, and you are told to enter. For a minute or two you can see nothing, so deep is the gloom. The coldness of the place chills you to the bone; and there is a damp mouldy smell like that of a charnel house or an ill-ventilated cellar. The only light comes from a little dormer window, looking toward the counterscarp of the bastion. The panes are dark gray, being overlaid with a thick covering of dust, which seems to have lain there for ages. When your eyes have become accustomed to the obscurity, you perceive that you are the tenant of a cell a few paces wide and long. In one corner is a bed of straw, with a woollen counterpane—as thin as paper—nothing else. At the foot of the bed stands a high wooden pail with a cover. This is the *parashka*, which later on will poison you with foul stenches. For the prisoners of the Troubetzkoi bastion are not allowed to leave their cells for any purpose whatever, either night or day (except for the regulation exercise), and the *parashka* is often left unemptied for days together. You are thus obliged to live, sleep, eat and drink in an atmosphere reeking with corruption and fatal to health. In your other cell you had a few requisites, generally considered indispensable for all men above the level of savages, such as a comb, a hair-brush, and a piece of soap. You were also allowed to have a few books, and a little tea and sugar, obtained, of course, at your own expense. Here you are denied even these poor luxuries, for by the rules of the Troubetzkoi ravelin prisoners are forbidden the possession of any object whatever not given to them by the administration, and as the administration gives neither tea nor sugar, neither brush nor comb nor soap, you cannot have them. Worse still is the deprivation of books. In no part of the fortress may books be brought from without. Ordinary prisoners must content themselves during all the years of their solitary confinement with such as are contained in the prison library, a few hundred volumes, consisting, for the most part, of magazines dating from the first quarter of the century. But to the doomed captive of the Troubetzkoi—doomed to a fate worse than death—are interdicted books of every sort. "They may not read even the Bible," says the letter. No occupation, either mental or manual, beguiles the wretched monotony of their lives. The least distraction, the most trifling amusement, is as strictly forbidden to them as if it were an attempt to rob their gaolers, who exact from their victims all the suffering which it is in the power of the latter to give. A prisoner, named Zoubkovski, having made some cubes of bread crumbs wherewith to construct geometric figures, they were taken from him by the gendarmes, on the ground that a prison was not a place of amusement. According to the regulations, the prisoners of the Troubetzkoi should have precisely the same amount of walking exercise as any other prisoners of the fortress. In point of fact, however, they are taken out only every forty-eight hours, to breathe the fresh air for ten minutes—never longer—and it sometimes happens to them to be left three and four consecutive days in the fetid atmosphere without break, as would appear for no other cause but the neglect of the warders.

The rations allowed by the Government are quite insufficient, and of poor quality; but, bad as they are, the prisoners do not get them, for the purveyors (who are also managers of the prison), in order to economize on the official allowance, buy the worst and cheapest food they can lay their hands on—of course stealing the difference.* The flour is always bad, the meat seldom fresh. In order to make the bread weigh heavier, it is so insufficiently baked, that even the crust is hardly eatable, and when the inside of a loaf is thrown against the wall, it sticks there like

---

* In past times things were managed differently. The fortress, being then an aristocratic prison, the prisoners had dinners of three courses, with white bread and even wine, and the linen was clean and fine. This went on, by routine, after the aristocratic prisoners were succeeded by the first Nihilists. But towards the latter end of the last Tzar's reign the fortress was democratized, and placed on the same footing as all the other prisons.

mortar. Here is the daily *menu* of a Troubetzkoi prisoner: Three pounds of black bread, quality as described; in the morning, a jug of yellowish water, supposed to be tea; at 11 o'clock, half a jug of kvas;* at noon, a plate of soup made of bread crusts and sour cabbages, porridge of damaged Indian meal, and—except a few bits of meat, never exceeding three-quarters of an ounce, mixed with the soup—nothing more; in the evening, another plate of sour soup, much diluted with water and without the least trace of meat.

The prison is no better warmed than the prisoners are fed, a terrible hardship at sixty degrees of north latitude in the winter time. The cells are always cold, the walls always damp. When the inspector makes his round he never takes off his fur pelisse. The prisoners, who have no furs, shiver even in their beds, and all through the long winter their hands and feet feel like lumps of ice. Even in summer the prisoners are not in much better plight, for during the warmer months St. Petersburg, built on a marsh, is more unhealthy than at any other time. The unfavorable hygienic conditions of the fortress, the dampness of the cells, the lack of sunlight, the continual presence of the malodorous *parashka*, the bad and scanty food (worse in summer than in winter), aggravate the misery of the prisoners and fatally injure their health. The mortality among them is frightful. The most robust are unable to resist the unwholesome influence to which they are exposed; they wither like flowers deprived of water and air. While their bodies lose flesh, their faces become swollen and blotched, and the extremities, especially the hands, are in a continual nervous tremble. It might be supposed that the deprivation of books and the gloom of their cells would tend to preserve their eyesight. But it is the very reverse. Their eyes be-

---

* The national drink; a sort of sour cider, or rather, acidulated water.

come inflamed, the lids swell and are opened only with great difficulty. But the maladies most fatal and frequent—which cause the greatest mortality and entail the most cruel suffering—are dysentery and scurvy, both caused solely by the insufficient and unsuitable dietary of the prison. Yet the sick are treated in exactly the same way as the whole; get the same food—same sodden black bread, same sham tea, even the same sour soup, which in their condition is nothing less than poison. No wonder that under such a regimen and without proper care—without any care at all—patients suffering from these disorders die quickly. They lose the use of their legs, they cannot reach the *parashka*, the warders refuse to change the straw of their wretched beds, and they are left to perish and rot in their own corruption. But these are horrors that defy description—that only the pen of a Dante could adequately portray.

"Oh, if you could see our sick!" exclaims the writer of the blood-written letter. "A year ago they were young, healthy, and robust. Now they are bowed and decrepit old men, hardly able to walk. Several of them cannot rise from their beds. Covered with vermin, and eaten up with scurvy, they emit an odor like that of a corpse."

"But is there no doctor?" it may be asked; and "What is he doing all this time?" Yes, there is a doctor; there are even two doctors. One, however, is past fourscore and past work. He comes to the fortress only occasionally. The other is young, and probably kind enough in intention, but not very resolute in character, and standing in great awe of the officers of the gaol. When he visits his patients he is invariably accompanied by a brace of gendarmes, lest he should surreptitiously convey letters to prisoners. He enters a cell with a troubled countenance, as if he were afraid of something; never goes further than the threshold, much less approaches the sick man's bed or makes any examination of him, feels his pulse or looks at his tongue.

After asking a few questions he delivers his verdict, which is almost always couched in the same words: "For your illness there is no cure."

And what better can the poor man do—what else say? According to the regulations enforced in the Troubetzkoi no indulgence can be shown to the sick; they must have the same food as the others—or none; no extra service is offered, no nurses are allowed them. The water is, moreover, so bad that, if other conditions were favorable, this cause alone would almost render recovery hopeless.

"No mercy is shown even to the mad," says another of the letters, "and you may imagine how many such there are in our Golgotha. They are not sent to any asylum, but shut up in their cells and kept in order with whip and scourge. Often you hear down below you, or at some little distance, the sound of heart-rending shrieks, cries, and groans. It is some wretched lunatic, who is being flogged into obedience."

The following extracts from the Troubetzkoi regulations fully confirm the prisoners' statements concerning the stringency of the discipline imposed upon them, and the barbarous treatment to which they are exposed:

"Prisoners of the Troubetzkoi, as bagnio slaves, are placed under the administration of the fortress. For slight offences the administration may order a prisoner to be put from one to six days in a penal cell, on a diet of bread and water, or sentence him to corporal punishment, the said corporal punishment to consist of not more than 20 stripes of the knout, or 100 strokes with a whip. In cases of serious offences (attempted escape, or resistance to authority) the culprit is relegated to the military tribunal, which may order the infliction of 100 stripes of the knout, 100 strokes with a whip, and as many as 8,000 blows with a stick."

Thus the political prisoners of the Troubetzkoi ravelin, mostly men of culture and refinement, and belonging to the higher grades of society, have ever before them the possibility of being compelled to undergo corporal punishment in its cruellest and most degrading form. "We have every reason to believe," says one of the letters in question, "that the threat (of a flogging) is no empty one. Zlatopolsky was flogged for carrying on a secret correspondence with the help of a gendarme."

"Is it possible to remain quiet," exclaims the writer of another letter, "while the menace of such an outrage hangs continually over your head; while every cry you hear makes you feel as if one of your friends was being knouted before your eyes!"

Nor is this the worst. There are women in the Troubetzkoi.

"What is most frightful," continues the writer, "is the position of the women, condemned like ourselves. Like us, they are at the mercy of their gaoler's caprices. No consideration is shown their sex. Their beds, like ours, are searched every day by men. The linen which they have just taken off is examined, at all times, by gendarmes. Nor is this all. Gendarmes may enter their cells day or night, just as they please. It is true that a rule forbids one gendarme to enter the prisoners' cells save in the company of another gendarme. But who cares for the infraction of such a rule? The relations between the various gaolers being of the most cordial nature, nothing is easier for them than to come to an understanding among themselves. Cases of rape are therefore very possible. At any rate attempts of this sort are common enough. Quite recently a young girl (one of the accused in the Odessa trial, L. Terentieva), has died most mysteriously. It is reported that she was poisoned by some venomous substance, administered by mistake in her medicine. There was, however, a rumor that this unhappy young girl, after being violated, was poisoned to prevent her from exposing the crime. It is, at any rate, certain that her death was for a long time kept secret from the superior police and gendarmery, that no inquiry has been instituted, and that the doctors have retained their posts."

Such are the horrors of prison life in the Troubetzkoi ravelin!

Shut out from all, surrounded by cruel and insolent gaolers, who never speak except, perchance, to answer a harmless question with a gross insult, the captives become at last utterly cowed and moodily silent, living in their lonesome dens without a thought, without a future, and without a hope. If a prisoner can hold no secret communication with his friends, he loses count of the days, then of the weeks, then of the months. If he be sick and unable to leave his cell for exercise, he even ceases to observe the seasons; for whatever may be the weather outside, his dreary abode is always cold, gloomy, and damp, and his existence becomes a chaos which can end only in madness or death.

And even yet all the terrors of the Troubetzkoi are not told.

Under the first floor, and below the level of the Neva, are other cells far worse than those I have described—real underground vaults, dark at noonday and infested with loathsome vermin. They are the condemned cells, provided by the Government for those it most hates, and whom it has doomed to die either in lonesome darkness, or on the scaffold and in the light of day. Let us see what the letter has to say about this pandemonium:

"The small windows are on a level with the river, which overflows them when the Neva rises. The thick iron bars of the grating, covered with dirt, shut out most of the little light that else might filter through these holes. If the rays of the sun never enter the cells of the upper floor, it may easily be imagined what darkness reigns below. The walls are mouldering, and dirty water continually drops from them. But most terrible are the rats. In the brick floors *large holes have been left open for the rats to pass through.* I express myself thus intentionally. Nothing would be easier than to block up these holes, and yet the reiterated demands of the prisoners have always been passed by unnoticed, so that the rats enter by scores, try to climb upon the beds and to bite the prisoners. It is in these hideous dungeons that the condemned to death spend their last hours. Kviatkovsky, Presniakoff, Scukanoff, passed their last nights here. At the present moment, among others, there is a woman, with a little child at her breast. This is Jakimova. Night and day she watches over her babe lest he should be devoured by the rats."

"But," I hear my readers exclaim, "can these things be? Is it possible that at the end of the nineteenth century, in a great capital which wears at least the outward semblance of civilization, deeds so monstrous and cruel can be perpetrated? These letters, written by men languishing in a wearisome captivity, and dwelling continually on their sufferings, are they not unconscious exaggerations?"

I should be glad to think so. I have no desire to paint with too dark a brush. But, as there is abundance of direct and indirect evidence to show, the statements set down by these necessarily nameless prisoners with their own blood are unfortunately only too true.*

From October 25 to 30, 1880, there were tried at St. Petersburg sixteen Terrorists, six of whom were condemned to death and eight to hard labor for different terms. Two of the former were executed and four reprieved. When the procurator, Aksharamoff, informed the four that the Emperor had been pleased to commute their sentences to penal servitude for life, his news was received with such unmistakable manifestations of disappointment and displeasure, that he retired in confusion, observing that he could not, unfortunately, change the decrees of the sovereign. And the prophetic souls of the prisoners did not deceive them. The greater part of these young and vigorous men (including those who were sentenced to hard labor) either died or went mad before they had been in the fortress two years. Isaieff, Okladsky, Zuekerman, and Martynovsky are mad, Schiraeff is dead, Tichenoff is dying.

From facts like these only one inference is possible.

What must be the system that produces so dire results!

---

* It is well to remember that the extracts from the letter in question, published in the *Times*, went the round of the European Press, and that the Russian Government has never ventured either to dispute their genuineness or disprove their statements.

Even if the blood-written letters were not there to tell us, we could have no doubt.

Another fact. On July 26, 1883, there arrived at Moscow a number of political convicts of both sexes deported to Siberia, who had been imprisoned in the Fortress of St. Peter and St. Paul; and the following is the description given by an eye-witness—eminently trustworthy—of the condition to which these prisoners, whose crimes, it should be borne in mind, despite their severe sentences, were not deemed serious, had been brought by one year's detention in the cells of the Troubetzkoi ravelin:

"The arrival of the St. Petersburg train caused great commotion amongst the officials and others who were in the station. Most of the prisoners could not alight without help, some even were unable to move. The guard wanted to transfer them straightway to our train, so as to conceal their condition from the public. But this was quite impossible. Six of the prisoners fainted outright. The others could hardly stand. On this the chief of the escort ordered litters to be brought. But as the litters could not be got into the carriages, the unconscious prisoners had to be lifted out, like corpses, and carried on men's shoulders.

"The first man brought out was Ignat Voloshenko (sentenced first to ten years' hard labor in the Osinski trial, secondly, to fifteen years' hard labor for attempting to escape from Irkoutsk, then transferred to Kara, and afterwards to the fortress, where he had been kept one year). It is difficult to describe the horrible appearance and condition of this man. Eaten up with scurvy, he was more like a putrefying corpse than a living being. Torn every moment by convulsion—dying. . . . But it is useless. I am utterly unable to speak of him more.

"After Voloshenko was lifted out Alexander Pribylev (condemned in the trial of June 17, 1882, to fifteen years' penal servitude). He had no scurvy, but long abstention from food and complete derangement of the nervous system had so reduced his strength that he could not stand and frequently fainted.

"Next came Fomin (a former military officer sentenced for life).* He looked like a corpse, and for nearly two hours several doctors tried in vain to bring him round. It was not until evening that he was sufficiently restored to resume his journey.

"Fomin's successor was Paul Orlov (first sentenced to ten years at the hulks, subsequently to twenty-one years for trying to escape, and put with Voloshenko in the fortress, where he had been kept a year). Only twenty-seven years of age and once remarkable for his stature and strength, he was now hardly recognizable. He was bent like an old man, and one of his feet was so crippled that he could scarcely walk. He had scurvy in its most terrible shape, blood was continually oozing from his gums and flowing from his mouth.

"The fifth was a woman, Tatiana Lebedeva,† whose sentence of death (February 15, 1882) had been commuted to penal servitude for life. But imprisonment for Tatiana, whether long or short, had lost its terrors. Her days were numbered, and the greatest boon her enemies could bestow on her would be speedy death. Besides being in the last stage of consumption and torn with a terrible cough, she was so eaten up with scurvy that her teeth were nearly all gone, and the flesh had fallen away, leaving her jawbones quite bare. Her aspect was that of a skeleton, partly covered with parchment-like skin, the only sign of life being her still bright black eyes.

"After Lebedeva came Yakimova, holding in her arms

---

* In 1882 he was at Geneva, a strong man, the very picture of health. —S. S.

† Some twenty-eight years of age. She was of delicate constitution, but before being arrested, in 1881, in excellent health.

an eighteen months' old babe born in the Troubetzkoi ravelin. The most hard-hearted could not look at that poor child unmoved. It seemed as if every moment would be its last. As for Yakimova, she did not appear to have suffered very much, either morally or physically, and, notwithstanding the penal servitude for life which was before her, bore herself with composure and firmness."

In view of facts like these it is impossible to delude ourselves with the hope that the pictures of their lives, drawn by the prisoners of the fortress in the letters I have cited, are in the least overdrawn, even unconsciously.

* * * * * * *

If the *régime* of preventative detention and interrogation is virtually a reproduction of the judicial tortures of the Middle Ages, that of penitential imprisonment is an altogether new and original system, begotten of the baseness and cruelty of the Russian Government. Too craven to execute men and women publicly and by the dozen, it kills by inches—yet none the less surely—those of whom, either out of policy or revenge, it desires to rid itself. Torture daily repeated is the means, death not too long delayed the end. Because, if solitary confinement at Novo-Belgorod be, as the prisoner Zizianoff avers, and there is abundant evidence to prove, *slow* death, the same cannot certainly be said of incarceration in the black holes of the Troubetzkoi.

It is a portentous fact that the system of punitive or penitential imprisonment we have described has ceased to be an exception. It is becoming generalized throughout the empire, and the Russian Government are adopting it as part of a settled policy in their dealings with political offenders. Since 1878 no political convicts have been consigned to the Central Prison, and the less seriously compromised alone are now transported to Siberia. Among the Terrorists none but those guilty of offences against State functionaries—

and chiefly those of them who are women—are sent to the northern hulks; yet not until, like Tatiana Lebedeva and others, they have been brought to death's door by a term of penitential imprisonment. And still there are exceptions, for some, like Hesse Helfmann, Vera Figner, and Ludmila Volkenstein, were kept in the fortress. Hesse died there.

As for the Terrorists implicated in plots against the Emperor (of whom the majority naturally consists), they were consigned to the fortress one and all; yet how many of them are "finished," to use a Russian expression, or are in the course of being finished, we have no means of knowing, that being one of the secrets of the prison-house.

The Fortress of Peter and Paul is great. But there is a limit to everything—even to the capacity of a Russian Bastile—and to meet the ever-increasing demand for more accommodation, the Government of Alexander III. has deemed it desirable to provide another purgatory for its political prisoners—the fortress of Schlüsselburg. It is a second Troubetzkoi—no worse—and surely nothing can be worse! What still could the Government do more?—roast its prisoners alive, or do with them as the Roman emperors were sometimes wont to do with their enemies—throw them into holes swarming with vipers?

But Schlüsselburg possesses in official eyes this priceless advantage—there is no chance of its horrors being exposed like those of the Troubetzkoi. Because Schlüsselburg is not in the middle of a great city, where there are thousands of sympathizers eager to communicate with the prisoners, and who, despite all the vigilance of the authorities, sometimes succeed in doing so. At Schlüsselburg nature herself acts as sentinel, for the new Castle of Despair is simply a huge block of granite covered with fortifications and surrounded by water. No news can be received, no secrets torn from that accursed prison. All who enter therein must abandon hope. From St. Peter and St. Paul volumes of clandestine letters have been received. The ravelins most jealously guarded—even the Alexis and the Troubetzkoi—have yielded their secrets to energy and perseverance. But from the prisoners in the Schlüsselburg—though they have been there for years—not a word, not a line ;. only vague rumors. Yet it is thither that were sent the noble heroes of the latest trials—Lieutenant-Colonel Ashenbrenner, Captain Pokitonoff, and Lieutenant Tichonovitch. In Schlüsselburg, too, they have shut up fourteen propagandists, lately returned from Siberian hulks.

Here, also, let me add, there has been immured for two years a man whose name I will not mention—the friend of my boyhood, my fellow-worker in the struggle. On the eve of his removal to the Schlüsselburg he sent to us from the depths of the Troubetzkoi ravelin this sublime farewell: "Fight on until the victory is won. For me henceforth there is but one measure ; the more they torment me in my prison the better is it with the struggle."

By what ferocious language, by what fresh tortures has he learnt the subsequent successes of his friends? Does he still continue to hear of them? Or is he, perhaps, with so many others, where there is no more to be suffered, no more to be learnt?

CHAPTER XX.

SIBERIA.

SIBERIA ! The word sends a thrill of cold through our very bones, and when we think of the unfortunate exiles lost in icy wastes and condemned to life-long servitude in chains, our hearts are moved to pity and compassion. Yet, as we have seen, this word of horror is to some people suggestive of consolation and hope. To them it is a promised land, a place of security and rest. We know, too, that thither are sent men and women who, though reduced to the last extremity, their gaolers do not as yet want quite "to finish."

What, then, is this paradise of the lost, this enigmatical Siberian place of punishment, converted by a strange evolution into a Nihilist Kurort—a revolutionary sanatorium—as in a legend of the Plutonic realm its liquid fire is said to be turned into a cool and refreshing drink?

Let us, taking the wings of imagination, cross the Uralian mountains, and flying far, far from the confines of Europe, descend in the region of Zabaikalia, beyond Lake Baikal, on the banks of the river Kara, see for ourselves what manner of life these Siberian transports lead.

But if we travel like ordinary mortals—and political convicts—we must, after leaving Irkoutsk by the Zabaikalia road, pass through Chita and Nertchinsk, celebrated for their "penitential mines," to Detensk. Here you take one of the Amour Navigation Company's steamers and journey by one of that river's affluents (the Shilke) to the little village of Oust-Kara, at the mouth of the river Kara, where there are several houses of detention for ordinary criminals and one for political convicts of the weaker sex. These prisons are detached buildings, standing on the river's bank, at intervals of from five to eight miles. All these prisons are under the general direction of a single chief; but the political prison, which consists of four buildings, has its own special organization and management. Twelve miles from Oust-Kara, and up stream, is the Lower Kara prison. Next comes that of Higher Kara; and, about the same distance further on, the Amour—that is to say, the prison on the river Amour.

A political prison is recognized by a characteristic peculiarity. Other places of the sort—those destined for ordinary convicts—have outer walls or palisades on three sides only, the fourth being unenclosed, with the front windows facing the road. Political prisons are arranged differently. Built in the middle of a court, they are surrounded on every side by walls so high that you can see only the roof. When the erection of these prisons was first proposed the architect designed them on the ordinary plan of similar structures in Siberia. But General Anutchin, at that time governor of Eastern Siberia, issued a special order that all gaols for political offenders were to be enclosed within lofty palisades in such a manner that the horizon of the inmates should be bounded by the wooden walls of their dreary abode. He thought this quite good enough for political prisoners.

The political prisons of Kara were organized at the same time as the Central Prison of Kharkoff. Their first tenants were Biberhal, Semenovsky, and others, of the first propagandists of 1872 and 1873. Next were sent thither the least compromised convicts of the trial of the 193—Sinegoub, Tcharushin, and others.

From 1879 onwards prisoners arrived in crowds. In 1882 came the twenty-eight "centralists" (Kharkoff prisoners) liberated by Loris Melikoff from their worse than Babylonian servitude. In May of that year there were at Kara more than a hundred political prisoners, not counting women.

At the beginning of their confinement the Kara prisoners were treated precisely in the same way as other convicts are treated in Siberian lock-ups. The only exception was that, whereas ordinary criminals were allowed to walk freely in the yard during the day, the others were locked up in their rooms day as well as night—save, of course, when they were at work in the mines. These mines are the Emperor's personal property, and the prisoners are employed in removing the earth which overlays the auriferous sand. At Kara, as in Siberia generally, there exists a regulation very favorable to convicts under sentence of penal servitude. After having passed a third of their time in prison "under probation," they are allowed to join a "free gang," which gives them the privilege of living outside the prison walls, in towns and villages—always on condition that they remain there. At first, political prisoners enjoyed this privilege equally with other prisoners. Sinegoub, Tcharushin, Semenovsky, and others were provisionally set free in this way. It is a matter of everyday occurrence for ordinary convicts to profit by their comparative freedom to try to escape and join the great horde of vagabonds who throng Siberian roads. But it never occurred to the administration to curtail, on this account, the privileges of those who remained, or make them jointly and severally responsible for the conduct of their comrades. As touching the politicals, however, extreme precautions were adopted. The "free gangs" of "politicals" were told that at the first attempt on the part of any of their number to escape, the "free gang" system, so far as they were concerned, would be abolished. The administration, on the other hand, undertook that, so long as the political prisoners faithfully observed the regulations, this and all the other privileges should be respected.

Though the prisoners, on their part, entered into no formal engagement to comply with these conditions, they did in effect faithfully observe them. Not once during the prevalence of the "free gang" system did there occur any disorder or any attempt to escape. Nevertheless the administration broke its word and withdrew the privileges.

This breach of faith was instigated by Loris Melikoff. At the very time the dictator was pretending to better the lot of political prisoners, posing as a man of exceptional benevolence and humanity, and, with a great flourish of trumpets, transferring people from the Central Prisons of Kharkoff and Mzensk to Kara, a peremptory order was issued withdrawing, as regarded political convicts, the "free gang" system, and remitting to gaol those who had been provisionally liberated. A strict interdict was laid on all correspondence between themselves and their kindred and friends.

The men who had only just been set at liberty, and were looking forward to permanent, if somewhat restricted freedom, had therefore to return to prison. This was very hard on the poor fellows, yet keenly as they felt the wrong they were compelled to resign themselves to their fate. The evening before they separated and went back to their cells they had a last supper. The meeting was sad, and their hearts, as may be supposed, were very heavy. For one member of the company it was indeed a last supper, and ended in a terrible tragedy. Semenovsky, maddened by despair, blew out his brains. In ill health, nervous, and with spirits broken by long confinement, the idea of returning to prison was intolerable to him. He preferred death. A man of high principle and wide culture, once an advocate in St. Petersburg, Semenovsky was sentenced on October 20, 1876, to a long term of penal servitude for simple propagandism. The administrator telegraphed the news of his tragic death to St. Petersburg. But it had no effect on the Government.

Semenovsky was buried, and his companions were again put in prison.

Nor was this all. They were not only remitted to confinement, but annoyed and teased past bearing, and harassed with all sorts of petty vexations. New restrictions were placed on the visits of the devoted wives who had followed their husbands to this far-away and dreary land. It was made more difficult for the sick to obtain admission to the hospital. But the greatest grievance of all was denying them the solace of labor. They were forbidden to work in the mines. In the spring of 1882 this privilege, for as such they esteemed it, was denied to them, a measure which greatly aggravated the hardship of their lot. The hardest labor—even the toil of the mines—was a lighter punishment than the sedentary and solitary monotony of life within the four walls of their prison house. Muscular exercise, besides doing them good physically, made time pass less slowly and more pleasantly. But all the efforts of the prisoners, and they were many, to obtain the hard work to which they were condemned proved abortive. It seemed as if the administration was resolved to let them perish slowly for want of air and exercise, like their friends in the central prisons. If we consider that most of these men were sentenced to very long terms—twenty, thirty, and even thirty-five years—it is easy to understand how ardently they must have longed for freedom, how eager they were to escape. No wonder that attempts to get away became thenceforth more frequent than before. How these attempts were dealt with by the authorities the following chapter will show.

CHAPTER XXI.

MUTUAL RESPONSIBILITY.

During the first May night of the year 1882 the sentinels of the political prison of Lower Kara noticed a man attempting to escape by the workshop window opening on the fields. Twice they fired on him, and twice they missed aim. An alarm was sounded, the prisoners were immediately mustered, and it was found that eight of them, among whom was Myshkin, had escaped. When informed by telegraph of what had come to pass, the Minister of the Interior was so angry that the governor of Zabaikalia, General Iliashevitch himself, feared that he should be dismissed for not exercising due vigilance, the more so as about ten days before he had inspected the prison together with the Senator Galkin-Vrasski, and reported everything to be in perfect order. Fearing for their places, the local administration resolved to provoke a riot among the prisoners in order to redeem their characters by its suppression, and to atone for the neglect that had caused the escape—which could then be explained by saying the rules were too lax, and that for prisoners so intractable ordinary supervision was not sufficiently severe.

On the 4th of May the prisoners were ordered, without further explanation, to shave their heads. They replied that, according to the rules they were allowed to wear their hair, and the rules being drawn up by the Minister of the Interior, he only, and not the director, had a right to change them.

On the 6th of the same month the political prisoners were officially informed that they would not be roughly dealt with, that all would go on as heretofore, and that they might make themselves easy. Five days passed in this way, and the prisoners were beginning to forget the incident. But they were reckoning without their host. The 11th of May was fixed for the riot and its suppression. About three in the morning six hundred Cossacks, under the command of General Iliashevitch himself, supported by Colonel Roudenko, surrounded the prison, occupied all the issues with platoons, and ordered the bulk of the force to rush upon the sleeping prisoners—of whom, it should be added, there were only eighty-four.

So soon as they were awake they were searched, and all their belongings, down to the merest trifles—books, clothes, combs, brushes—seized, and thrown pell-mell into a corner. This done, the prisoners were attired in convict dresses and taken into the courtyard. Here twenty-seven "promoters" and "instigators" of the "riot" were picked out, and led under the escort of Cossacks to Upper Kara, a distance of some ten miles. Encouraged by their officers, the Cossacks grossly insulted and ill-used the prisoners during the journey, and when a few tried to defend themselves, Colonel Roudenko said, "Tie their hands behind them, and if one of them says anything impertinent give him a knock on the head with the butt-end of your guns." Meantime the prison of Lower Kara was being pillaged. Before the struggle began Colonel Roudenko addressed the Cossacks thus: "If I order you to beat them, do so; if I order you to fire, shoot them. When you have taken the prison you shall have everything belonging to them." And the Cossacks, having subdued the sleeping rioters, set about pillaging their possessions. The officers, not to be outdone by their men, appropriated some of the best things—even carrying off tables, chairs, stools, which had been made by the prisoners themselves, and giving them to their friends.

After they had passed some time in the empty room, with no other clothing than the gray regulation cloaks, the deputy-director, Boutakov, appeared before the prisoners, one of whom asked:

"Is it possible that we are to remain in this state much longer?"

"Yes, always," answered Boutakov. "You were formerly treated well, but now, after these escapes, we see that your conduct——"

Orloff observed that the administration itself had provoked the escapes, not the prisoners, and that in any case it was unjust to make those who remained suffer for those who had escaped.

This modest and polite answer put the deputy-director into such a rage that he ordered the Cossacks to seize Orloff, beat him, and drag him to the punishment cell. Some of his comrades wished to prevent this, but he besought them to offer no resistance. When he was outside the door, Colonel Boutakov rushed at him, began to strike him, and ordered the Cossacks to do the same. A little later—while the prisoners were dining—the director came in person, mustered them, and told them to "get up." Some did not obey with sufficient promptitude. "Make them get up with blows," ordered the director, and a fresh summary execution began. "This is the way to muster," said he, with great satisfaction, going out after the disturbance. In the next room a similar scene was being enacted, under the command of the captain of the guard. When he entered, the student Bobokhov was lying on the plank. The captain, turning to his Cossacks, ordered them to "drag him up by the hair," and by the hair he was dragged up.

Rodionoff, quite a young man, was also beaten by the director himself, who, when he was tired, handed the victim over to his Cossacks, telling them to "give him as much as he could carry." After this Rodionoff was put into the black hole for thirty days.

This took place at Lower Kara; but the men who had

been taken to the two other prisons came off no better, save that in one instance, at Upper Kara, the soldiers, to their honor, absolutely refused to beat them. Those at the Amour prison were more complaisant, thereby suggesting Gerasimoff's grim *bon mot*, "We are beaten twice a day, and fed once."

In the summer of 1882 the Lower Kara lock-up was rebuilt on a new plan. The large common rooms were divided into small cells, where five and six men were made to sleep together on the same bed, so tightly wedged that it was difficult to move, and impossible to turn. The prisoners who had been dispersed in the other gaols were brought back (except fourteen sent to Schlüsselburg as "promoters"), and everybody was put in irons. Three were chained (the chains being fastened with rivets) to wheelbarrows, which they had, of course, to drag with them everywhere. Then, to render flight more difficult—or rather, recapture more easy—the left half of each man's head was clean shaven, an operation which was effected with some circumstance, the authorities probably fearing that the indignity might be forcibly resisted. The prisoners were called one by one into a room, as they supposed, to be questioned touching their knowledge of the escape. The victim was then surrounded by soldiers, and asked if he would submit quietly; if not they threatened to tie his hands and shave his head by force. Resistance in these circumstances was, of course, not attempted.

All the work of the prison was done by the convicts themselves; they cleaned their own rooms, washed their own linen, and prepared their own meals. But whatever they did they were under strict and continual supervision, being never left a moment to themselves. Then, as if to fill the measure of their misery to the full, a common malefactor, named Ziploff, was brought amongst them. He had carried letters between some of the political prisoners, an offence which, as the administration chose to think, qualified him for their company. Yet, so far from approving of the change, Ziploff begged and prayed to be allowed to go back to his old quarters. But the administration had other views. One day he was called into the office, charged with some trifling breach of descipline of ancient date, and ordered to be flogged. The punishment was duly inflicted under the personal supervision of Commandant Kaltourin himself. What this meant the others knew only too well. It was a warning, an intimation made in the most forcible way possible, that the political prisoners were no longer to enjoy immunity from corporal punishment; and shortly afterwards it was rumored that the fugitives, all of whom had meanwhile been recaptured (Myshkin at the very moment when he had got on board an American ship at Vladivostock, bound for San Francisco), would be publicly flogged. The cup of their sufferings, already full to the brim, now ran over. The prisoners resolved that, rather than submit to this new degradation, they would die; and, notwithstanding the desire of a considerable minority to adopt a more energetic form of protest, it was decided that they should die of hunger.

Then began a long fast, a terrible ordeal for men weakened with hardship and by confinement. All went to bed, and were soon reduced by abstinence to a state of utter prostration. In seven days they had almost lost power of speech, and could not answer to their names at roll call, a formality which takes place three times a day. Then the directors, who had hitherto cherished the hope that the prisoners, tormented by the pangs of hunger, would give up the contest, saw that matters were come to a crisis. They entered the cells, regarded in silence the inanimate forms of the sufferers, and the gravity of their looks showed how much they were concerned. Next came Commandant Kaltourin, who, after asking what they wanted, had their demands put in writing, and promised to communicate immediately by telegraph with the governor of the province, Iliaschevitch. He assured them, moreover, on his own responsibility, that there was neither truth in the rumors they had heard, nor any intention to abolish the rules which proscribed the flogging of political prisoners. But as no confirmation of this statement was received from General Iliaschevitch the voluntary famine continued. But it could not go on much longer. The fasters were on the point of death. They suffered from convulsions, sleeplessness, and dysentery. A few, who from the first had objected to this form of resistance and taken no part in it, now adjured their companions to abandon the contest before it was too late. Their persuasions, together with something else that happened of great importance—the nature of which, however, our correspondent did not feel himself at liberty to mention—prevailed at last on the strikers to terminate their fast—on the thirteenth day after it had begun. This terrible struggle, which permanently injured the health of most of the prisoners who engaged in it, had no other result than a few concessions, and a not very definite assurance from the administration that their exemption from corporal punishment would be continued.

In this way did the administration avenge on the prisoners the abortive flight of a few of their companions. Nor was this the full extent of their punishment. Sixteen men, who at the time of what is known as "the revolt of the 11th of May" had finished their term, and were entitled, according to the regulations, to become free Siberian colonists, were kept in prison another year. Even political prisoners elsewhere (Kviatkovski, Zoubrilloff, and Frangeoli), who did not even know of the escapes, were dealt with in like manner. In 1883, however, they were released, those first set free being sent as colonists to the province of Baikal. But when Shoubin, the new commandant of the political prisons, reported to Governor Iliaschevitch that the Kara prisoners still manifested "a spirit of indocility," he ordered the colonists, and thirteen others whose terms had also expired—"by way of giving them a lesson"—to be exiled to a village in the far north, the region of the polar night, among the savage Yakutes, where life is, if possible, even harder than in the prisons. This is what they call in Russia "mutual responsibility."

Among the colonists was a young woman of the name of Maria Koutitonskaia, who, after the affair of May 11th, had been released from jail and "interned" in a village of the province. That is to say, she was free to go about but not to go away. This girl-heroine resolved with her own hand to avenge the cruel outrages inflicted by the authorities on innocent and helpless prisoners. After obtaining a small revolver, she started secretly for Chita, where lived General Iliaschevitch, the Governor. Arrested as a fugitive, she was taken to Chita—exactly where she wanted to go. On her arrival thither she asked to see the Governor, saying that she wanted to explain to him personally why she had left Aksha. There being no reason why this request should not be complied with, she was taken straightway to the palace; and as General Iliaschevitch came out of his cabinet, Maria drew her revolver, and with the words, "This is the answer to the 11th of May," fired at him point blank. The ball struck the Governor in the abdomen, and he fell, badly wounded, to the ground. Maria was, of course, immediately arrested and put in prison. She was afterwards tried and condemned to death, but the Government deemed it expedient to commute this sentence to one of hard labor for life.

It is hardly necessary to say, however, that this incident had very little effect on the lot of the prisoners of Kara. The barbarities and cruelties we have described went on without surcease.

Such is life in the political prisons of Siberia, the promised land toward which revolutionists under sentence of penal servitude turn longing eyes. And it is certainly an improvement on the Fortress. On the other hand, it is very little, if any, better than detention in a Central Prison. If in this latter place of punishment the torture inflicted on prisoners is more sustained and systematic, in Siberian jails they are more exposed to the violence and brutality of warders and guards; for long-continued immunity, the absence of all control, and the evil traditions of despotism, have transformed the jailers of our hyperborean prisons into veritable tyrants. "For you I am Chief, and Tzar, and God," is a stereotyped expression in the mouths of these Cerberuses, when addressing a prisoner.

Time fails me to recount a hundredth part of the known atrocities inflicted on the victims of despotism in every part of Siberia, and on every possible pretext. And how much greater is the number of those we do not, nor ever shall know!

But an instance of the sort of treatment which women receive at the hands of the Siberian servants of the Tzar is too relevant and characteristic to be omitted.

The victim on this occasion was Olga Lioubatovitch, one of the heroines of the trial of the fifty propagandists who, as the reader may possibly remember, won to so remarkable a degree the sympathy of the public. On August 30, 1883, as Olga (who once escaped from Siberia, reached Geneva, then returned to Russia, only to fall a second time into the toils) was passing through Krasnoiarsk on her way to her destination in Eastern Siberia, she was called before the *ispravnik* (local chief of police) and ordered to change the dress she wore for the costume of a convict. But having been condemned to transportation by administrative order—not to hard labor—she had a right to wear her own clothes, and this she tried to make the *ispravnik* understand. At her first words, however, he became furious, and repeated that she must not only change her dress, but do it there and then in the bureau, before everybody. To this monstrous request Olga Lioubatovitch answered by a plump refusal. Then at a sign from the *ispravnik* his subordinates took hold of the prisoner and proceeded to undress her by force. A shameful struggle ensued. Several men set on this defenceless woman, beat her, pulled her hair, and tore off her clothes. So long as she kept her feet she defended herself as best she could, but the chief of the police by a violent kick felled her to the earth. What follows is best described in her own words:

"I fell into a kind of stupor. I remember confusedly how the heavy boot of the *ispravnik* struck my chest. Some one was pulling my hair, another was striking my face with his fists; the rest were tearing off my clothes, and at last, naked, crucified on the floor, in the presence of a crowd of men, I felt all the shame and horror of a woman violated. Alarmed by their own deed, the cowards fled, and when I recovered consciousness I saw around me only my companions, pale as death, while Fanny Moreiness was writhing in hysterical convulsions."

But enough, enough! The sufferings of the Nihilists are truly terrible, and, as being the noblest holocaust ever offered by patriots on the altar of a country's redemption, worthy of all sympathy and respect. Yet compared with the trials and sufferings of Russia at large they are only a drop—a bitter and burning drop, but not to be compared with the ocean of which they form so small a part.

Let us explore this ocean.

PART III.
ADMINISTRATIVE EXILE.

CHAPTER XXII.

INNOCENT THEREFORE PUNISHED.

The judicial procedure, of which the complete cycle—from arrest to punishment—we have already described, is far from including all the means employed by the Russian Government in its struggle with revolution.

Tribunals from their very nature must deal with facts. However great may be their severity, however willing they may be to conform to orders, impute motives, and visit trifling misdeeds with draconian punishments, they must, at least, have something to go upon. In other words, they cannot convict a man because he is innocent. If a person be found in possession of a revolutionary proclamation, or if he lends his room for revolutionary purposes, he may be condemned to death; but if no overt act, no equivocal expression, no compromising conduct whatsoever can be brought home to him, they are obliged to pronounce a verdict of acquittal. This depends not on the quality of the judges but on the nature of tribunals.

The ordinary methods of prosecution are therefore essentially circumscribed. They can be used only against offenders who have given some manifest sign of hostility to the existing system, or openly or covertly attacked the Government.

How, then, are those to be dealt with who have done none of these things, yet who, there is every reason to believe, will do them sooner or later?

Let us take an example. A man who has had secret relations with the revolutionary party and falls under suspicion is arrested, questioned, and badgered in the usual fashion, and kept in prison several months. But neither in his own admissions nor in any other way can a scintilla of evidence be found against him. In no single respect can he be considered a compromised person, and it is impossible, by any stretch of ingenuity, to include him in the indictment of those who are supposed to be his confederates and friends. So he is let out on bail, and subpœnaed as a simple witness. But by his conduct under examination and before the tribunal, by his unwillingness to testify against the accused and his eagerness to testify in their favor, he shows only too clearly that he is a sympathizer with them in spirit if not a confederate in fact.

Against another man, perhaps, the public prosecutor has succeeded in gathering some miserable scraps of equivocal evidence, and so includes him in the indictment. So equivocal is it, indeed, that the tribunal, with all the will in the world to oblige the procurator, has no alternative but either to acquit the prisoner altogether or give him a nominal sentence. There is nevertheless good reason to believe that this individual is just as *perverse* as those of his friends who have allowed themselves to be taken in the act, and been sentenced to penal servitude. Who can say that this absence of proof is not the result of pure accident? And even if he has done nothing so far, what signifies that? It is only because he has had no opportunity—that is all. Being a revolutionist in intention, he is sure to take action on the first favorable occasion. It is merely a question of time. Put him outside the court certainly, but only that he may be forthwith re-arrested.

For how can the police let these men, whom they have the chance of collaring, depart in peace? It would be as bad as letting prisoners of war rejoin the enemy. It cannot be done.

But let us leave judicial considerations to lawyers and experts, and regard the question in another aspect and from a general point of view. Let us take the case of a man so free from reproach that he can neither be arraigned as a prisoner nor called as a witness. But "from information it has received" (the reports of spies), the Government feels sure that he is a revolutionist. When this conviction is entertained about a man, absence of proof is held of no account. The police and procurators have a very high opinion of the integrity of their country's revolutionists. They firmly believe that these men always possess the courage of their opinions and act according to the dictates of their conscience. Want of evidence serves only to increase their suspicion. None who have had dealings with our procurators and gendarmes can fail to have heard, twenty times, the stereotyped phrase: "We know quite well there are no proofs against so and so—your husband, brother, sister, or friend—but that only makes them the more dangerous; it shows that they have arranged matters so cleverly that the police can find nothing out."

Once the wolf has been discovered under the lion's skin measures must be taken to disarm the enemy of order and society. If these words, "order" and "society," were understood in their accepted signification, an ordinary government might deem it expedient to wait a while and defer somewhat to considerations of general utility and public decency. But if "order" means its own skin, and "society" its own pocket, this becomes a psychological impossibility. A government ruling a nation as a conquered country, a government hemmed in by enemies on every side, with every thought concentrated on its own defence, and possessed of unlimited power to make that defence good—such a government as this was sure, sooner or later, to supplement the ordinary judicial procedure with another, a prompter, and a more subtle system, designed to redress its failures and correct its shortcomings—to do that which, in the nature of things, it was out of the question the former should do.

This system is known as the "administrative procedure." It involves a division of labor. The tribunal punishes, the administration prevents. The tribunal deals with acts, the administration with intentions. The tribunal searches people's houses and pockets, the administration looks into men's hearts and reads their thoughts.

When the administration has decided that a man has it in his mind to do them an ill turn, they place him under the supervision of the police.

In this, taken by itself, there is nothing extraordinary or extreme—at any rate, on the Continent, where it is quite in the common course of things to submit people to police surveillance. But between the practice of Germany and France and the practice of Russia there is this great difference: in the former countries only malefactors who have been tried and convicted are placed under supervision, whereas in Russia men are treated after this fashion who have been tried and acquitted, as also men who never have been tried or even accused. But wide as is this difference, it is not all. There is supervision and supervision. In its common acceptation the word means that the police will keep its eye upon you. How they do this is their affair and that of their spies. All that is required of you is to inform them of any change in your address. In Russia, however, it is very much otherwise. In Russia the marked man is required so to arrange matters that the supervisors shall have every facility for performing their task and be able to watch their man without giving themselves too much trouble. Suppose, for instance, that a man living at Odessa is ordered to be placed under supervision. The police, in that case, would probably declare it to be quite out of their power to supervise him effectually except at a place some thousand versts or more away. On this, our man would be promptly sent to the locality designated and forced to remain there until the police had done with him. Hence police supervision in Russia is but another name for administrative exile.

The right of putting people under surveillance, which the Russian criminal code, like the codes of France and Germany, reserves exclusively to the courts of justice as a penitential measure, the administration exercises arbitrarily without the least scruple. It orders into exile with equal indifference persons who have been tried and acquitted, witnesses who have testified truly, and citizens who, for some inscrutable reasons, are simply suspected of latent sedition. We therefore come to this—that the liability of Russian subjects to be exiled is limited only by the good pleasure of the gendarmery and the police. Under the pretext that an exile's conduct has not been satisfactory, moreover, the term of his banishment may be indefinitely prolonged. Thus in the affair of the Netchaeff Society (autumn, 1871), when of eighty-seven prisoners thirty-three were convicted and thirty-four acquitted, the latter were exiled with hardly an exception, as also several witnesses whom the procurator had not ventured to indict. Among the exiled, as is well known, was Miss Vera Zassoulitch. She passed several years in exile, and only recovered her liberty by flight. Mr. Nikiforoff, a kinsman of hers, and one of the witnesses on the trial, was also exiled, and though fourteen years have elapsed is in exile still.

Administrative exile played an important part even during the first period of the revolutionary movement. The thing was so common that when it was mentioned that these or those persons had been acquitted at this or that trial, the first question asked was invariably, "And whither are they exiled?" This observation implied neither irony nor doubt —was so natural, indeed, that only the fact of their not being exiled would have called forth an expression of surprise. Sometimes the police play with their victim after the manner of a cat with a mouse. In 1878 Mr. Alexander Olkhin, a member of the St. Petersburg bar, being suspected of having secret relations with the revolutionary party—albeit there was not a shred of evidence against him—was exiled to Kholmogori in the government of Archangelsk. Two years later, the police imagined they had found the desired proof, whereupon Mr. Olkhin was brought back to St. Petersburg and put on his trial. But the police had been in too great haste. The proofs were too flimsy even for the most pliable of tribunals; the prisoner was pronounced not guilty (the Mirsky trial, November, 1879). But this result had not the slightest effect on the police, they exiled Mr. Olkhin afresh, and his second condition was worse than his first.

To finish, I will cite a well-known name, that of Prince Alexis Krapotkin, brother to Prince Peter, a mathematician and astronomer who never concerned himself with politics. His fault was being akin to Peter and not showing sufficient respect for the gendarmes. In the autumn of 1876 the post-office having intercepted a letter which, as the police suspected, was destined for a political refugee whose acquaintance Alexis had made while travelling abroad, they searched his house. No confirmation of their suspicion was forthcoming, but the prince imprudently showed annoyance at this proceeding, treated the procurator and gendarmes with scant courtesy, and, to use an idiomatic Anglicism, "gave them a piece of his mind." Imprisonment produced no change in his demeanor, and in the end they sent him to Siberia. This came to pass nine years ago, and he is in Siberia still, ruined in health and bereft of his only son.

All the exiles of this period were banished by subterfuge. While nominally placed under police surveillance as a measure of precaution, they were sent to the confines of the empire as a matter of fact, and there detained. Thus was committed a double wrong. In the first instance, these people were punished without trial, in itself a gross illegality; in the second instance, they were not alone placed under surveillance without warrant, but this surveillance, equally without warrant, was converted by a piece of casuistry into a sentence of unlimited transportation. The code, it may be well to mention, recognizes no such thing as administrative exile. This, however, is a consideration which has little interest for Russians, and, save legists, few ever give it a thought.

In 1879, however, the reproach in question was removed, and for six years administrative exile has been a recognized bulwark of order and a regular Russian institution. On April the 2nd of the year in question, Solovieff attempted the Tzar's life. On the 6th—three days later—a new law was ordained whereby all Russia, habited and habitable, was divided into six regions, under the rule of six generals, each in his own region clothed with despotic powers. The local civil authorities were ordered to render these satraps the same obedience which they would render in a state of war to a general-in-chief. The six dictators, moreover, had the same powers as are wielded by a commander-in-chief in war time over all the inhabitants of their respective districts. These powers included (*a*) the right to exile by administrative order all persons whose continued stay in the district might be considered prejudicial (to public order); (*b*) to imprison at their discretion all persons, without distinction of rank or title, whenever they might find it advisable; (*c*) to suppress, or provisionally suspend, any journal or review the tendencies of which might seem to them dangerous; and (*d*) generally take such measures as they might deem necessary for the maintenance of tranquillity and order in the regions over which they were placed.

This in Russia they call a law! Since April, 1879, therefore, administrative exile has become perfectly legal. In the same way, when the six satrapies were abolished, the country was placed in "a state of surety" (for surety read "siege"), and the exceptional powers intrusted to the generals were permanently conferred on the ordinary governors.

Since that time the system of administrative exile has received a great extension and become the favorite weapon of the Russian Government in its contest with the nation—so much so that *de facto* juridic procedure is relegated more and more to the background.

When Solovieff's attempt was followed by several others, the Government fell into a very paroxysm of panic and passion. It felt the ground shaking under its feet, it tried to spread terror everywhere, to strike hard, to tear up sedition by the roots. For this end exile was far more effective than the tribunals, with their forms, ceremonies, and delays; and on the least suspicion, real or feigned, the least sign or the flimsiest pretext, it was applied right and left. It became a pest, a devastation.

If, however, the reader were to ask me to define, more or less precisely, the signs and pretexts which the administration deem sufficient to justify the infliction of so severe a punishment as exile, I should find it difficult to give a satisfactory answer. Everything has its measure, even the susceptibility of the Russian police. As in chemistry there are substances whose presence is manifested by very energetic reactions, but the detection of which defies the most delicate scales, so it is with the police. Except in cases where personal antipathy or private vengeance is the motive (cases which are far from being exceptional), the police, before they tear a man from his family and his business, deprive him of his livelihood, and send him to the other extremity of the empire, must have *something* against him. What this something may be we can form an approximate idea from incidents that have actually occurred, cases in which it has been possible to obtain information as to the motives of the police in sending people into exile. In many instances it is impossible even to conjecture these motives, and I purposely confine myself to cases in which the victims have been of good social position, for to them the Government generally shows somewhat more consideration than to people of inferior rank.

We will begin with Mr. Petrounkevitch, landowner, member of the Zemstvo of Tchernigoff, and president of the justices of peace of his district. In May, 1879, this gentleman was arrested by order of the Minister of the Interior, the ground assigned for the proceeding being his dangerous opinions as manifested in an official report of the local Zemstvo, drawn up by a commission, of which Mr. Petrounkevitch was the chairman, in answer to a ministerial circular. He was taken in open day while busied with his official duties; and, without being allowed to say a word to his family, hurried off under police escort to Moscow, and sent thence to Varnavin, in the government of Kestroma.

About the same time was arrested Dr. Bely, the medical officer of the same Zemstvo. As his name was not appended to the report in question, and he took no part in the proceedings of the Zemstvo, the "perversity" imputed to him could not be inferred from his acts or his words—it had to be divined by intuition, read in his heart. This duty was undertaken by the parish priest of Ivangorod, a sort of duty for which priests in general have a decided predilection. He denounced Dr. Bely as "evil-intentioned and a suspect" on the following grounds (which I give textually): "That the doctor was personally acquainted with Petrounkevitch, upon whom he was in the habit of calling (in which, seeing that they lived within a few miles of each other, there was surely nothing very extraordinary), and whose opinions, the perversity of which was well known, he shared." The priest alleged further that Dr. Bely showed a decided partiality for the company of peasants; that he seldom went into the town, where there was good society, preferring rather to remain in the village among his peasant neighbors; that he did not bestow sufficient care on the health of the local nobility, neglecting his patients of that class in order to give more time to his humbler patients; that in his hospital were two young ladies, one of whom wore the national folks' dress (this was Miss Bogolubova, who had been a Sister of Mercy in the army of the Balkans. She was arrested a few days after Dr. Bely, and exiled nobody knows whither). The facts set forth by the priest, leaving no doubt as to the doctor's perversity, Mr. Malakhoff, the *pristav* (subaltern officer of police), had him arrested on July 19th. He was first sent under escort to Vychny-Volotchek, and then exiled to Eastern Siberia—neither more nor less.

Mr. Jujakoff, a distinguished press writer and publicist, son of a major-general and rich landowner of the south of Russia, was exiled by Todleben to Eastern Siberia on the following grounds (textual): (1) because he belonged to a dangerous family, all the members of which (except the general) were imbued with perverse ideas. (His mother had been arrested and kept in prison for ten days for refusing to reveal the name of the owner of a socialist book; his sister was in prison, and is now in Siberia.) (2) Because it was owing to his influence that certain leaders against the Socialists *were not printed* in the *Odessa Listok* after the attempt of April 2nd!

Mr. Kovalevsky, an officer of the Odessa municipality, was exiled to Eastern Siberia because (1) he was his wife's husband. (Madame Kovalevsky, while living at Kieff, away from her husband, became implicated in the Terrorist doings there, and was sentenced in May, 1879, to a term of hard labor.) (2) Because he had been heard to say, in the presence of some of his fellow-officers of the municipality, that he had no very high opinion of the Government; and (3) because he exercised a bad influence over his friends.

The case of Mr. Belousoff, professor in one of the colleges at Kieff, is still richer. He was arrested in the summer of 1879, dismissed from his post and exiled to the north, all owing to a pure "misunderstanding," as they say in Russia, on the part of the police, and pure misfortune on his; the head and front of the poor man's offending being the name he bore—the name of Belousoff. So did somebody else with whom the police confounded him. Five years previously this somebody else had been accused, or suspected, of carrying on a propaganda among the workmen of Kieff, but succeeded in escaping. Thus Mr. Belousoff was made to suffer for the sins of a namesake whom he neither knew nor had ever seen. Already, in 1874, he had been brought before the police under a similar misapprehension, and the error being explained, dismissed—presumably, "without a stain on his character." In 1879, however, he was less fortunate, for this time the police (who had doubtless on overhauling their records found his name thereon) condemned him to an indefinite term of administrative exile.

It may be remarked, by way of parenthesis, that this sort of *quid pro quo* is far from being uncommon in Russia. At Kharkoff a student named Semenovsky was arrested for no other reason than that, three years before, an advocate, similarly named, had been tried and convicted of propagandism. At Odessa, again, the police wanted a certain Mr. Kohan; but there being "two Richmonds in the field," they hesitated at first which to take, but got over the difficulty by arresting both.

But let us continue Mr. Belousoff's story. When the mistake was explained to General Tchertkoff, Governor of Kieff, and he was requested to revoke the sentence passed on an admittedly innocent and therefore deeply wronged man, he answered in these words: "I quite believe that what you say is quite true; but in a time of trouble like the present, the administration cannot afford to make mistakes. So let him go into exile, and in a little while he may petition me for a revocation!"

Another example in conclusion. Mr. Isidor Goldsmith was for eight years editor of two high-class monthly reviews. When, in 1879, the rigors of the censorship obliged him to abandon the career of letters, he betook himself to Moscow, of which city his wife (a member of the well-known and highly popular Androusoff family) was a native, and began practice at the bar. But an untoward, yet all too common, incident thwarted his plans, and involved himself and his wife in interminable trouble. They were denounced by a spy, who accused them to the police of having come to Moscow for nothing else than to organize a central revolutionary committee. Search and arrest followed as a matter of course, and, equally of course, nothing whatever was found to justify the statement of the spy and the action of the police. All the same, a formal inquisition was opened, and in ordinary circumstances the accused would have been kept in prison during the six months over which an examination generally extends. But having friends in high quarters and the absurdity of the charge against them being self-evident, the Governor-General of Moscow, Prince Dolgorouky, was prevailed upon to interest himself in their favor. The consequence was that, instead of being locked up in gaol, they were placed under domiciliary arrest in their own house. But on September 24th they were arrested a second time, and without more ado sent under escort to Archangelsk, on the shores of the White Sea, the chief town of the province of that name. After a stay there of two months, they were transferred to the little town of Kholonogory in the same district. Before being conveyed to their new destination, Mr. Goldsmith had the good fortune to get sight of the document in which the grounds of the action taken against himself and his wife were set forth. It ran as follows:

"The gendamerie department of Moscow accused Mr. Isidor Goldsmith and his wife Sophia of having come to Moscow intent on founding a central revolutionary committee. After a minute domiciliary search and an examination for the discovery of proofs, the charges brought against the before-mentioned persons were found to be quite without justification. Consequently the Minister of the Interior and the chief of the gendarmerie decree that Isidor Goldsmith and Sophia his wife be transported to Archangelsk, and there placed under the supervision of the local police."

Could logic more exquisite be imagined? These people are innocent, *therefore* let them be punished, a result so incredibly and grotesquely absurd that the uninitiated may well be excused for preferring to ascribe it rather to an error of transcription than to deliberate intention. But the reader, who is beginning to understand the spirit which animates the Tzar's bureaucracy, and has had time to familiarize himself with the manners and customs of official Russia, will find no difficulty in filling up the hiatus which seems to disconnect the syllogism from the conclusion in this remarkable and, unfortunately, by no means exceptional document.

The charge being false, says, in effect, the Third Section, there can be no ground for a formal prosecution. But as people who have once been accused are always looked upon with suspicion, this gentleman and his wife, in accordance with the usual custom in such cases, must be sent into exile.

And I repeat it, the cases I have adduced are neither exceptional nor extreme. The victims whose experiences we have narrated were able to ascertain, directly or indirectly, the causes to which their exile was ostensibly due. In every instance the cause was political. But there is ample room for the play of other and even more darker causes; the methods of the police especially binding themselves to the gratification of private malice and personal revenge. For they not only protect and support their own creatures—spies by profession—but do all in their power to encourage the spontaneous denunciations of amateur informers. An accused person is never, in any circumstances, allowed to know the name of his accuser, and the charge is always so worded as to throw you off the scent, and prevent you, as far as possible, from guessing the name of your secret enemy. For instance, the police will protest that they are in possession of evidence showing that you have distributed revolutionary proclamations; but where, when, or in what circumstances, they will no more tell you than they will divulge the name of their informant. It is, moreover, a positive fact that a great many persons ordered into exile are neither told the reason why, nor informed what they have done amiss. A few years later, perhaps, they may learn, by some indirect means, that they owe their ruin to a rogue whom they had threatened with prosecution, or *chantagist* (I use the French word because there is no English equivalent) to whom they had refused black-mail. As I have already had occasion to mention, the Revising Commission appointed by Loris Melikoff discovered so many cases of exile arising from false evidence, that the Government itself was seized with horror. So at least the censured journals of the day emphatically affirmed. That the number of these cases was something enormous we can well believe. Under the existing system it would be surprising if they were not. But it may be permitted to doubt the sincerity of the horror ascribed to the Government. In any event it did not last long, and was speedily forgotten in the greater horror inspired by the dread spectre of revolution. For the system flourishes in full vigor even now, and in every city of the empire the best, the bravest, and the ablest continue to be torn from work profitable to themselves and useful to the country, and sent into hopeless exile.

But what, it may be asked, is this administrative exile? We know that in ordinary parlance it means simple deportation, and that a man sent to a far country may possibly gain by the exchange. We know, too, what the supervision exercised by the police of continental countries over common criminals whose offences are considered not to have been sufficiently expiated by their previous punishment is like— an onerous and vexatious system that tends only to increase crime, and is strongly disapproved by the best authorities of the countries in which it prevails. But the Russian system of political exile is altogether *sui generis*. The person exiled is much more than a political malefactor. The crime he is credited with a desire to commit is speech—the utterance of words. Worse than a malefactor, he is a centre of contagion. Because, when you come near a man he talks—and if his disposition be perverse and his political views unsound, he will inevitably poison with his venom all with whom he comes in contact—if you let him. Hence he must be isolated, even in the place of his exile. Nor is this all. A man of culture can infect even at a distance. By means of letters and the press he may corrupt people whom he never sees. It is therefore imperative to cut him off from the entire world.

And this is the principle acted upon, as the following extracts (textually rendered) from the Regulations for Administrative Exiles (March 12-25) will show:

"To exiles is forbidden:—Every sort of pedagogic occupation, such as the teaching of arts and trades, the reading (or giving) of public lectures, participation in the proceedings of scientific societies, and all public activity whatsoever!"

They are forbidden further to act as "typographers, lithographers, photographers, or librarians, or to serve in any such establishments as agents, clerks, overlookers, or simple workmen." The vending of books, or other printed matter or product of the press, is likewise forbidden to exiles (paragraph 24).

All other employments (?) not forbidden by the law (say, manual labor, for which the average political exile is little apt) are open to exiles, with the reservation, however, that the local governor may veto the occupation selected in the event of the exile using it for the carrying out of perverse intentions, or if, owing to special circumstances, it is likely to endanger order or disturb the public tranquillity (paragraph 28).

By paragraph 21 it is forbidden to employ exiles in government offices or local public establishments, except as copyists, and by special permission of the Minister of the Interior. Paragraph 27 lays an interdict on medical or pharmaceutical practice by exiles, except, as in the former case, by special permission of the Minister. But as such permission is as hard to obtain as a revocation of the decree of exile, the interdict is practically absolute.

As the Government deprives exiles of almost every possible way of gaining a livelihood, it is only just that it should keep them. And this it does—after a fashion. In the central provinces they are allowed the pittance of six roubles (about eighteen shillings) a month; in the northern provinces, where life is more costly, the allowance is eight roubles—in both cases for exiles of the nobility. Members of the non-privileged classes receive exactly half this sum, and, as may be supposed, it is almost more than any of them can do to keep body and soul together.

And then comes paragraph 37, which reads like the bitterest irony: "Exiles who shirk work, either from idleness, bad conduct, or lazy habits, will be deprived of their governmental stipend!"

Finally, we have paragraph 29, which is, perhaps, the cream of the collection. It runs thus:

"The Minister of the Interior is empowered to forbid to

any exile the direct delivery of his letters and despatches which, in that event, are to be handed by the post office to the chief of the local police or the gendarmes. These latter, after reading them, may give them to the exile, if they find nothing prejudicial therein. In the contrary case, the confiscated correspondence must be immediately forwarded to the gendarmerie. In the same way all letters or dispatches which the exile proposes to send away must be first read by the aforementioned authorities."

Practically, as we have good reasons to know, these rules are applied in the inverse sense—all our exile's correspondence is submitted to the censorship of the local police. The contrary is the exception.

It is not difficult to picture to ourselves what life must be like under conditions such as these. But as an illustration, and by way of facilitating the process, I will, with the reader's permission, tell the story of a company of my exiled friends. Those who prefer to trust to their own unaided imaginations are, of course, at liberty to skip the following chapter. Let us, then, abandoning laws, regulations, and paragraphs, deal for a moment with creatures of flesh and blood, and study a deeply interesting but little known phase of human life.

CHAPTER XXIII.

LIFE IN EXILE.

ON an early June day, in the year 1879, all the exiles of Gorodishko, a wretched little town on the northern coast, are gathered near the landing-place. They number about thirty, and are of all sorts and conditions—young and old, vigorous and decrepit, some dressed like gentlemen, others like peasants, some in paletots, others in smock frocks, plaids, and jackets—pacing to and fro, leaning against the piles, sitting on bales of merchandise, standing in little groups and talking with the absent manner of men who are thinking of something else. From time to time they turn curious and eager eyes toward the upper reaches of the river. For it is thence will come the steamer, whose arrival all are waiting.

There have been serious troubles in a university town of Southern Russia. Beginning in the university itself, and arising, as usual, out of a misunderstanding with one of the professors, the disturbance speedily involved the entire city. A hundred of the students were expelled, and most of them —as also some others who, although they had been arrested, it was not considered expedient to keep in prison—were immediately ordered into exile. According to the accepted usage in such cases they were divided into little groups, the leaders being sent to a dozen different places in Siberia, the less compromised to the northern littoral. One of these groups was coming to Gorodishko—an event on which our exiles were warmly felicitating each other. It was not, perhaps, very much to their credit to rejoice over the misfortunes of others, and the addition of six persons to thirty who were dying of *ennui* did not promise to be much of a distraction. But the lives of these thirty were so terribly dull that any event, however trifling, was regarded as a blessing. And the new arrivals came from without—"from liberty," as runs the mocking phrase, which sounds strangely from Russian lips. They bring with them a ripple of new life, as a prison door, opening for a moment, lets in a breath of fresh air! So the exiles were gay, and prepared to give their new *confrères* a warm welcome.

They had long to wait, for the poor fellows in their eagerness had assembled on the wharf two hours before the time fixed for the steamer's arrival, and, as is generally the case in Russia, she was behind her time. But patience had become a habit with these involuntary waiters on Providence, and it never occurred to them to murmur.

A young man from Odessa of the name of Ursitch, recently exiled for taking part in a "demonstration," had stationed himself, binocular in hand, on the top of a pile of wood. Every now and then those near him inquired if he could "see anything."

At length, towards three o'clock in the afternoon, he uttered the long-expected cry—"The steamer." And far away on the horizon could be seen a faint black line, surmounted by a thin gray column. A boat beyond question. But so small that a doubt arises whether it is *the* boat. May it not be some merchant steamer? The binocular is passed from hand to hand. Everybody stares with all his might into the double tube, but none can decide. The glass does not carry far enough.

"Uskimbai the sultan!" shouts one of the exiles, "get up there quickly on the pile."

As if in answer to the summons a strange figure comes pushing through the crowd—large and solid—clad in a long gray capot, with a deep, yellow, hairless face, little Mongol eyes, a big flat nose, and a square neck, the latter covered with short black hair as crisp and bunchy as a horse's mane.

This was Uskimbai the sultan—a veritable sultan, not merely so dubbed in sport or derision. For all the chiefs of the Nomad Kirghis tribes under Russian domination bear this high-sounding designation. It is recognized by the Russian authorities, and after some dozen years' service these wandering sultans receive the commission of third lieutenant in the army of the Tzar. But instead of the insignificant epaulettes usually worn by officers of this rank, they are allowed to don the epaulettes of a major, the long tassels of which, when attached to the *khalate*—the sort of dressing-gown which constitutes their sole costume—have a remarkably brilliant effect. But Allah had not decreed that Uskimbai should receive this coveted mark of distinction. One night when he and some men of his tribe were quietly driving off a flock of sheep belonging to the garrison of a Russian post, they were caught by some Cossacks *in flagrante delicto*. The sultan, who fell into their hands, was taken in bonds to the nearest town, and exiled by administrative order to the northern provinces.

He moved with the rolling gait peculiar to men who have passed much of their lives at sea or on horseback.

"Get up and tell us what thou seest, sultan," said the owner of the binocular.

Uskimbai gave an affirmative nod, and did as he was asked. He knew they could not do without him; a large smile broke his great beardless face in halves, exposing under the yellow skin two splendid rows of strong white teeth.

Pushing scornfully aside the glass tendered to him by Ursitch, and turning his eyes, or rather the two narrow slits in which a pair of brilliantly black cockchafers seemed to be hidden, towards the horizon, he declared, after a moment's earnest gaze, that the boat was the steamer. He said further that he could see three men on the bridge, one of whom wore a white hat, and was looking into a machine like that they had just offered him.

This seemed rather too much, and the declaration of the Kirghis chief was greeted with a shout of incredulous laughter, which evidently annoyed him.

"Thou Russian sees nothing ; Kirghis sees everything. Thou'rt blind fowl," exclaimed the child of nature from his "coign of vantage" to the crowd below—"thouing" in the fashion of his country, whose language admits of their using "thou" in the plural.

This sally was received with great good humor, and the sultan, descending from the timber with a dignified air, took a seat, singing the while a Kirghis song of triumph composed of only two notes, which he repeated continually in a slow and monotonous measure as if it were a funeral dirge.

Uskimbai's eyes had not deceived him, as fifteen minutes later everybody, with the help of the binocular, were able to see. The steamer was the steamer, and on the bridge stood the three men exactly as the sultan had described them. They were shortly afterwards joined by two others, whose costumes alone, even if they had not been accompanied by a brace of gendarmes, would have proclaimed their quality. When, doubling the wood-covered promontory which impeded the view, the steamer appeared in her majestic grace rushing with her black prow through the white foaming water, a great shout went up from the landing-stage, and the exiles made tumultuously for the gangway.

The passengers came ashore, and the new arrivals found themselves in the midst of a noisy exiled crowd. Greetings are exchanged, and in a few minutes strangers and old stagers have made each other's acquaintance, and are on the footing of familiar friends. Three of the new-comers are students, and as each in turn mentions the cause of his exile, the old stagers learn that the offence of their young comrades was putting their names to a petition. The other two are more advanced in years, and evidently not students. The first introduced himself as "Podkova Taras, advocate —for a shirt."

"How? You are indeed a cheap advocate to accept a shirt as retainer," laughed the others.

"No, no, I don't mean that. I mean that a shirt is the cause of my exile."

In this answer there lurked a touch of Ruthenian humor, Podkova's supposed offence being Ukranian separatism, the evidence against him being, according to the statement of an informer, that he was in the habit of wearing the national shirt affected by the peasantry of his native province.

His companion, Dr. Michel Losinski, a professor of the healing art, was less fortunate. He had not been able to learn the cause of his exile.

"It was perhaps out of consideration for these gentlemen," he said, smiling and pointing to his companions, "the police did not think it right to let them make so long a journey without their own physician."

The introductions over and the formalities in the police office completed, the new comers were led by their new friends to one of the large communes, where a modest— a very modest—meal had been prepared in anticipation of their arrival. It consisted of fish, seasoned with powdered horse-radish, specially brought from the garden of a monastery, six miles away, the sole possessor of this culinary treasure. For dessert they had a dish of carrots—in that land of ice a rare gastronomic delicacy—the whole washed down with yellow water, dignified with the name of tea, and drawn from a capacious samoven which seemed to contain an inexhaustible supply.

Conversation, the chief burden of it being naturally borne by the new comers, was kept up during the repast with great animation. The doctor was in vein. With characteristic Polish spirit (though born on the left bank of the Dnieper, and therefore "Russianized," he was a Pole by origin) he described the more comic incidents of his examination and preliminary detention, and told several racy anecdotes about the gendarmes of K—— and their proceedings generally. Orshine, one of the students, was called upon for a history of the troubles in which they had been implicated. Podkova spoke little. He had been a rising lawyer, of great ability and promise; but in the society of strangers his manner was timid and constrained. Orshine, who had made his acquaintance on the way, and was becoming warmly attached to him, said that Podkova after one of his speeches reminded him of a discharged electric needle.

The exiles did not separate until late in the evening. But as the new comers had neither told all their news, nor exhausted their stock of suppositions, opinions, and conjectures, the divers communes, great and small, took possession of them as if they had been prisoners of war, and led them away. The distribution was, however, amicably arranged, and every commune had its man.

But what is a "commune" in this sense? the reader will ask.

It is a common institution of Russian university life. In all the universities and superior schools a great part of the students form themselves into societies, each numbering from eight to twelve men, who hire rooms, make a common purse, and live together in full fraternity. In the common purse every man puts all that he receives from home or earns by teaching, without thinking or knowing whether his comrades contributed more or less than himself. It is only by means of this system that so many poor scholars are enabled to study at the capital, and maintain themselves on their often very limited resources. But useful as is this system of mutual help to Russian students, to Russian exiles it is simply a matter of life and death. For without this sort of brotherly union and co-operation hundreds of exiles would every year perish of privation and want.

* * *

If the Russian Government were less besotted with fear it would surely let the unfortunate suspects live in peace whom it sends to eat out their hearts in holes like Gorodishko.

Imagine a town "of about 1,000 inhabitants," occupying from 150 to 200 houses, the latter in two rows parallel with the river and forming a single street. The spaces between the dwellings serve as short cuts to the forest and the river. All the buildings are of wood—except the church, which is of brick. If you ascend the steeple to take a survey of the country, you see on every side dense and wide-stretching pine-forests, broken in the neighborhood of the river by great clearings covered with the blackened stumps of departed trees. If the time be winter, you have no need to mount so high; for you know beforehand that you will see only an immense ocean of snow, whose billowy surface is oftener traversed by hungry wolves than by Esquimaux sledges. In that inclement climate and almost polar region agriculture is out of the question. Bread is imported and therefore dear. The few inhabitants occupy themselves with fishing, hunting, and charcoal-burning. The forest and the river are the sole sources of their existence. Among the people of Gorodishko there are probably no more than a dozen who can read and write. These are the *tchinovniks*—Government *employés*—and even they are half peasants. Little time is given to bureaucratic formalities in this icy desert; and if you should happen to require the services of the chief magistrate, you would probably be told that he was away on a journey, engaged in the transport of merchandise, for the man acts as a common carrier. When he returns in two or three weeks and with his great fat fingers signs your papers, he will be happy, for a very moderate consideration, to drive you to your destination.

The intellectual horizon of these *tchinovniks* is not much wider than that of their peasant neighbors. No man of education and capacity could be persuaded to take service in so remote and wretched a place. They are either creatures without spirit or rogues sent thither by way of punishment; service in these regions being a sort of exile for the *tchinovniks* themselves. And if among the latter there chance to be some young *employé* ambitious of promotion, he is careful to avoid all contact with the exiles; for to be friendly with political pariahs would of a surety draw upon him the suspicions of his superiors, and probably ruin his prospects for life.

* * *

For ten or twelve days after their arrival the new comers had no fixed abode. The others wanted to make their acquaintance thoroughly—to know them—and they wanted to know the others. So they lived first in one commune and then in another, changing about as the fancy took them. After a while three of their number—Losinski, Taras, and Orshine—together with Ursitch, the Odessa man, formed themselves into a little commune of their own. They hired a small suite of rooms. Each member of the society acted in turn as cook, all their domestic work being, of course, done by themselves. The question of daily bread—naturally the first which presents itself—was their greatest difficulty. It was the means, too, of getting Taras into bad repute with the local police. The exiles brought, as they thought, enough money to last them until they should receive more. But the authorities did them an ill turn—made them pay out of their own pockets the travelling expenses of their escort to Gorodishko! And all their cash being in the hands of the chief gendarme, they were powerless to resist this curious and unexpected exaction. When Ursitch heard of the incident, he tried to console his newly made friends by telling them that the corps of cadets of which he had been a member were treated even worse. At the termination of the course, every graduate was made to contribute twenty-five roubles toward the expense of the canes consumed during their pupilage. But this anecdote, amusing though it was, did not seem to reconcile the victims to their loss. As for Taras, he was furious, swearing roundly that if he had known what the gendarmes were going to do, he would have thrown all his money into the sea rather than let them have it.

All were in great straits. Some even had not a sufficiency of clothing. People are arrested wherever they may happen to be—as likely as not in the street—thrown into prison, and in some instances sent away without being allowed time either to make provision for their journey or say farewell to their friends. This had happened to Taras. His fellow exiles placed their wardrobes at his disposal, but he refused to profit by their kindness.

"You have need of all these things for yourselves," he said. "The Government has brought me here by force, and deprived me of my means of living, and the Government must feed and clothe me—I will spare it nothing."

Not a day passed that he not go to the office to ask for his eight roubles, always receiving the same stereotyped reply. The local authorities had written to headquarters, but the necessary authorization had not yet arrived. He must have patience. Nothing that he said or did seemed to produce any impression, and his companions asked him to desist from his labor in vain. He need not expect anything for several months to come, and to bother the officials would only set them against him.

"They shall pay me that money," was the only answer Taras vouchsafed to their kindly meant counsel.

One fine afternoon, when the other exiles were going out for their usual walk, Taras went out also, but so strangely dressed that all the children ran after him, and the place was quite in a commotion. He had nothing on but his night clothes, and a counterpane. Before he had marched up and down the single street half a dozen times, the *ispravnik* (to whom somebody had hurried with the news) appeared on the scene in a state of great excitement.

"Mr. Podkova, what on earth are you doing?" he said, in a tone of admonition. "Just think! an educated man like you making a public scandal. The ladies can see you from the windows!"

"That is not my fault. I have no clothes, and I cannot remain for ever within the four walls of my room. It might injure my health. I must take a walk occasionally."

And for a whole week he promenaded every day in precisely the same guise, paying no heed whatever to the *ispravnik's* remonstrances, until by his persistency he fairly vanquished official inertness and got his wretched stipendium. But from that moment he was looked upon as a "turbulent man."

* * *

The short summer, which in that far northern region lasts but two months, passed only too quickly. Autumn came and went almost unperceived, and then the long polar winter, with its interminable nights, reigned over the land. The sun, after showing himself for a brief space on the southern extremity of the horizon as a small arch of a few degrees of amplitude, went down into the long line of snow, leaving the earth in a night of twenty hours dimly lighted by the faint and distant reflections of the aurora borealis.

At this time, as may be supposed, the exiles of Gorodishko did not find life very amusing. Enforced idleness amid an environment destitute of everything that can fix the attention of a civilized man, must of necessity deaden the faculties and stupefy the mind. In summer it is not quite so bad. There are berries and mushrooms to be gathered in the neighboring woods, the authorities being good enough to wink at the slight infractions of the regulations which forbid exiles to put a foot outside the boundaries of the town. A man can read, too; a resource which in winter is far from being always available. Candles being expensive and exiles poor, they can afford only rush-lights made of fishes' fat, or the *loutchina*, a splinter of resinous wood, whose flickering and uncertain light ruins the eyesight of those who use it for reading. For these unfortunates the winter, which lasts three quarters of the year, is a period of misery and inaction, a season accursed. The only way in which they can kill time is by exchanging visits among themselves—in the circumstances, however, a poor and altogether insufficient distraction. True, they are like a family. They would divide with each other their last crust of bread. But always the same faces, always the same talk, always the same subjects, their lives never presenting a new feature—and they end by having nothing to say. Men drag themselves first to one house and then to another, hoping that here or there they will find something less stale, flat, and unprofitable, only to go away disappointed, and repeat the experiment elsewhere with the same result. And this goes on for days, weeks, months.

One winter evening a company of exiles were gathered as usual around the samoven, sipping tea, yawning wearily, and staring at each other in dull silence. Everything—faces, positions, movements, even the room itself, half lighted by a single candle stuck in a big rustic chandelier of wood—bespoke the very extremity of weariness. From time to time somebody half unconsciously lets a word or two drop from his lips. A minute or two afterwards, when the speaker has forgotten what he said, there suddenly comes from a dark corner another word or two, which, with some effort, the listeners understand to be an answer to the previous observation.

Taras does not speak at all. Stretched full length on a bench of pine wood, covered with dry moss, which serves both as bed and sofa, he smokes incessantly, watching with a dreamy air the little blue cloudlets of smoke as they hover over his head and lose themselves in the gloom, and seems quite satisfied with his occupation and his thoughts. Losinski is balancing himself on a chair hard by. Whatever might be the cause, whether worried by his friend's imperturbable phlegm, or rendered nervous by the electric influence of the aurora borealis, he is evidently more than usually hipped and unhappy. Though the evening differed in nothing from other evenings, it seemed to him exceptionally unsupportable. All at once he broke out.

"Gentlemen!" he exclaimed, in an excited and energetic voice, which, by its contrast with the languid tone most in vogue, awakes immediate attention. "Gentlemen, the life we lead here is detestable! If we live on in this idle, purposeless way a year or two longer, we shall become incapable of serious work, utterly unnerved, and good for nothing at all. We must bestir ourselves, we must do something; if we do not, we shall grow so weary of this sordid, vegetating existence, that we may be tempted to drown our *ennui* and seek oblivion in the degrading bottle."

At these words the blood mounted hotly to the face of a man who sat opposite the speaker. They called him *Starik*, "the old one." He was the senior member, the *doyen* of the colony, alike by his age and the greatness of his sufferings. He had been a journalist, and was banished in 1870 for some articles which had displeased people in high quarters. But this happened so long ago that the true cause of his exile had in all probability been forgotten even by himself. To the others it seemed as if Starik must have been born a political exile. Yet he lived in hope, looking always for some change in the higher spheres that might bring about an order for his liberation. But the order never came, and when he could bear the suspense no longer he would grow utterly desperate, and drink furiously for weeks, so that his friends were forced to effect a provisional cure by putting him under lock and key. After a bout of this sort he would quiet down, and for months together be as abstemious as an English teetotaler.

He lowered his head at the haphazard allusion made by the doctor, who continued to talk in the same strain. Then a shade of displeasure passed over his face as if he were vexed at being ashamed, and looking up he interrupted Losinski bluntly with this point blank question—

"What the devil would you have us do, then?"

For a moment Losinski was disconcerted. When he began his remarks he had nothing in his mind very definite or practical. He started on the impulse of the moment, like a spurred horse. But his confusion endured only a moment. An emergency with him never failed to suggest an idea, and the very next instant he conceived a happy thought.

"What would I have you do!" he repeated, in his ordinary manner. "Why, for instance, instead of sitting stupidly here catching flies, do we not go in for mutual instruction, or something of that sort? There are thirty-five of us. Every one knows something that the others don't know. Every one can give lessons in his own specialty turn about. That will occupy the listeners, and stimulate the lesson-giver."

Here was at least something practical, and a discussion naturally followed. Starik observed that the sort of thing suggested would not be very amusing either, and that they would soon be more *ennuyé* than before. There were of course *pros* and *cons*, and the speakers grew so animated that they wasted their powder, several talking together, and nobody understanding what they said. It was a long time since the exiles had spent so agreeable an evening. On the evening following the proposal was discussed by all the communes together, and accepted with enthusiasm. A study plan was drawn up, and a week later Losinski opened the course with a brilliant lecture on physiology.

This promising enterprise was, however, of very short duration. The whole town was thrown into a ferment by the news of a proceeding at once so curious and so unprecedented. The *ispravnik* sent for Losinski, and gravely informed him that his lectures were in contravention of the regulation which expressly forbids exiles to engage in any sort of public teaching.

The doctor answered with a laugh, and tried to make the timid *tchinovnik* understand that the article in question did not apply to the exiles as amongst themselves. So long as they were allowed to meet and converse with each other, it would be too absurd to forbid them to instruct each other. Though the point did not seem quite clear to the *ispravnik*, he was for once persuaded to listen to reason, or at least to act as if he did. He had fortunately as secretary a young fellow who, having almost completed a course at a gymnasium, was regarded by the people of Gorodishko as a prodigy of learning. It so happened, moreover, that the youth, having a brother in the "movement," was a secret sympathizer with the exiles, and always willing to do them a good turn whenever it lay in his power. He had already rendered them many services ; but for reasons easily understood they seldom appealed to him. Such help as he gave was generally spontaneous. It was he who, in this instance, interceded on their behalf and decided the *ispravnik*, after some hesitation, to grant their request. But they little suspected that adverse influences were at work, and that danger threatened the project from another quarter.

* * *

A day or two afterwards, just when the shadows of night

were beginning to descend on Gorodishko, that is to say, between two and three o'clock in the afternoon, a strange-looking figure walked rapidly down its single street towards a little gray house hard by the church, a figure covered entirely with hair. The lower limbs are hidden in huge and heavy boots of double fur—hairy within and hairy without—making the legs look like the forelegs of a bear. The body is enveloped in a *savok*, a sort of blouse or surplice, having long sleeves, and a hood, all of deerskin, with the hair outwards. The hands are lost in enormous *roukavitsi*, gloves of calf-skin—hoof-shaped sacks rather, because the hands would freeze in fingered gloves after the European fashion. As the temperature is forty degrees (Centigrade) below zero, and there is a piercing north wind, the hood is lowered, completely hiding the face. So every part of the body—head, arms, and feet—is covered with red-brown hair, and the figure is more like a wild animal which has learnt to walk on its hind legs than a human being. If it were to go on all fours the illusion would be complete. But as the figure is that of one of the most elegant in Gorodishko's beauties the suggestion is perhaps a little ungracious, if not positively ungallant. The lady is none other than the judge's wife, and she is just now bent on paying a visit to the *Popadia*—the wife of the parson of the parish.

On reaching the little gray house, she enters the court and mounts quickly to the ante-chamber. Here she throws back her hood, showing a square face with large jaws, and eyes as clear and blue as those of the fish of the country, and shakes herself energetically like a dog fresh out of the water, to get rid of the snow which has fallen on her furs. Then she enters the next room and finds the *Popadia* at home, whereupon the visitor takes off her outer garments, and the friends embrace.

"Have you heard, mother, what the students are about?" says the judge's wife, excitedly.

In the far north political exiles are called "students" indiscriminately, albeit not more than a fourth of them are so.

"Oh, don't mention them! I fear so much that they will do me an ill turn, that every time I pass one of them in the street I make a sign of the cross under my *savok*. Every time, I assure you. It is that alone which has so far kept me from harm."

"I fear now, though, it will protect you no longer."

"Oh, the very Holy Virgin! What do you mean by that? You make me tremble all over."

"Sit down, mother, and I will tell you. Matrena, the fish-wife, came to see me half an hour ago, and told me all about it. As you know, she lets them two rooms, and she has heard something through the key-hole. She did not understand everything—you know how stupid the woman is—but she understood enough to enable us to guess the rest."

Whereupon the judge's wife, with many exclamations, interruptions, and asides, repeated all the terrible things she had heard from the eaves-dropping fish-wife—and something more.

"The students, according to this account, had conceived a diabolical project. They wanted to take possession of the town and destroy everything. But as they are not allowed to do this they are angry. The doctor, that Pole, you know, is the ringleader; and, as you know, a Pole is capable of anything. He had the others in his room yesterday, and he showed them things—such things! And he told them things —such things! It would make the very hair stand on your head to hear them."

"Oh, the saints of paradise! Tell me quickly or I shall die of fear!"

"He showed them—a skull—a dead man's skull!"

"Ah! ah!"

"And then he showed them a book full of red pictures, dreadful enough to dry up your bowels."

"Oh! oh! oh!"

"But, listen; there is something still more terrible. After showing them all these things, after speaking words that a Christian cannot repeat, the Pole said this: 'In seven days,' he said, 'we shall have another lesson, then another, and so on for seven times. And then, after the seventh lesson——'"

Here the speaker raised her voice, and paused for a moment to watch the effect of her words.

"Oh, oh!" exclaimed the *Popadia*, "the powers of the holy cross protect us!"

"'After the seventh lesson,' said the Pole, 'we shall be strong and powerful, and able to blow up the city with all its inhabitants to the very last man.'"

"To the last man—oh!——"

And the *Popadia* made as if she were going to faint; but, remembering the imminence of the danger, she refrained.

"And the *ispravnik*, what does he say?"

"The *ispravnik* is an ass; or, perhaps, he has been won over by these plotters—sold himself to the doctor."

"Do you know what we must do, then, mother? We must go to Mrs. Captain. Come!"

"Yes, that is it. Let us go to Mrs. Captain."

Ten minutes later the two friends were in the street, both attired in the same grotesque costume, and if they had tumbled about among the snow they might easily have been mistaken for a couple of frolicsome young bears. But they were too much concerned about the fate of their native town to think of amusing themselves in this or in any other fashion. They hurried on to their friend to pour into her sympathetic ear the story of Matrena, the fish-wife, a story, we may be sure, not likely to lose anything in the telling.

"Mrs. Captain" was the wife of the captain of gendarmerie, who had been a resident at Gorodishko for several years. So long as the exiles were few the *ispravnik* had been in sole charge. But when the number rose to twenty and went on increasing, it was thought necessary to provide him with a colleague in the person of a captain of gendarmerie. The exiles were thus placed under the supervision of two rival authorities who were always on the watch to trip each other up, and, by a great show of zeal, ingratiate themselves with their superiors at the expense, it need hardly be said, of the unfortunate objects of their solicitude. Since the captain arrived at Gorodishko not one political exile had been released. If the *ispravnik* gave a good account of a man the captain gave him a bad one, whereas if the latter had reported favorably of any one the former reported unfavorably.

It was the captain of gendarmerie who on the present occasion checkmated his adversary. A well-drawn up denunciation was forwarded to the governor of the province by the first courier. The answer, the nature of which it was easy to foresee, was not long in coming. The *ispravnik* received a severe reprimand, and a threat of dismissal "for his careless supervision of the political exiles," and the license he had allowed them.

This rap on the knuckles so terrified the chief of police, that not alone were the exiles forbidden to give each other lessons, but placed under something like a state of siege. If there were too many of them in a room at the same time the gendarmes knocked at the window as a summons to disperse. They were also forbidden to form groups in the streets—in other words, to walk together—an order in a town of one street somewhat difficult of execution, and which led to several misunderstandings with the police.

* * *

Ties are early formed in exile, for exiles, exposed as they

are to vexations on every hand, to all sorts of annoyance and ill-will, naturally cling to each other and take refuge in their own little world. Like people in colleges, prisons, barracks, and on board ship, they are thrown so much together that the least similarity of character and sentiment leads to intimacies which may grow into lifelong friendships.

After the setting in of winter our friends' little commune received an accession in the person of the *starik*, who had become much attached to them. They lived together like a family, but the two that seemed to form the strongest intimacy were Taras and young Orshine.

In the growth of friendships there is something strange and not easily definable. Perhaps it was the very contrast of their natures—the one concentrated and self-possessed, the other expansive and enthusiastic—which drew these men together; or perhaps it was the need of having somebody to support and protect that attracted the strong and energetic Taras to the frail boy, tender and impressionable as a woman. Be that as it may, they became almost inseparable. Yet when the others rallied Taras on their friendship he seemed annoyed, saying it was only habit, and in his manner with Orshine there was often a certain measure of reserve and restraint. They did not even "thou" each other, common as is this practice among young Russians. Nevertheless Taras, while hiding his feelings under a variety of pretexts and subterfuges, watched over his friend with the solicitude of a loving and devoted mother.

One day at the beginning of spring—in the monotony of exile, albeit the days drag as if they would go on forever, the months pass quickly—the friends came in from a walk. They had been repeating for the thousandth time the same conjecture as to the probability of a speedy ending of their exile, and citing for the hundredth time the same signs in support of their hopes. They had also discussed, as usual, the expediency of trying to escape, and decided, as usual, in the negative. Neither of them that at time was bent on flight. They thought it better to wait. The revocation was sure to come. Both were socialists, but Taras was all for influencing society largely and on the mass. He was conscious of being an orator, loved his art, and had tasted the first-fruits of success. He had no wish to sacrifice the future of his dream —the only one to which he aspired—for the underground activity of a member of the Terrorist party. He resolved therefore still to wait, although his lot became even harder to bear and patience less easy to practise. Orshine, on the other hand, had not a spark of personal ambition. It was a sentiment he could not even comprehend. The youth was a genuine type of a class of young men common in Russia and known as *narodnik*—enthusiastic admirers of the peasantry. It had been his wish to leave the university and take the position of school-master in some obscure village, and there pass his life, not in influencing the peasants (that would have been unwarrantable presumption), but in giving them the rudiments of culture. Though his plans were temporarily thwarted by the troubles at the university, in which he could not avoid taking part, and which had caused his exile to Gorodishko, he had not renounced them. He even desired to turn his enforced leisure to account by learning some handicraft which might help him to "simplify" himself, and enable him the better to study the peasantry whom, as yet, he knew only in the poems of Mekinssoff.

When the friends reached the town it was already late, and the peasant fishermen were going out for their hard night's work. By the rosy light of the setting sun they could see a number of them preparing their nets. One was singing.

"How these fellows work, and yet they sing!" said Orshine, pityingly.

Taras, turning his head, looked vaguely in the direction indicated.

"What a fine song!" went on Orshine. "It is as if something of the soul of the people vibrated in it. I find it very melodious, don't you?"

Taras shook his head and laughed lightly. But his attention had been roused, and when he came near the singer he listened. The words of the song struck him. It was evidently an old ballad, and he conceived on the instant an idea. He thought he had found an occupation which would help to while away the time. He would make a collection of popular songs and traditions, a collection which might possibly form a valuable contribution to folk-lore and literature.

When he communicated his idea to Orshine, the latter found it splendid, another got the peasant to repeat his song, and made a note of it there and then.

They both went to bed in high spirits, and the next day Taras set out in search of the treasures which he proposed to gather. He did not think it necessary to make any secret of his intention. Twenty years before a company of exiles had openly undertaken a similar work, and enriched science with specimens of the folk-lore of Northern Russia previously unknown. But that was one time, this was another. The *ispravnik* had not forgotten the affair of the lessons. When he heard of the exile's new enterprise he was furious, and sent for Taras to his office, when a scene took place which the latter did not soon forget. The *ispravnik*, that brute with a thief's wages, dared to insult him, Taras; dared to threaten him with a dungeon for "disturbing people's minds"—as if these stupid scandal-mongers ever had any minds! All the pride of his nature was thoroughly roused. He would have liked to knock the fellow down. But he refrained; they would have shot him on the spot; that would have been too great a triumph for the blackguards. So Taras spoke never a word; but when he left the police office, his deadly paleness showed how sharp had been the conflict and how much it had cost him to keep his temper.

The same evening, when he and his friend were returning from a long and silent walk, Taras said suddenly—

"Why should we not go away? The one can be no worse than the other."

Orshine made no reply. He could not as yet make up his mind. Taras understood. He understood also why Orshine demurred to his proposal; for exiles, like long-married couples, know each other so well that answers are often unnecessary; they can divine their companions' thoughts and interpret their unspoken words.

The younger exile, moreover, was in good spirits. A school had been opened at Gorodishko; a governess of the new style was on her way to take charge of it, and Orshine awaited her arrival with impatience. It pleased him to think that he would make her acquaintance, and take lessons from her in the art of teaching. He could have consented to stay a long time at Gorodishko if he might have had permission to help her. But of that there was no question.

At length the new teacher came. She had gone through a course of pedagogy, and was the first to begin the new system of teaching at Gorodishko. All the fashionable people of the place went to see the young woman at work with as much curiosity as if the school had been a menagerie and she a tamer of wild beasts. Orshine could not help making her acquaintance, and when he waited on her he met with a very cordial reception. Passionately attached to her calling, the young teacher was delighted to meet with somebody who shared in her enthusiasm and sympathized in her views. Orshine left her house with a pile of pedagogic books under his arm, and his visit was followed by several others. But one day when he called he found the young woman in great trouble. She had been summarily dismissed from the situation "for having relations with political exiles."

Orshine was in dispair. He protested energetically against the teacher's dismissal, and pleaded warmly in her favor, pointing out that it was he who had sought her acquaintance, not she who had sought his. But all was in vain; the authorities were not to be moved from their purpose, and the unfortunate teacher had to go.

As Taras and Orshine returned from the wharf, whither they had been to see her off, the former repeated the question he had so often put before—

"Well, don't you think I am right?" he said. "One can be no worse than the other."

"Yes, yes," answered the younger man passionately. He had borne the wrongs inflicted on himself with a patience and forbearance which to his friend was simply exasperating. But now the cup had run over.

"If we are not liberated this winter we will escape," resumed Taras. "What do you say?"

"Yes, yes; by all means."

The winter brought only new troubles.

* * *

It was mail day. Writing and receiving letters were the only events that broke the sameness of that stagnant world. It might almost be said that the exiles lived only between one mail day and the other. The post arrived at Gorodishko every ten days—that is to say, about three times a month. Although, according to the regulations, an exile's correspondence is not of necessity censured, none of the Gorodishko exiles were spared the infliction, for the administration shrewdly calculated that the privilege of exemption, if granted to one, must be granted to all. They therefore granted it to none, and all the letters addressed to the exiles, after being read by the *ispravnik*, were resealed with his own seal and forwarded to their owners. Their friends never, of course, thought of writing to them anything of a compromising character, any more than if they had been actual prisoners, everybody being aware that all their letters passed through the hands of the police. But owing to the crass ignorance of the officials of that remote region, the censorship of correspondence gives rise to innumerable vexations. A scientific phrase, or a word of foreign origin, is enough to put them into a paroxysm of suspicion, and a long-looked-for and ardently-desired letter is lost in the bottomless pit of the Third Section. The greater part of "misunderstandings" with the police are caused by the confiscation of correspondence. Letters written by the exiles of Gorodishko were treated in the same way. To prevent them from evading the humiliating obligation, a policeman was always stationed by the single letter-box the place possessed, and he seized without scruple any mail matter that an exile or his landlady attempted to post. A few copecks might have closed one of the fellow's eyes—perhaps both of them. But what would have been the use? The people of Gorodishko are so little given to correspondence, that the postmaster knows the handwriting of every one of them, and can recognize an exile's letter at a glance. Nor is this all. The correspondence of the natives is confined to Archangelsk, chief town of the province and head-quarters of its trade. Letters addressed to Odessa, Kieff, Caucas, and other distant cities, belonged almost exclusively to the exiles.

To evade the censorship, then, it was necessary to hit on some special expedient, and it one day occurred to Orshine to utilize for this purpose a book he was returning to a comrade at Odessa. He wrote a long epistle on the margins, so arranging the book that, as he thought, it would not easily open at the part where he had written. He had practised the stratagem before, and always with success. But this time an accident led to its discovery, and there was a terrible to do. It is hardly necessary to say that Orshine had written nothing very particular or serious. What that is serious or particular has an exile to say? But Orshine, when he penned the epistle, being in a bantering vein, drew a picture more sarcastic than flattering of the fashionable and official world of Gorodishko, in which, as may be supposed, the *ispravnik* and his wife occupied a prominent place. The chief of police, who had discovered the secret of the book, was beside himself with rage. Running across to our friends' quarters, he threw himself among them like a bombshell.

"Mr. Orshine, put on your clothes at once. You must go to prison."

"Why, what has happened?" said the young man, in great surprise.

"You have been sending clandestine correspondence to the papers with the object of exposing the established authorities to ridicule and disrespect, and shaking the pillars of rule."

On this the friends perceived what had come to pass, and were very much disposed to laugh in the *ispravnik's* face. But it was hardly a time for laughter. They had to protect their friend and assert their rights.

"Orshine shall not go to prison. You have no right to put him there," said Taras, firmly.

"I did not speak to you. Shut your mouth. Make haste, Orshine."

"We shall not let you take Orshine to prison," repeated Taras, looking the *ispravnik* full in the face.

He spoke resolutely and slowly, a sign with him of growing anger.

"He is ill," put in Losinski.

All took the same line, and thus followed a hot dispute. Meanwhile the other exiles, having got wind of what was going on, hurried to the spot and joined in the remonstrances of their friends. Taras took the lead, and despite Orshine's pressing and reiterated request, that they would not compromise themselves on his account, they refused to let him go.

"If you put him in prison you must put us all there," they shouted.

"And then we will knock the old carcass in pieces about your ears," said Taras.

The affair began to look ugly, for the *ispravnik* threatened to call his men to arms and use force. In the end Orshine insisted on giving himself up, and his friends reluctantly allowed him to be taken away.

He was kept in the lock-up only two days, but the incident embittered still further the relations between the exiles and the police. The former took their revenge in the only way open to them. It so happened that the *ispravnik* had a morbid and almost superstitious dread of newspaper criticism. The exiles resolved to strike the man in his tenderest point. They wrote a sarcastic letter about him, and contrived to send it to a St. Petersburg paper by a roundabout way. The letter duly reached its destination and appeared in print, not only hitting its mark, but causing considerable excitement. The governor himself was annoyed, and ordered an inquiry. Many of the exiles and their lodgings were searched "for traces of the crime;" and as the guilty man could not be detected, all were suspected in turn, and submitted to every sort of petty persecution, especially as touching their correspondence. The police insisted on the strict observance of every article of the regulation, in the application of which the exiles had hitherto succeeded in obtaining considerable indulgence. Losinski was the first to suffer from this change of policy. The eternal question of his medical practice again came up. A contention on this subject had been going on ever since the doctor's arrival at Gorodishko. The last pretext on which he had been refused permission to practise was that he might profit by it to make a political propaganda. Yet when one of the officials or some member of their families fell ill, he would often be called in. In this way his professional activity came to be practically tolerated, if not openly recognized. But he was now roundly informed by the *ispravnik* that if he did not strictly comply with the regulations his disobedience would be reported to the governor. The chief of police had no idea of risking the loss of his place in order "to give Dr. Losinski pleasure."

Nor were the others more tenderly dealt with. The supervision exercised over them by the police was almost past bearing. They were not allowed to extend their walks beyond the limits of the wretched little town, which thus became their prison. They were continually annoyed by visits of inspection, equivalent to the roll-calls of the prisons. Not a morning passed that a policeman did not call to inquire about their health. Every other day they had to call at the police office and enter their names in a book kept for the purpose. Virtually they were in a jail—a jail without cells, yet surrounded by a vast desert which cut Gorodishko off from the world of the living more effectually than granite walls. The police, moreover, had the exiles continually in view; the latter could never appear in the street without being followed by one or more gendarmes. Whether they went in or out, whether they paid a visit or received a friend, they were always under the eye of the *ispravnik* or his agents.

This was all the more discouraging as there was little prospect of a change for the better. On the contrary, the chances were rather in favor of an aggravation than an amelioration of their lot, for, as they learned from the *ispravnik's* secretary, a storm was brewing against them at Archangelsk. They were in bad odor with the governor, and it was probable that some of their number would be sent before long to a town still more to the north.

In these circumstances further hesitation would have been foolish, and Taras and Orshine informed their companions of the commune, and afterwards the entire colony, that they had decided to attempt an escape. Their resolution met with general approval, and four of their fellow-exiles determined to follow their example. But it being out of the question for six men to go away at once, it was arranged that they should leave two at a time. Taras and Orshine were to be the first pair, Losinski and Ursitch the next, while the third was to be composed of two of the older exiles. The colony talked of nothing else. The whole of the common fund was placed at the disposal of the fugitives, and to increase it by a few roubles the exiles imposed on themselves the greatest privations. The remainder of the winter passed in discussing the various projects which were suggested, and preparing for the great event.

* * *

In addition to the political exiles, Gorodishko possessed about twenty ordinary transports—pickpockets, petty forgers, larcenous *tchinovniks*, and other rogues of divers grades. These malefactors were all far more indulgently treated than the politicals. Their correspondence was not censored, and so long as they were occupied were let alone. But they did not much care to be occupied, preferring rather to live by begging and pilfering. The authorities, who are "dogs and wolves" with the politicals, show great forbearance towards the rogues, with whom they have evidently a fellow-feeling, and take tithe of their plunder. These commune transports are the scourge of the country. Sometimes they form themselves into organized gangs. There was one town, Sheukoursk, which they actually put in a state of siege. Nobody was allowed either to go out or come in without paying them black-mail. At Kholmogori their conduct rose to such a height that the governor, Ignatieff, had to proceed to the place in person before they could be reduced to order. He called the rascals before him, and gave them a paternal lecture on their misconduct. They listened with the utmost respect, promised to behave better in the future, and, as they left the audience chamber, stole his samovar. As it was a very fine samovar, and the police were unable to recover it, a message of peace was sent to the thieves, and negotiations were opened for the return of the stolen property. In the end the governor ransomed his samovar with a payment of five roubles.

The relations between the two classes of exiles are somewhat peculiar. The rogues profess great respect for the politicals and render them many services—a respect, however, which does not prevent them from cheating their fellow-exiles and taking their money whenever opportunity offers.

As the thieves were less closely watched than the politicals, it occurred to Ursitch that they might be turned to good account in the matter of the contemplated escape. But though this plan had many advantages, it had one great drawback. The thieves, most of whom were confirmed drunkards, could not be trusted. Yet the co-operation of somebody outside their own body, if not absolutely necessary, was very desirable, and the question arose as to what they should do.

"I have it!" exclaimed Losinski one day. "I have spotted my man—Uskimbai!"

"The Sultan?"

"Yes, the Sultan. He is the very man!"

The doctor had cured him of an affection of the chest, to which the wild men of the steppes are always liable when transported to the frozen north, and from that moment Uskimbai had shown for his benefactor the blind affection of a dog for his master. He was a man upon whom they could count—honest and simple, a very child of nature.

The commune invited the Sultan to tea, and explained

what they desired him to do. He agreed without hesitation to everything they proposed, and entered heartily into the exiles' plans. Being under a much more liberal *régime* than the politicals, he was allowed to carry on a little trade in cattle, and from time to time visited the neighboring villages, where he had several acquaintances, and would be able to conduct the fugitives to the first stage. In his anxiety to oblige the doctor and his friends, who alone at Gorodishko had befriended him, the poor fellow made little of the danger of detection.

It is unnecessary to dwell on the details of the escape. It was effected under the best auspices. Uskimbai acquitted himself of his task to admiration, and brought back the news of the fugitives' safe arrival at the first relay (stage) and their departure for Archangelsk. A week passed quietly; another, and unwonted activity was observed among the police. It was a bad sign, and the exiles feared that some ill had befallen the fugitives. This foreboding was only too quickly realized. A few days later they heard from the *ispravnik's* secretary that at Archangelsk their friends had fallen under the suspicion of the police, and that, although they succeeded in getting away, they were followed, and after a chase of five days, during which they underwent terrible hardships, they fell, faint and exhausted with hunger and fatigue, into the hands of their enemies, who treated them with the utmost brutality. Orshine was struck and rendered almost insensible. Taras defended himself with his revolver, but was overpowered, disarmed and fettered. The two were then thrust into a carriage and taken to Archangelsk, where Orshine had been placed in the hospital to be cured of his wounds.

This was a thunder-stroke for the exiles, and plunged them into the deepest distress. For a long time they remained in mournful silence, every man fearing to look his neighbor in the face lest he should see there the reflection of his own despair. And yet every object, every incident, recalled these unfortunate friends, whom a community of suffering had made as dear to them as their own kin. It was only when they were gone that they knew how much they had loved these lost ones.

On one of the three remaining members of the commune this new trouble had an unlooked-for effect. The evening of the third day after the arrival of the fatal news, Starik, who had been much depressed, was persuaded to make a visit to one of his old friends of another commune. He was expected back about eleven. Yet eleven came and went, and no Starik; but at the stroke of twelve the outer door opened, and the tread of halting footsteps was heard in the corridor. It could not be Starik; he was not wont to walk unsteadily. Ursitch went outside, holding a candle over his head, to see who the intruder was, and by its fitful light perceived the figure of a man leaning helplessly against the wall. It was Starik, blind drunk—the first time he had been in such a state since he had joined the commune. The others brought him in, and the work of looking after their unfortunate friend served in some measure to lighten the burden of their affliction.

* * *

The year following was marked by many sorrowful incidents. Taras was tried for armed resistance to the police, and sentenced to hard labor for life. Orshine, before he had recovered from his hurts, was transported to an Esquimaux village in seventy degrees of north latitude, where the ground thaws only six weeks in the year. Losinski had a letter from him, full of sadness, a letter that left no doubt as to what the end would be. The poor fellow was very ill. His chest, he said, was in such a state that he felt fit for nothing, "and you are not here to make me listen to reason." His teeth were playing him traitor, and showed a great desire to leave his mouth. This was in allusion to the scurvy, a disease peculiarly fatal in polar regions. In the same hamlet with Orshine was another exile, sent thither, like himself, for attempting to escape. They were evidently very wretched, being often without either meat or bread. Orshine had abandoned all hope of ever again seeing his friends. Even if a chance of escaping were to present itself he could not profit thereby, so utter was his weakness. He concluded with these words: "This spring I hope to die." And he died before the time himself had fixed. About his death, moreover, there was something mysterious. It was never exactly known whether he died naturally, or shortened his sufferings by suicide.

In the meanwhile the lives of the exiles had become more and more insupportable. After the attempted escape of the two friends the tyranny of their custodians increased, and their hope of being restored to liberty and civilization vanished almost to nothingness. For as the revolutionary movement extended, the severity of the Government towards those whom it retained in its power became greater; and as a further check on attempts to escape it was decreed that every such attempt should be punished by exile to Eastern Siberia.

But all the same, escapes continued to be attempted. The Gorodishko police, fatigued with their own zeal, had hardly begun to relax their precaution when Losinski and Ursitch made off. It was a desperate enterprise, for they were so ill-supplied with money that success was almost out of the question. But Losinski could not wait. He was on the point of being transferred to another town because he had not been able to refuse the appeal of a mother to visit her sick child and of a husband to attend his fever-stricken wife. Fortune, moreover, did not favor them. They were compelled to separate on the way, and from that time forth Losinski was heard of no more. He disappeared without leaving a trace behind. His fate is therefore a matter of conjecture. Having to traverse the forests on foot, he probably lost his way, and either died of hunger or fell a prey to the wolves which infest that part of the country.

Ursitch, in the beginning, was more fortunate. Not having enough money to pay his way to St. Petersburg, he engaged himself at Vologdb as a common laborer, and worked there until he had saved enough to continue his journey. But at the very moment he entered the train he was recognized and recaptured, and subsequently condemned to lifelong exile in the land of the wild Yakoutes.

As he marched along the tear-bedewed road to Siberia, escorted by soldiers and surrounded by companions in misfortune, he met, not far from Krasnoiarsk, a post-carriage drawn by three horses and going at full speed. The face of the principal occupant, a well-dressed man in a cocked hat, seemed familiar to him. He looked more attentively, and could hardly restrain a cry of joy as he recognized in the traveller his friend Taras—Taras himself. He could not be mistaken. This time, at least, Taras had succeeded in escaping, and was now on his way to Russia as fast as three fleet horses could take him.

Quickly the carriage came on, passed like a flash, and disappeared in a cloud of dust. But in that brief moment—was it illusion or was it reality?—it seemed to him that he had caught his friend's eye, and that a gleam of recognition and pity swept over his energetic face.

As Ursitch looked backward towards the fast-flying carriage, all the sorrowful past which that face recalled rose before him; and he saw, like an impassable gulf, the dark future which awaited him and his fellow-captives. But he wished all success to the fugitive, whom he knew to be brave and strong, and made him in thought the bearer of his hopes and the executor of his vengeance.

Whether Taras really recognized his friend in the fettered

convict by the wayside we are unable to say. But we know that he faithfully accomplished the mission mutely confided to him. At St. Petersburg he joined the party of action, and for three years he fought on—without resting either head or arm—wherever the battle was hottest. When at last he was taken and condemned to death, he could say proudly and with all justice that he had done his duty. But they did not hang him; his sentence was commuted to imprisonment for life, and he was left to perish in the Fortress of St. Peter and St. Paul.

Thus, at the end of five years, there remained of the little family by adoption, which had first met in that remote northern village, but one "living"—that is to say free from chains. This solitary survivor was Starik. He is still in the same place, without hope and without future, not desiring even to quit the wretched town where he has stayed so long, for in the state to which he is reduced what is he fit for, the unfortunate?

* * *

My story is finished. Though it may not be cheerful or diverting, it has at least the merit of being true. I have simply tried to reproduce the reality. The scenes I have described are being continually repeated in the hulks of Siberia and other northern towns which the Government has transformed into veritable prisons. Even worse things than I have told come to pass; for I have narrated only ordinary cases, not wishing to take advantage of the right given me by the form I have adopted in this sketch to darken my colors for the sake of dramatic effect. To prove this I need only make a few extracts from the official report of a personage whom none certainly will accuse of exaggeration—General Baranoff, formerly prefect of St. Petersburg, now Governor of Riazan, and who for a short time was governor of the province of Archangelsk. Let the reader himself read between the lines of this matter-of-fact document the tears, the sorrows, and the tragedies which its every page reflects.

I translate, of course, literally, retaining the conventional expressions employed by a Russian *employé* when addressing the cabinet of the Tzar.

"From the experience of past years, and my own personal observation," says the general, "I have arrived at the conclusion that administrative exile for political causes tends rather to exasperate a man and infect him with perverse ideas than to correct him (correction being the officially declared object of exile). The change from a life of ease to a life of privation, from life in the bosom of society to separation from all society, from an activity more or less active to an enforced inaction—all this produces an effect so disastrous that often, especially of late—(observe !)—there have occurred among the exiles cases of madness, of suicide and attempted suicide. All this is but the direct result of the abnormal conditions of life under which exile places educated and intelligent men. We know no instances of a man exiled for motives based on serious suspicion of his political convictions leaving his exile reconciled with the Government, purged of his errors, and converted into a useful member of society and a faithful servant of the throne. On the contrary, we can affirm that very often a man sent into exile by misunderstanding—(observe again ! what an exemplary confession is this)—or by an error of the administration, becomes—partly owing to personal exasperation, partly by the influence of men really hostile to the Government—himself hostile to the Government. As for the man in whom are already implanted the germs of anti-governmental tendencies, exile, by the whole of its conditions, will favor the growth of these germs, sharpen his discontent, and transform his theoretic opposition into practical opposition ; *i. e.*, into an opposition extremely dangerous. Among citizens who have no connection with revolution it develops, in consequence of the same conditions, revolutionary ideas, thus producing results diametrically opposed to those to obtain which exile was instituted. And whatever may be the outward conditions of an exile's life, exile itself gives the victim the idea of arbitrary administration, which alone is sufficient to exclude all possibility of reconciliation and amendment."*

The outspoken general is quite right. All who have succeeded in escaping from exile have almost, without exception, entered the ranks of the extreme Terrorist party. Administrative exile, as a correctional measure, is an absurdity. General Baranoff must be truly unsophisticated if he believes that the Government is not fully aware of this, or believes for a moment in the reformatory efficacy of the system. Administrative exile is at once a punishment and a formidable weapon of defence. Those who escape it become, it is true, determined enemies of the Government. But it is an open question whether this result would not equally come to pass if they were not exiled. There are numbers of revolutionists and terrorists who have never undergone this ordeal. For every one who escapes from exile, moreover, there are a hundred who remain and perish irrevocably. Of the hundred the great majority are entirely innocent; but ten or fifteen, or perhaps twenty-five, are really enemies of the Government, or likely in a short time to become so; and those of them who perish with the others are so many taken from the devil—so many foes the fewer.

The only practical conclusion Count Tolstoi could draw from the general's *naïf* report would be that a decree of exile should never be revoked; and this in effect is the principle on which the Government consistently acts.

---

* *The Moscow Juridic Review.* October, 1883.

CHAPTER XXIV.

A DESTROYED GENERATION.

WE have so far restricted ourselves to a description of administrative exile in its mildest form, as it exists in the northern provinces of European Russia. We have said nothing of Siberian exile in general, of which the peculiarity consists in the senseless and despotic brutality of the least and lowest police functionaries, who have been made what they are by the system of penitential colonies which has prevailed in Siberia since its annexation to the empire of the Tzars.

In the latter part of the reign of Alexander II. there came into vogue another form of exile—that to Eastern Siberia. It still endures, and though considerations of space forbid us to treat the subject at length, it is too important to be altogether ignored. The reader will remember that most of the men whose cases we have cited as examples of the extreme arbitrariness of the punishment of exile (Dr. Bely, Jujakoff, Kovalevski, and others), were banished to Eastern Siberia—the country of the Yakoutes—a country apart, differing much more from the rest of Siberia than Siberia differs from European Russia.

We will not weary the reader with descriptions of this almost unknown land, but simply give the translation of an article which appeared in the *Moscow Zemstvo* of February 4, 1881. This article gives the substance of several letters on the subject published, with the permission of the official censors, during the brief period of liberalism which began with the dictatorship of Loris Melikoff.

" We know and we are accustomed," runs the article in

question, "to the hard conditions of administrative exile in European Russia, thanks to the bovine patience of our Russian people. But as to the conditions of Siberian exile beyond the Ural we have, until lately, known next to nothing. Our ignorance on this score arises from the fact that before 1878–79 instances of administrative exile in Siberia were extremely rare. In former times we were much more humane. The instinct of morality, not yet stifled by political passion, did not permit the sending of untried people by administrative order to a country in which exile is regarded by Russians as equivalent to penal servitude. But after a while the administration, stopping at nothing, began to banish men to places the very name of which excited horror. Even the wild country of the Yakoutes is beginning to be peopled with exiles. It might be supposed that those who are sent thither are criminals of deepest dye. But so far the public has heard nothing of the nature of their offences, while, on the other hand, the Press has published communications which remain without contradiction, proving that these men have been exiled on grounds as strange as they are incomprehensible. Thus M. Vladimir Korolenko relates in the *Molva* his sad history, with the object, as he says, of ascertaining wherefore and for what cause he so narrowly escaped being exiled to the land of the Yakoutes. In 1879 two searches were made in his lodgings absolutely without result. This, however, did not hinder him from being sent to the province of Kiatka for reasons which he has been unable to discover. After passing five months in the town of Glasvo, he was one day honored with an unexpected visit from the *ispravnik*, who, after making a search of his lodgings without finding anything suspicious, informed our exile that he would be forthwith deported to the Huts (*polchinki*) of Beriosoff, a place altogether unsuited for a civilized being.

"After he had passed some time in these miserable Huts there suddenly arrived several gendarmes—functionaries who had never been seen there before—took Mr. Korolenko and his slender baggage, and marched him off to Viatka. Here he was kept fifteen days a prisoner without receiving any explanation, or undergoing any examination, and then taken, under escort, to the jail of Vishne Volotchkov, whence there is only one road—that to Siberia. Fortunately for him this jail was visited during his detention by a member of the Commission of Revision, Prince Immeretenski, whom Mr. Korolenko prayed to inform him whither, and for what crime, he was to be exiled. The prince was complaisant and humane enough to give him the particulars of the case set forth in the official documents. According to these papers Mr. Korolenko was to be deported into the country of the Yakoutes for attempting to escape, an offence which he had never committed. The Commission of Revision was just then inquiring into the system of political exile, and a multitude of cases of revolting injustice was brought to light. A happy change now took place in the fate of Mr. Korolenko. At the Tomek *étape* (Western Siberia) he and several other unfortunates were informed that five of them were to be fully liberated, and five others sent to European Russia. But all are not equally fortunate. There are men who continue to enjoy the pleasures of life in the polar circle, albeit the crime imputed to them differ in no essential respect from that imputed to Mr. Korolenko. Thus the *Rousskia Vedomosti* gives the history of a young man now at Verkoiansk, whose adventures are truly remarkable. He was a student at Kieff university. For complicity in some disorders that took place there in April, 1878, he was exiled to Novgorod, which, as being a not very remote province, is reserved by the administration for persons whose offences they regard as venial. Even the severe administration of that period did not attribute to this young man any political importance, as is proved by the fact that a little later he was transferred from Novgorod to the province of Kherson, which is much warmer and better in every respect than the former district. It is necessary to add, moreover, that, according to the directions of Count Loris Melikoff, all the students of Kieff university who were exiled to towns in European Russia for participation in university disorders, have been liberated and allowed to resume their studies. Yet one of these same students is at present living in the Yakoute country, really because the higher administration thought fit to ameliorate his lot by transferring him from Novgorod to Kherson. The fact is that when Count Todtleben, the Governor-general of Odessa, undertook to purge the region under his charge of its noxious elements, he exiled to Siberia, without exception, everybody who was under the supervision of the police; and to this fate the *ci-devant* Kieff student had to submit for no other reason than that it was his ill-fortune to be placed under supervision in the province of Kherson (forming part of the southern district) instead of that of Novgorod!

"Another equally astounding instance of exile to Eastern Siberia is related by the *Moscow Telegraph*. According to the particulars set forth, this fate befell Mr. Borodine, a gentleman who had published in the St. Petersburg papers several articles on local economic questions. He lived at Viatka under police oversight. One evening at the theatre he had a dispute with the deputy *pristav* (officer of police), Mr. Filimonov, about a place, in the course of which the latter struck Mr. Borodine in the presence of several onlookers. The blow had a decisive influence on the fortunes not of the insulter, but of the insulted. Though the officer was not so much as reprimanded, Mr. Borodine was put in prison, and it required great efforts on his own part as well as on that of his friends to procure his liberation. His freedom, however, was of brief duration, for shortly thereafter he was sent by *étape* (that is to say, on foot, and with a gang of common malefactors) to Eastern Siberia.

"But how came it to pass that Mr. Borodine was exiled, seeing that his quarrel with the deputy *pristav* ended satisfactorily in his release from prison ? We do not err in saying that the answer to this question is found in the communication addressed to the *Rousskia Vedomosti* on the exile to Viatka of the author of certain articles printed in the *Annals of the Country*, the *True Russian Word*, and other periodicals. Yet his name was not mentioned. It is only said that while living at Viatka he committed, in the eyes of the local administration, a great crime. When the administration affirmed that the province was prosperous, he proved by facts and figures that, so far from this being the case, the people were dying of hunger. The consequence was this turbulent and disagreeable man—to the administration—had to submit to two police visitations ; and at last they found among his papers the manuscript of an article intended for the Press, and the supposed cause of the writer's exile to Eastern Siberia. After a long journey on foot, in the costume of a convict, with a yellow ace on his back, our author arrived at Irkoutsk. Here he had the pleasure of receiving the *Annals of the Country*, wherein was printed at length, without either abbreviations or omissions, the article to which his exile was ascribed.

"Let us see now what is the life of a man exiled in the country of the Yakoutes. Here we have to notice, in the first place, the facilities for communication with the Central Government. If an exile living at Kolimsk should think fit to petition Count Loris Melikoff for a revocation of his exile, the petition would reach St. Petersburg in a year. Another year must pass before the minister's inquiries touching the exile's conduct and political opinion can reach the local police. The third year will be taken up with the conveyance of the answer from Kolimsk to St. Petersburg that the police see no objection to the petitioner's liberation. Finally, at the end of the fourth year, the minister's order for the prisoner's release will reach Kolimsk. If the exile has no personal or hereditary property, and if before his banishment he lived by intellectual work, for which there is no demand in the Yakoute country, he will risk death by famine at least four hundred times during the four years while the post is making the four journeys between St. Petersburg and Kolimsk. The administration allows nobles by origin six roubles a month; while a *poud* (40 lbs.) of black bread cost at Verkhoiansk five to six roubles, and at Kolimsk nine roubles. If physical labor, hard and ungrateful to men of education, or the help of relatives and friends, or, lastly, alms given in the name of Christ, save the exile from death by hunger, the terrible polar cold will give him rheumatism for all his life, and if he has not strong lungs conduct him to the tomb. In such towns as Verkhoiansk and Kolimsk, the former of which has 224 inhabitants of both sexes, the latter a few more, there is no such thing as civilized society. Nearly all are Yakoutes or Russian Yakoutes. Yet the exile who is allowed to live in any town whatever may esteem himself fortunate. In the Yakoute country there exists another sort of exile still more cruel and barbarous, an exile of which the Russian public has no idea, and is informed for the first time by the *Rousskia Vedomosti*. This is the exile by *oulousses*—that is to say, the placing of men administratively exiled one by one in Yakoute *jourtes* (huts), distant from each other several kilometres. The correspondent of the *Rousskia Vedomosti* cites the letter of an exile living in one of these *oulousses*, which vividly describes the terrible position of an intelligent man thrown pitilessly into the hut of one of these northern savages.

"'The Cossacks who escorted me from Yakoutsk,' he writes, 'are gone, and I am left alone among the Yakoutes, who know not a word of Russian. They watch me continually, fearing that if I go away they will be held responsible by the administration. If you leave the *jourta*—where you are suffocated—for a walk, the suspicious Yakoute follows you. If you take an axe to cut some wood the timid Yakoute tells you by signs to put it down and return to the *jourta*. You return and find sitting before the fire a stark-naked Yakoute catching fleas—a fine tableau! During the winter the Yakoutes live with their cattle, often not separated from them by the slightest partition. The accumulation of excreta of every sort inside the *jourta*, the phenomenal filth and dirt, rotting straw and noisome rags, the multitude of insects on the beds, the insupportable atmosphere, the impossibility of speaking a word in Russian—all this is truly enough to make a man mad. And the food of these Yakoutes it is almost impossible to touch. It is always very dirty, often putrefying, and without salt. If you are not used to food in this state it causes sickness and vomiting. The Yakoutes do not know how to make either pottery or clothes. They have no baths, and during the long winter of eight months you become yourself as dirty as a Yakoute. I cannot go away anywhere, much less to a town, the nearest of which is 120 miles distant. I live with the Yakoutes—turn and turn, about six weeks in one hut, six weeks in another, and so on. I have nothing to read, neither papers nor books, and I know naught of what is going on in the world.'

"Further cruelty cannot go except by fastening a man to the tail of a wild horse and sending him into the steppe, or chaining him to a corpse and leaving him to his fate. It is hardly credible that without trial and by a simple administion order a man can be submitted to sufferings which European civilization does not inflict on the worst of malefactors whose guilt has been pronounced by competent tribunals. Still more incredible seems the assurance of the *Rousskia Vedomosti's* correspondent, that even yet the lot of exiles in the Yakoute country has been in no way bettered, and that even recently there had arrived ten more administrative exiles, who for the most part are sent to the *oulousses*, and that further arrivals were shortly expected."

One word as to the pretended incredulity of the writer of the foregoing article. It is a common subterfuge of the censored Russian Press to express thus quietly and indirectly its disapproval of the proceeding of Government. The *Moscow Zemstvo*, as every Russian who read the account knew, did not doubt for a moment either the reported arrival of the ten exiles in question, or the expected further arrival mentioned by the correspondent of the *Rousskia Vedomosti*.

We have thus reached the utmost limits of the official system of administrative exile as established in Russia. The *Zemstvo* was quite right—it is impossible to go further. After the facts I have exposed it is only figures that can speak. Let us then call figures in evidence.

The havoc wrought by administrative exile is far greater than that wrought by the tribunals. According to the particulars set forth in the almanac of the *Narodnaia Volia* for 1883, there took place between April 1879, when Russia was put under martial law, and the death of Alexander (March, 1881), forty political prosecutions, the accused numbering 245 persons, of whom twenty-eight were acquitted and twenty-four sentenced to trifling punishments. But according to documents in my possession there were exiled to divers places—Eastern Siberia included—from the three satrapies of the south alone (Odessa, Kieff, and Kharkoff) 1,767 persons.

The number of political prisoners sentenced in the 124 trials of the two reigns was 841, a good third of the penalties being little more than nominal. Official statistics relating to administrative exile are not procurable, but when, during the dictatorship of Loris Melikoff, the Government desired to refute the accusation of having exiled the half of Russia, it admitted that in various parts of the empire there were 2,873 exiles, all of whom, with the exception of 271,[*] were exiled in the short period between 1878 and 1880. If

---

[*] See M. Leroy Beaulieu's work on Russia, vol. ii. pp. 445, 446.

we make no allowance for the natural reluctance of the Government to acknowledge the extent of its own shame; if we forget that, owing to the number of authorities who can issue decrees of administrative exile at their discretion without giving information to anybody,* the Central Government itself does not know the number of its victims—if, ignoring all this, we reckon these victims at about three thousand, the true number exiled in 1880, we should double this rate for each of the five years of relentless persecution which followed. In assuming that during the two reigns the totals range from six to eight thousand, we shall not be exceeding the reality. According to information received in the office of the *Narodnaia Volia*, Mr. Tichorimoff computed the number of arrests made in the first half of 1883 at 8,157, and in Russia arrests, nine times out of ten, are followed by exile, or worse.

But we need not dwell on the statistics of punishment. A thousand exiles more or less makes little difference. The great fact is that in a country so poor in intellectual strength as Russia, all that is most noble, generous, and intelligent is buried with these six or eight thousand exiles. All her vital forces are in that great crowd, and if the number be not twelve or sixteen thousand, it is because the nation is unable to furnish so many.

The reader has seen what are the motives deemed by the Government sufficient to justify a man's exile. It is no exaggeration to say that the spies and collaborateurs of Count Tolstoi alone can count on immunity from this fate. To merit exile it is not necessary to be a revolutionist; it is sufficient not to approve fully and entirely the policy and proceedings of the Government. Under conditions such as these an honest and intellectual man is more likely to be exiled than to escape.

Exile in any of its forms—whether banishment among the

---

* See M. Leroy Beaulieu's work on Russia, vol. ii. pp. 445, 446.

Yakoutes or exile in the northern provinces—means, with few exceptions, complete ruin to the victim and the utter destruction of his future. For a mature man, having some profession or occupation—a scientist or writer of reputation—exile is necessarily a great hardship, involving sacrifice of comfort, destruction of his home, and loss of work. Yet if he has energy and strength of character, and does not perish of drink or privation, he may possibly survive. But for a young man, who is generally a scholar, who has not yet acquired a profession, or reached the maturity of his powers, exile is simply fatal. Even if he do not perish physically, his moral ruin is inevitable, and the young alone form nine-tenths of our exiles, and are treated with the greatest rigor. Revocations, moreover, are rare, and generally only granted in cases of " misunderstandings." And if among political exiles there be a few who, after a few years' detention, are reprieved through some fortunate chance, or by the help of influential friends—without being obliged to purchase their liberty by the cowardly hypocrisy of a feigned repentance—the suspicion pursues them from the very moment of their return to active life. On the least occasion they are struck once more—this time forever.

How many are the lives this exile has ruined!

The despotism of Nicolas crushed full-grown men. The despotism of the two Alexanders did not give them time to grow up. They threw themselves on immature generations, on the grass hardly out of the ground, to devour it in all its tenderness. To what other cause can we look for the desperate sterility of modern Russia in every branch of intellectual work? Our contemporary literature, it is true, boasts of great writers—geniuses even—worthy of the highest place in the most brilliant age of our country's literary development. But these are all men whose active work dates from the period of 1840. The romance writer, Leon Tolstoi, is fifty-eight; the satirist, Schedrin (Saltykoff) sixty-one; Goutcharoff, seventy-three; Tourgueneff and Dostorevsky, both recently deceased, were born in 1818. Even writers of the second rank, such as Oushensky in *belles lettres*, Mikenlovsky in criticism, belong to the generation which, beginning life in 1860, was far less harassed than its successors. The new generation produces nothing, absolutely nothing. Despotism has stricken with sterility the high hopes to which the splendid awakening of the first half of the century gave birth. Mediocrity reigns supreme. We have not a single genius; not one man of letters has shown himself a worthy inheritor of the traditions of our young and vigorous literature. As in letters, so it is in public life. All the leaders of our Zemstvo, modest as are their functions, belong to an older generation. The living forces of later generations has been buried by the Government in Siberian snows and Esquimaux villages. It is worse than the pest. A pest comes and goes; the Government has oppressed the country for twenty years, and may go on oppressing it for who knows how many years longer. The pest kills indiscriminately, but the present *régime* chooses its victims from the flower of the nation, taking all on whom depend its future and its glory. It is not a political party whom they crush, it is a nation of a hundred millions whom they stifle.

This is what is done in Russia under the Tzars; this is the price at which the Government buys its miserable existence.

CHAPTER XXV.

HIGHER EDUCATION.

I.

At length we are out of the darkness and away from the abysmal depths in which despotism immures its countless victims. We have finished our excursions into that nether world where we heard at each step cries of despair and impotent rage—the death-rattle of the moribund, and the maniacal laugh of the insane. We are on the surface of the earth and in the full light of day. True, the revelations we have still to make are not gay; the Russia of to-day is a very unhappy country, dear reader. But we shall have no more to do with wasted lives and blood-curdling horrors. We are about to speak of the inanimate, of institutions which do not suffer, although they are falling in pieces. After crushing the living —the man, the artisan—the Government naturally and inevitably attacks the institutions which are the framework and support of human society.

We propose, then, to describe briefly the struggle of the Government with the most vital institutions of the country, institutions to which, because they favor the cultivation of the mind, it is instinctively hostile—the Schools, the Zemstvo, and the Press. The policy pursued by the autocracy towards these three cardinal elements of national well-being will show us what part it plays generally in the life of the State.

I have already had an opportunity of laying bare this policy to the English public. The five chapters on Education and the Press, which form the main part of this section of my book, have been published as special articles in the most influential of European journals (April and September, 1884). I take this opportunity of thanking the *Times* for its appreciative comments on the articles in question, and the proprietors for their permission to reproduce them in the present work. I should have liked to enrich these chapters with examples and citations drawn from that ocean of sadness which Russia now presents to us. But this the limits of my space forbid, and with the exception of some slight changes of phrase and a few interpolations they appear in their original form.

It is well to observe at the outset that Russian universities occupy a position altogether peculiar and exceptional. In other countries universities are places of learning and nothing more. They are frequented by young men, all of whom, save the idle, are busied with their studies, and whose chief if not the sole desire is to pass their examinations and obtain a degree. Though they may take an interest in politics they are not politicians; and if they express sympathy with this or that idea, even albeit the idea be extreme, nobody is either surprised or alarmed, the fact being regarded as evidence of a healthy vitality, fraught with hope for the future of the nation.

In Russia it is altogether different. There the universities and the public schools are the *foci* of the most intense and ardent political life, and in the higher spheres of the Imperial administration the name of student is identified, not with something young, noble, and aspiring, but with a dark and dangerous power inimical to the laws and institutions of the land. And this impression is so far justified that, as recent political trials abundantly prove, the great majority of the young men who throw themselves into the struggle for liberty are under thirty, and belong either to the class of undergraduates or to those whose academic honors are newly won. This, though it may surprise Englishmen, is neither unprecedented nor unnatural. When a government in possession of despotic power punishes as a crime the least show of opposition to its will, nearly all whom age has made cautious or wealth selfish, or who have given hostages to fortunes, shun the strife. It is then that the leaders of the forlorn hope turn to the young, who, though they may lack knowledge and experience, are rarely wanting either in courage or devotion. It was thus in Italy at the time of the Mazzinian conspiracies; in Spain at the time of Riego and Queroga; in Germany at the time of the Tugendbund, and again about the middle of this century. If the transfer of the centre of political gravity to the young is more marked in Russia than it has been elsewhere, it is that the determining causes have been more powerful in their action and more prolonged in their duration. One of the most potent of these causes is the conduct of the Government, whose ill-judged measures of repression exasperate the youth of our universities and convert latent discontent into flat rebellion. That this is no mere assertion, the facts I am about to adduce will sufficiently prove.

Towards the end of 1878 there occurred among the students of St. Petersburg University some so-called "disorders." They were not serious, and in ordinary circumstances would have been punished by sending a few score of young fellows to waste the rest of their lives in some obscure village of the far north, and neither the Ministry nor the University Council would have given the matter further thought. But this time there was a new departure. After passing judgment on the rioters, the Council appointed a commission of twelve, among whom were some of the best professors of the university, to institute a searching inquiry into the cause of these troubles, which recur with periodical regularity. After discussing the question at length, the Commission prepared a draft petition for presentation to the Emperor, demanding his sanction for a thorough reform of the disciplinary regulations of the university. This proposal did not, however, find favor with the Council, and instead of it they drew up a report to the Ministry "on the causes of the disorders and the best means of preventing a renewal thereof."

The document, which is of the highest interest, was published neither in the annual report of the university nor by the Press. Any journal which had dared even to refer to it would have been promptly suspended. But a few copies were printed in the clandestine office of the *Zemlia i Volia*, and those of them that still exist are prized as rare bibliographic curiosities. From a copy in my possession I make the following extracts, which, as will be seen, give a vivid description of the rule under which the students are compelled to live, and the irritating treatment to which they are expected to submit.

"Of all departments of the administration the one with which students come most in contact is the Department of Police. By its proceedings they naturally form their opinion of the character of the Government. It is, therefore, in their interest, and that of the State, that the conduct of the police towards the members of our universities should be kind, considerate, and reasonable. But what we see is precisely the reverse. For most young men intercourse with comrades and friends is an absolute necessity. To satisfy this necessity there exists in all other European universities (as also in those of Finland and the Baltic provinces, which enjoy considerable local liberties) special institutions, such as clubs, corporations, and unions. At St. Petersburg there is nothing of the sort, although the great majority of the students, being from the country, have no friends in the city with whom they can associate. Private reunions might, in some measure, make up for deprivation of other opportunities of social intercourse were it not that police interference renders the one almost as impossible as the other. A meeting of several students in the room of one of their number draws immediate attention and gives rise to exaggerated fears. The porters, and even the proprietors of the rooms, are bound on their peril to give prompt information of the fact to the police, by whom such meetings are often dispersed. Besides being practically forbidden to enjoy each other's society, students, even in the privacy of their own chambers, are not free from annoyance. Although they may lead studious lives, meddle with nobody, and receive and make few visits, they are none the less submitted to a rigorous oversight. (The professors observe, not without malice, that *everybody* is under police supervision. Everything, however, depends on the form it takes and the extent to which it is exercised; and the supervision exercised over the students, ceasing to be a measure of public security, became an interference with their private life.)

"'How does he pass his time?' 'Whom does he associate with?' 'What time does he generally come home?' 'What does he read?' 'What does he write?' are among the questions put by the police to porters and lodging-house keepers, people generally of little or no education, who carry out their instructions with scant regard for the feelings of impressionable youth." (Read between the lines this means that during the absence of the students their books and papers are overhauled, and anything in them that may appear suspicious brought under the notice of the police.)

This is the testimony of the heads of the University of St. Petersburg, speaking in confidence to the Ministers of the Tzar.* But these worthy gentlemen told only half the truth.

* Shortly after the appearance of the article which forms the substance of this chapter in *The Times*, Mr. Katkoff, in a warm and eloquent leader in the *Moscow Gazette*, roundly accused me of having invented both the commission of professors and their report; neither of which, according to him, ever existed. As the facts are rather of old date and almost forgotten by the public, and as the charge may be repeated, I am constrained, in my own justification, to mention certain details and to give the names which, in the first instance, I omitted. The commission nominated by the University is no more a myth than the twelve professors of whom it was composed, and who took part in its proceedings. MM. Beketoff, Faminzine, Butleroff, Setchenoff, Gradovsky, Serguevitch, Taganzeff, Vladislavleff, Miller, Lamansky, Khoolson, and Got-

Their remarks apply only to the treatment of students outside the university. A natural feeling of delicacy restrained them from dwelling on the things that are done within the walls where learning and science should reign supreme. The interior oversight of the undergraduate is entrusted to a so-called "Inspection," composed of an inspector, appointed by the Ministry, several sub-inspectors, and a number of agents. The students, like the professors, live outside the precincts of the University, and meet in the *aulas* only at appointed hours, and for the sole object of attending the lectures that are there given. The professors are quite competent to maintain order in the schools.

And what good purpose can be served by submitting this noble and pacific activity to special police oversight? As well organize a special force of spurred and helmeted sacristans to supervise the faithful when they meet for Divine worship. In Russia, however, it is precisely because universities are laboratories of thought and ideas in constant action, that their supervision is deemed, above all things, desirable ; and that inspection in this element of their domestic life is kept most in view. Having nothing to do with study, in no wise subject either to the management or to the University Council, depending only on the high police, and the Ministry, this heterogeneous element, like a foreign body introduced into an organism, deranges all the natural functions of a scholastic institution.

Three-fourths of the so-called "university disorders" are caused by the meddlings of the divers agents of the inspection. The inspector—and herein lies the chief cause of the universal detestation in which he is held—is a delegate of the general police; an Argus sent into the enemy's camp to sow the seeds of sedition. A word whispered in the ear may entail conse-

---

stunsky. I hope these gentlemen, most of whom are still professors in St. Petersburg University, are in good health. Their report was drawn up on December 14, 1878. It is not very long since. They doubtless remember the circumstance, and the question can easily be put.

quences the reverse of agreeable, not alone on an unfortunate student but on a college don of high rank.

These hated spies, moreover, enjoy the most extensive powers. An inspector can do almost anything. With the approbation of the Curator, that is to say, of the Minister who directs his proceedings, he may expel a student for one or two years, or forever, without any sort of inquiry or trial. The same functionary controls the scholarships and bursaries, so numerous in Russian superior schools, and by his mere veto can deny them to the destined recipients by classing the latter as *neblagonadejen*—a word for which the English language has no equivalent, but which means that, albeit the victims are not yet under suspicion they cannot be regarded as altogether impeccable. The inspector wields another power. By a stroke of the pen he can deprive a host of students of the means of livelihood in forbidding them to give private lessons. Many of the students are very poor, and depend on work of this sort for their daily bread. No one can give private lessons without police authorization, and authorization is never given without the approval of the inspector, and then only for a limited time. The inspector may, at his own good pleasure, prevent the renewal of the authorization, or even cancel it before the expiration of the term for which it was granted. This officer, and each of his agents, is also empowered to punish refractory students by imprisonment in a dungeon for any time not exceeding seven days. He may reprimand them for coming late to a lecture, for wearing clothes he does not like, for the cut of their hair and the pose of their hats, and otherwise torment them with any puerilities it may please him to inflict.

II.

These petty tyrannies are, if possible, more keenly felt and more bitterly resented by Russian students than they would be by students of other nationalities. Our young men are precocious. The sufferings they witness and the persecutions they endure bring them rapidly to maturity. A Russian student unites the dignity of manhood with the ardor of youth, and feels the outrages to which he is exposed, all the more acutely that he is powerless to resist them. The students belong for the most part to the lower nobility and the lower clergy, both of whom are poor. All are familiar with the literature of Liberalism and free-thought, and the great majority are imbued with democratic and anti-despotic ideas. As they grow older these ideas become intensified by the conditions under which they live. They are compelled either to serve a Government which they detest or betake themselves to callings for which they may have no aptitude. Russia has absolutely no future for young men of noble natures and generous aspiration. Unless they consent to don the livery of the Tzar, or become members of a corrupt bureaucracy, they can neither serve their country nor take part in public affairs. In these circumstances it is no wonder that seditious notions are rampant among the students of Russian universities, and that they should be ever ready to take part in demonstrations against authority in general, and, above all, against their enemies of the police—demonstrations which in official phraseology become "disorders" and "troubles," and are ascribed to the machinations of the revolutionary party. The charge is false; for the revolutionary party gains nothing by this warfare. On the contrary, they are weakened; because those who are lost to the cause by a university squabble might have used their energies to better purpose in a truly revolutionary struggle. The disorders in our universities are entirely spontaneous; they have no other cause than latent discontent, which, always accumulating, is ever ready to vent itself in a "manifestation." A student is unjustly expelled from the university, another is arbitrarily deprived of his bursary, an unpopular professor requests the inspectors to force undergraduates into his lecture-room. The news spreads, the students are excited, they gather in twos and threes to discuss the matter, and, finally, a general meeting is called to protest against the action of the authorities, and demand reparation for the injustice they have committed. The rector appears and declines to make any explanation; the inspector orders the meeting to disperse forthwith. The students, now in a white heat of indignation, refuse to obey; whereupon the inspector, who had anticipated this contingency, calls into the room a force of gendarmes, Cossacks, and soldiers, and the meeting is dissolved by main force.

An incident that occurred at Moscow in December, 1880, affords an apt illustration of the trivial causes from which disorders sometimes arise. Professor Zernoff was giving a lecture on anatomy to an attentive audience, when all at once a loud and unusual noise was heard in the next room, and most of the students ran out to see what had happened. Nothing particular had happened, but the professor, annoyed by the interruption of his lecture, made a complaint to the authorities. The next day it was stated that the complaint had led to the expulsion of several members of the anatomy class. A punishment so severe for an offence so venial kindled general indignation. A meeting was called and a resolution passed calling upon the rector for an explanation. But instead of the rector came the chief of the Moscow police, followed by a great array of gendarmes, Cossacks, and infantry, who ordered the meeting to disperse. The young fellows were now greatly excited, and, though they would have listened to reason, refused obedience to the behests of brute force. On this the *aula* was surrounded by the soldiers, all the issues were beset, the students, to the number of four hundred, were taken prisoners, and amid a square of bayonets marched off to jail.

Affairs of this sort do not always end with simple arrests. At the least show of resistance the foot soldiers make free use of the butt-ends of their muskets, the Cossacks ply their whips, the faces of the students stream with blood, some are thrown wounded to the ground, and there ensues a terrible scene of armed violence and unavailing resistance. It happened thus at Kharkoff, in November, 1878, when some troubles arose from a mere misunderstanding between a professor at the Veterinary College and one of his classes—a misunderstanding which a few words of explanation would have sufficed to remove. It was thus at Moscow and St. Petersburg during the disorders of 1861, 1863, and 1866; and in certain circumstances the law sanctions even grosser outrages. In 1878 an enactment, the cruelty of which it is impossible to exaggerate, was promulgated. "Considering," it ran, "the frequency of students' meetings in the universities and public schools, the law concerning seditious gatherings in the streets and other public places is applied to all buildings and establishments used as colleges and superior schools." Thus all students in Russia are placed permanently under martial law. A meeting or group of undergraduates, after being summoned three times to disperse, may be shot down as if they were armed rebels.

Happily, however, this monstrous law has not yet been applied in all its rigor. The police still limit their repressive measures to beating and imprisoning the students who contravene their commands or otherwise incur their displeasure. But the students, so far from being grateful for this moderation, are always in a state of simmering revolt, and lose no opportunity of protesting, by deed and word, against the tyrannical proceedings of the agents of the law. There is, moreover, a strong fellow-feeling among them, and "disorders" at one university are often a signal for disorders at half a dozen other seats of learning. The troubles which began at the end of 1882 extended over nearly the whole of scholastic Russia. They began in the far east, at the University of Kazan. Firsoff, the rector, deprived a young man named Voronzoff of his bursary, a thing which he had no right to do, the bursary having been granted by the Zemstvo of Voronzoff's native province. Voronzoff was so exasperated that he publicly boxed the rector's ears. In ordinary circumstances, and in a well-ordered university, an outrage so gross would have provoked general indignation, and the students themselves would have punished the offender. But the rector's despotic rule had rendered him so unpopular that on the day of Voronzoff's expulsion the students—some six hundred in number—broke open the assembly room, and held a tumultuous meeting, whereupon the Pro-rector Voulitch hurried to the spot and ordered the assembly to disperse. Nobody listened to him. Two of the students made speeches against Firsoff and defended Voronzoff. A former student of Moscow University, without giving heed to the presence of Voulitch, spoke in the most violent terms against the curator, the rector, and the professors generally. In the end the meeting voted and presented to Pro-rector Voulitch a petition demanding Rector Firsoff's immediate dismissal, and the revocation of Voronzoff's expulsion.

Then, before dispersing, the students resolved to meet again on the following day. On this the heads of the university applied to the governor of the province for the means of restoring order, and the great man promptly placed at their disposal several companies of infantry and a large force of police. A few days later it was announced that complete tranquillity reigned at the University of Kazan. But the papers that made this announcement were forbidden, under pain of suppression, to mention in what manner the pacification was brought about — that the rebellious students were beaten, whipped, thrown on the ground, dragged about by the hair of their heads, and many of them hauled to prison. Despite the interdict laid on the Press, these facts were quickly bruited about. On November 8th (as is set forth in the official report) hectographic copies of a letter from one of the Kazan students, giving a full account of the affair, were circulated among the students of St. Petersburg, and caused naturally a great sensation. On the 10th hectographic circulars were issued calling a general meeting of the St. Petersburg students to protest against the outrages inflicted on their comrades of Kazan. When the students presented themselves at the place of meeting, the police, who appeared in force, ordered them to disperse, an order which they refused to obey, and while the police were still there passed a vote of censure on the authorities and of sympathy with the students of Kazan. On this, force was ordered to be used, and 280 students were arrested and conducted to prison.

The next day orders went forth for the provisional closing of the university.

The outbreaks at St. Petersburg and Kazan were speedily followed by similar scenes in other university towns. On November 15th there were disturbances at Kieff, and on the 17th and 18th at Kharkoff. At the latter place they were so serious that the military had to be employed for their suppression, and many arrests were made. Almost at the same time troubles befell in the Juridical School of Yaroslavle, and a few days later at the Forest School of Moscow. At all these places events followed in the same order—agitations, meetings, forcible dispersions, arrests, and then provisional cessation of lectures.

Disorders are of frequent occurrence in all the universities and superior scholastic institutions of the empire. Not a year passes that several do not come to pass in different parts of Russia. And every one of these outbreaks, whether appeased by the exhortations of the professors or suppressed by Cossack whips, entails inevitably the expulsion of a crowd of students. In some cases fifty are expelled, in others one hundred, and even more than one hundred. The troubles of October and November, 1882, caused the expulsion of six hundred. The tribunal which orders the expulsions—that is to say, the Council of Professors—divides the offenders into several categories. The "leaders" and "instigators" are condemned to perpetual expulsion and denied the right of entering thereafter any superior school whatever. Others are expelled for a term varying from twelve months to three years. The lightest penalty awarded in these cases is "sending away," a sentence which, in theory at least, does not prevent the offender from entering at once some other university. In reality, however, there is very little difference between one sort of punishment and another. "The police," says the report of the St. Petersburg professors which I have already cited, "regard every disturbance that occurs in the university as a political movement. Every student who may be condemned, even to a slight punishment, becomes a political suspect, and to every Russian suspect there is dealt the same measure—exile by administrative order. Penalties inflicted for the merest breaches of scholastic discipline may be aggravated by administrative exile, as the disorders of March 18 and 20, 1869, clearly showed. All the students "sent away" for a year, as well as those definitively expelled, were immediately exiled, and after the late disturbances (December, 1878) the rector was asked to furnish the Chief of Police of the quarter with the names of all students who had ever appeared before the university tribunal, even though they might not have been punished (in order that they, too, might be exiled).

If in other parts of Russia the police are less severe than in St. Petersburg, students compromised by participation in university disorders are none the less dealt with in a way which renders impossible the resumption of their professional studies.

The minister himself undertakes the task of tracking and marking them. Here is an instance in point: In a weekly journal, published at St. Petersburg, there appeared, on November 9, 1881, under the heading "An Incomprehensible Decision of the University Council of Kieff," a communication to the following effect—

"The students provisionally expelled (rusticated) from Moscow University applied for admission to the University of Kieff. But the Council, after taking the matter into consideration, refused to receive them. This was virtually increasing, on their own motion, the punishment originally inflicted on the postulants. It was denying a right reserved to them by their judges."

And the Press generally blamed the Council for displaying a severity which was qualified as excessive and inexplicable. The explanation, however, was very simple. The minister, by a special circular, had forbidden all other universities to receive the expelled students from Moscow. This the papers knew better than anybody else, and these diatribes had no other end than to provoke the University of Kieff into an exposure of the double dealing of the Government, an object which, it is hardly necessary to say, was not realized. Similar circulars are almost invariably sent out after university disturbances wherever they may happen to occur.

The struggle between the Ministry and the universities is far from being limited to disorders and their results. These events, after all, are exceptional; they occur at comparatively long intervals, and are separated from each other by periods of apparent calm. But quietness brings the students no immunity from espionage and persecution. The police never cease making arrests; when clouds darken the political sky, and the Government, with or without reason, take alarm, they arrest multitudes. At these times students are naturally the greatest sufferers, for, as I have already shown, our Russian youths are nearly all eager politicians and potential revolutionists. A fraction of the arrested are condemned, even after trial, to divers penalties. Some eighty per cent. are exiled, without trial, to Siberia or to one of the northern provinces; a few, after a short detention, are allowed to return to their homes. A proportion of those sentenced to a term of imprisonment may also be allowed to resume their occupations, instead of being exiled by administrative order. But mercy is a quality unknown to the Russian police; they take back with one hand what they give with the other. On October 15, 1881, a law was made instituting a sort of double judgment and twofold penalty for students coming under the categories last named. Articles 2 and 3 of this law direct university councils to act as special tribunals for the trial of students who have been tried and acquitted by the ordinary courts, or who have expiated their offences by terms of imprisonment. This law prescribes that, in the event of the police certifying that a young man whose case is under consideration has acted " out of pure thoughtlessness and without evil intent," the council may either admit or expel him at their discretion. But should the police impute to him "perverse intentions," albeit in a measure so infinitesimal that they do not deem it necessary to proceed against him themselves, the council must, nevertheless, pronounce a sentence of perpetual expulsion and deprivation of the right to enter any superior school whatever. Article 4 explains that the preceding articles apply not alone to students who have fallen under the lash of the ordinary law, but also to those who have escaped undamaged from the exceptional "law of public safety"—in other words, from the martial law, which has become one of Russia's permanent institutions.

To obtain for those who have not fallen into the hands of the police any remission of their ostracism is a matter of excessive and almost insuperable difficulty. Requests for indulgence must be made to the Emperor personally (how many students have friends at Court?), and are only entertained when the suppliant can *prove* that during two years after his liberation, or the definitive expiation of his offence, *he has repented him of his errors*, and entirely broken with his old companions.

But apart from the juridic absurdity of a condition which reverses the accepted maxim that it is crime, not innocence, that must be demonstrated, how, we ask, can repentance be proved, if not by treachery or betrayal, or some service rendered to the police? And it may be safely affirmed that the law touching the expulsion of students acquitted by the courts, or who have undergone the punishments assigned to them, notwithstanding its deceptive indulgence, is absolute. The police never pardon; and even if that body and martial law allowed them to live freely in society, the interdict on their university career would still remain.

Such are the true forms assumed by the veritable war which, sometimes open, sometimes latent, has for more than twenty years been waged between the youth of our superior schools and the Government of the country.

III.

But these are the merest palliatives. What has this ruthless persecution of a quarter of a century effected? Nothing at all. Despite arrests and banishments the students are as hostile to the Government as before. The fate of those who go down in the struggle serves not in the least as a warning to the survivors. More than ever are universities breeders of discontent and centres of agitation; and is there not something in the nature of things which necessarily produces this result? For what is higher education if not the study of European culture—its history and its laws, its institutions and its literature? And a man who has gone through a university course and studied these things can hardly be kept in the belief that Russia is the happiest of all possible countries, and her Government the perfection of human wisdom. Hence to destroy the evil at its roots it is imperative to strike, not men alone, but institutions. This Count Tolstoi, as a far-seeing man, has long felt, though it is only of late that circumstances have permitted the practical application of his sagacious counsels. In the result the universities were attacked in two quarters—the high and the low. As a beginning Count Tolstoi made a strenuous effort to reduce the number of students by increasing academic fees and rendering examinations absurdly severe. When this measure did not suffice to abate the flood of young men eager for instruction, the Count (by a ministerial order under date of March 25, 1879) arbitrarily deprived seminary pupils (who formed a large proportion of the undergraduates) of the right of admission to the universities, a right they had enjoyed from time immemorial. At Odessa the proportion of these youths was from a third to a half of the total number of undergraduates. Thus the new law wielded by Count Tolstoi did yeoman service.

Yet still he was not satisfied, and other measures whose vandalism was cynical and complete were instituted, measures which mutilated to the verge of extinction the system of superior education.

The first to feel the effect of these measures was the Medico-chirurgical Academy of St. Petersburg. Than this there is no institution in the empire more useful to the State. It is under the Ministry of War, and supplies the army with surgeons, of whom during the conflict with Turkey there was so lamentable a lack. But the medical school, with its one thousand students, was a centre of political agitation, and an Imperial ukase, dated March 24, 1879, doomed it to complete transformation and semi-extinction. The number of students was diminished to five hundred, the terms reduced from five to three, and the first two courses, the undergraduates belonging to which were the most unruly, were abolished.

The only students now received are those who have passed two terms at a provincial university. They are paid, wear a uniform, take the oath of allegiance, and from the day of their admission are considered as forming part of the army, and held amenable to military law. At the instance of the Minister of War the five years' course has lately been re-established, but the other repressive measures are maintained in all their rigor.

On January 3, 1880, another ukase ordered a similar transformation of the Institute of Civil Engineers. This mutilation of a useful school lessened by one-half the few openings in life available for the pupils of our non-classical gymnasiums.

A little later came the turn of the Female Medical School of St. Petersburg. This school, founded in 1872, proved eminently useful. In Russia the supply of medical men is utterly inadequate for the needs of its vast population. Doctors, being much sought, naturally settle by preference in the towns where their services bring the best return. With rare exceptions, the rural districts are left a prey to blood-letters, bone-setters, quacks, and sorcerers. Women, on the other hand, settle by preference in the country, and are content with such moderate fees as the *zemstvo* can afford. The Female School of Medicine was thus a great boon ; requests for women doctors were continually being received from all parts of the country ; and when, in April, 1882, the Government announced that, "for pecuniary reasons," they would be compelled to close the school, there was a general expression of surprise and regret. The papers protested as much as they dared; the *zemstvo* remonstrated; the municipality of St. Petersburg and several scientific corporations offered annual subsidies; private individuals, both rich and poor, and even obscure villages, offered subscriptions towards the maintenance of so valued an institution. But the Female School of Medicine was doomed, and in August, 1882, appeared an ukase ordering its abolition. Students already admitted might complete their course, but no new pupils were allowed to be taken. The cause assigned for this proceeding was the shallowest of pretexts; the true reason being a fear on the part of the Government that the school might become a seminary of revolutionary ideas.

Not less characteristic was the conduct of the Government in the matter of the Polytechnic Institution of Kharkoff. The only establishment of the sort in Russia is that of St. Petersburg, and thither all youths desirous of being educated in the mechanical arts must proceed. In a country so vast this is highly inconvenient, and for a long time past Kharkoff had wanted to have a polytechnic of its own. At length, after repeated applications to the Minister of Public Instruction and negotiations extending over ten years, the authorization was granted; whereupon the municipality erected a suitable building, appointed a staff of professors, and all was ready to begin, when the Government suddenly changed their mind, withdrew the authorization, and forbade the school to be opened—on the ground that they saw no necessity for any establishment of the sort. Nor was this all. They offered the building, which had cost Kharkoff 50,000 roubles, as a present to the university; but the university, making common cause with the town, declined the offer. The building is still in the hands of the State, and will, it is rumored, be turned into a cavalry barrack.

At length, and only a few months ago, came the long-expected blow which struck our universities in another vital point—the regulation of September, 1884, whereby was definitely abolished the regulation of 1863.

There are a few recent questions which have so greatly excited public opinion in Russia, and given rise to so much heated polemic in the Press as that of the abolition of the regulation of 1863. It was a regulation which, by permitting the professors to fill up vacant chairs and elect the members of the managing body, conferred on the universities a fair measure of autonomy and independence. Mr. Katkoff, who is one of the most influential men in the empire, and whose particular friends of the Moscow University have not found this independence to their advantage, entertained for the unfortunate regulation of 1863 a mortal hatred. For years it was his *Delenda Carthago*. He protested against it in season and out of season. To hear him you would think this regulation was the cause of all the so-called "disorders" and most of the misfortunes of the last twenty years. Sedition (Nihilism) in his opinion derives its chief support from the autonomy of the universities. The process by which he arrives at this conclusion is short and simple. The majority of the professors being secret ministers of subversive ideas (rather a strange confession to be made by a friend and defender of the Government), to leave them free to choose their colleagues is to maintain at the expense of the State a permanent revolutionary propaganda. But this argument, however ingenious, was rather too far-fetched to be used by the administration. A more plausible if not a more truthful pretext was necessary, something that might enable the Government to say that in abolishing the obnoxious regulation they were promoting the best interests of the nation. The inventive genius of Mr. Katkoff was equal to the occasion. He developed from his inner consciousness the thesis that the abolition of the regulation of 1863 would give an extraordinary stimulus to the study of science, and raise learning in Russia to a level with that of Germany. The idea being eagerly caught up by the official Press, it was soon made to appear that, in the interest of knowledge as well as of order, a new regulation had become absolutely necessary.

Let us now examine a little this palladium of reaction, and see by what means it is proposed to effect the twofold object in question.

First of all, as to the police ; for whenever anything happens in Russia the police are sure to be to the fore, and nobody doubts that the object of the present measure is simply repression. This is avowed by its advocates. "The universities," exclaimed the *Novoie Vremia*, "will no longer be corrupters of our youth. The universities will henceforth be guaranteed against disloyal intrigues." But will the new regulation be really to the advantage of learning? timidly whispered the so-called Liberal papers. All alike recognized the true character and aim of the measure.

We pass by the proposals for the supervision of the undergraduates, as to which there nothing, or next to nothing, more remained to be done. That which gives a special savor to the new regulation is placing the professors themselves under stringent police surveillance and an arbitrary *régime*. Two institutions are charged with this ignoble duty. First of all the governing body, composed of professors ; next the police of the inspection. Under the old system the rector and the four deans were simply *primus inter pares*, elected by their colleagues for a term of three years, when others might be chosen to succeed them. Now they are masters, nominated by the Minister, and holding their lucrative places at his pleasure. As, moreover, among fifty or sixty men there must necessarily be some sycophants and self-seekers, the Minister has no difficulty in finding rectors who will take his orders and do his bidding. Under the new dispensation the rector, now become a Government agent, is clothed with extensive powers. He can convoke and dissolve at his pleasure the university council, once the supreme governing body. It is he alone who decides whether the proceedings of the council are according to rule, and by simply pronouncing it irregular he may quash any resolution to which he objects. The rector may also, if he thinks fit, preside with the same prerogatives at the meetings of the faculties. Like a commander-in-chief, wherever he appears he is supreme. The rector is also enjoined to make any observations to the professors he may deem necessary, and reprimand them whenever he sees fit. Every part of the administrative machine is open to his inspection, either in person or by deputy. Finally, paragraph 17 gives him, in cases of urgency, the right "to take any measures he may think expedient for the maintenance of order in the university, even if they exceed his powers." This article has evidently in view the so-called "collective manifestations," which it is the custom in Russia to put down by military force. But almost any construction might be placed upon the clause, and there is hardly any measure, however extreme, which it could not be held to sanction.

Thus Russian universities resemble fortresses whose garrisons are permeated by sedition, and ready at any moment to break into open mutiny, rather than homes of learning and temples of science. The rector is the commander-in-chief. Under his orders are four deans, rectors of faculties, each exercising in his own department analogous functions, but chosen by the Minister, not by the rector. It is chiefly to the deans that the task is intrusted of overseeing the professors of their respective faculties; and to render the latter more dependent the new regulation introduces important innovations in the method of their appointment. Before a man can become a professor he must henceforth serve three years as a tutor (*privat-docent*), and he can only become a tutor on the nomination of the curator of the province, or on the proposal of the council of professors of the faculty of his choice. In any event the appointment must be confirmed by the curator of the province, and this functionary, who is a high official of the Ministry, may revoke any tutor's appointment without assigning a cause. A tutor's pay is only about a third of that of a full-fledged professor; and as he is subjected to an incessant surveillance to guard him against the contagion of subversive ideas, the post cannot be considered a very desirable one; nor is it likely to attract young men of large views and independent mind.

To the rector and the deans falls the duty of seeing that the tutor's teaching is all that it ought to be. If his lectures are not in conformity with the dignity of his subject, or are found to be tainted with dangerous ideas, they must admonish him. Should the admonition prove ineffectual the rector will propose to the curator to dismiss this refractory tutor, and the curator will no doubt give prompt effect to the proposal. But if the curator should learn in some other way (through spies or a member of the inspection) that a tutor's lectures are showing subversive tendencies, he may be removed without reference to the rector. The new *privat-docents* have thus two or three sets of masters, and besides being at the mercy of the rector and his deputies, as also of the curator of the province, they are liable at any moment to be denounced by the inspector and his satellites. The least show of independence will insure their prompt dismissal, the more especially as being only young in the scholastic profession they are not likely to command the respect of their superiors. For promotion they depend entirely on the Minister and his agents. Formerly the professors were nominated by the council of the faculty. True, the Minister had the power of veto, but he had no power of appointment, and if one man was rejected the council had only to nominate another. According to the new scheme, however, the Minister can appoint to a vacant chair " any scholar possessing the necessary qualifications "—that is to say, one who has served the prescribed time as a *privat-docent*. The Minister may if he likes consult the heads of the university, but only if he likes. He may equally, if he likes, consult a private friend or a member of the inspection. The promotion of a professor from the second to the first class—a change which brings with it increased emoluments—also rests entirely with the Minister.

Nor does this exhaust the enumeration of the Minister's powers. He nominates professors to examinerships, which from a financial point of view, and having regard to the new system of paying examiners, is a highly important function. Under the old system every professor was *ipso facto* an examiner; under the present, examinations are conducted by special commissions nominated by the Minister. Under the old, students paid a fixed yearly sum which gave them the right of attending all the university lectures. According to the new regulations they have to pay each professor separately. In these circumstances, undergraduates, having the right of choice, naturally flock to the lectures of the professors by whom they are likely to be examined. Hence the placing of a professor on the examining commission is greatly to his pecuniary advantage—it brings him hearers and adds to his emoluments. The right of nomination is thus a very effective means of increasing the power of the Government over the teaching body. In a country such as Switzerland, where political motives are not allowed to influence collegiate appointments, this system produces no injurious results; but experience proves that in Prussia its consequences are bad, and in Austria nothing less than disastrous. It is easy to understand, therefore, the motives of our Government in importing the system into Russia, and the effect it is likely to produce there.

"But where, then," the reader may ask, "is the teaching strength—where the science and other branches of higher culture? In what consists the reform which is supposed to confer on the measure its pedagogic character? Are we expected to believe that it consists in the new discipline imposed on long-suffering rectors, deans, and inspectors, the appointment of *privat-docents* and payment by lesson?"

All these things being, in name at least, borrowed from Germany, they are expected in some mysterious fashion to render teaching more efficient. If we could have the freedom of German universities, their methods might perhaps be adopted with advantage, but the form without the spirit can profit nothing.

To all who are not blinded by self-interest, it is evident that the new regulation must prove fatal to all true learning—freedom and independence being as essential to its prosperity as atmospheric air to physical life. By making political orthodoxy the only sure qualification for all higher university appointments, the intellectual *élite* of the nation is almost necessarily excluded from their walls. The old system of Government interference drove from their chairs some of our best professors—Kostomarov, Stasulevitch, Pipin, Arseniev, Setchenov, and many others—all moderate men, who had retained their positions with honor for years, and were guilty of only one fault—that of maintaining their personal dignity and the dignity of their calling, and refusing to prostrate themselves before the despotism of a Minister. That which was formerly an exceptional abuse of power has now become a rule. The professors have been converted into *tchinovniks*—an odious name, despised by all our Russian youth—and their characters and qualifications will soon be in strict conformity with their new rank; one by one all true scholars will abandon their chairs, and the Government, in the exercise of their rights, will fill them with its creatures. In default of men of high scientific acquirements, the old professors will be succeeded by tutors and *soi-disant* scholars, whom the curators are at liberty to choose from among persons that have not even undergone the examinations ordained by the faculty, "provided they are favorably known by their works," as to the merit of which his excellency the curator is the sole judge.

CHAPTER XXVI.

SECONDARY EDUCATION.

I.

THE war of Russian Governments against higher education, described in a previous article, is of long standing. It began in the time of Alexander I., during the reaction that followed the murder of Kotzebue by the student Sand, which, originating in Germany, spread quickly over the whole of Continental Europe. In the reign of Nicolas, which was a period of uninterrupted reaction, the universities were always under the special care of the Third Section. In order, as he hoped, to counteract the pernicious effects of liberal culture, he organized the universities like battalions, and lectures in the class-room were followed by drills in the square. Knowledge he regarded as a social bane, and military discipline as its only antidote. The absurd regulation in question was suppressed by his son, whose reign began so brightly and ended so terribly. Alexander II. loosened the fetters which his father had imposed, and for some time after he had ascended the throne, learning breathed freely and made marked progress. But in 1860, when "disorders" and "manifestations" occurred in the universities of the two capitals, the authorities took alarm, repressive measures were adopted, and since that time the struggle between the State and the flower of our Russian youth has gone on with ever-increasing virulence. The war against secondary education—for war it has become—is of more recent date. On April 4, 1866, Karakosoff fired the fatal revolver shot which confirmed, as it would seem forever, the resolution of the Government to follow the dangerous path of reaction and repression.

"You are a Pole, are you not?" asked the Tzar, when Karakosoff was led before him.

"No; I am a Russian," was the answer.

"Then why did you try to kill me?" demanded the astonished sovereign. So difficult did he find it at that time to believe that any other than a Pole could make an attempt on his life.

But Karakosoff told the truth; he was one of the Tzar's own Russian subjects, and the subsequent inquiry directed by Mouravieff showed that many of Karakosoff's former fellow-students sympathized with his objects and shared in his ideas.

The effect of this attempt, and the discovery to which it led, were decisive. The Polish insurrection, as is well known, had converted Alexander II. to reactionary views. But it now became evident that the reactionary measures which were adopted in 1863 had proved abortive, and that the revolutionary fermentation was increasing. Yet, instead of inferring therefrom that the fault of this failure lay with the new policy of reaction, the very opposite conclusion was drawn—that the reins must be still further tightened. It was then that the reckless reactionary party brought forward the man of fate, Count Dmitry Tolstoi, whom posterity will call the scourge of Russia and the destroyer of the autocracy.

This paladin of absolutism was entrusted with plenary powers for the purification of the schools of the empire from social heresy and political discontent.

How he dealt with superior education we have already told. Yet he only strengthened and enforced the system which his predecessors had for a long time practiced. To him alone, however, belongs the questionable honor of "purifying"—according to his lights—first of all secondary, and afterwards primary education. It was especially in relation to the former of these branches that the inventive genius of the man shone the most brilliantly. His fundamental idea was perfectly just —that thoroughly to "purify" the universities he must go first to the fountain-head and purify the gymnasiums, from which they draw their yearly tribute of students. So Count Tolstoi set himself to purge these institutions, which, of course, meant handing them over to the tender mercies of the police ; and it is a positive fact that Russian schoolboys of from ten to seventeen years of age may now be punished for so-called political offences and for holding erroneous political opinions. No longer since than September of 1883, the Minister of Public Instruction issued a circular in which it was stated that in thirteen gymnasiums, one pro-gymnasium, and ten "real" schools, there had been discovered traces of a criminal propaganda, and that in fourteen other gymnasiums and four "real" schools there had taken place "collective disorders," whatever that may mean. All these establishments were ordered to be placed under special police oversight.

It is difficult for a stranger to realize the extent to which espionage is carried in our gymnasiums. The pedagogues who ought to enjoy the respect of their pupils, and imbue the rising generation with sentiments of honor, are transformed into agents of the Third Section. The boys are under continual supervision. They are not left in peace even in the houses of their kinsfolk. By a special law, tutors are ordered to visit the pupils at their own homes, or wherever they may be living. The Minister is not ashamed from time to time to issue circulars, as on July 27, 1884, cynically offering rewards and promotion to professors who show the greatest zeal in supervising the "moral dispositions" (read "political tendencies") of their pupils, and threatening that in the event of any antigovernmental propagandism being discovered in their classes, they will be held equally responsible with the directors and inspectors (*Rousskia Vedomosti*, July 28)—which means money and advancement for those who play the part of spies, dismissal for those who refuse to bow the knee to Baal.

II.

But measures of police are not enough; they must be backed up by measures of prevention. Boys must be removed from every influence which might predispose them to pernicious ideas, such as socialism, liberty, materialism, and so forth. To this end the pedants of the Third Section drew up a series of prescriptions known as the Gymnasial Regulations of 1871, which are still in force. The explanatory appendix to the regulations says roundly that "the less history is studied in the gymnasiums the better." The study of Russian literature is also banned by Count Tolstoi; and general geography, on account of its "dangerous tendencies," is proscribed by the Minister of Instruction. It may "suggest conflicting conclusions and give rise to useless reasonings." In other words, the study of geography may peradventure lead to discussions on political and social subjects. For these reasons the Regulations of 1871 diminished the number of lessons in history, geography, and Russian. The void made by these omissions has been filled up with the learned languages. The panacea is found in Greek and Latin. The gymnasiums have become classic, and nothing but classic. The first class of a Russian gymnasium (composed of boys of ten years old) has now eight Latin lessons a week; the third the same in Latin and as many in Greek. All other subjects are declared secondary, and though not ostensibly forbidden, persistently discouraged. However many bad marks pupils may receive in their mother tongue, in history, mathematics, geography, foreign languages, or even in religion, they never fail to obtain their promotion to a higher class, but backwardness in the classical languages is severely punished, often by expulsion.

Is it, however, the fact, that study of the classics serves as a safeguard against "perverse," in other words, liberal and humane, ideas? Certainly not. Great authorities hold, and John Stuart Mill has said, that serious study of the lives and history of the peoples of antiquity makes more for the development of moral and civic virtues than the study of modern history.

But we have no desire to discuss the advantages or disadvantages of classical education. Whichever way the balance may incline, it is quite certain that the classicism devised by Tolstoi, Katkoff, and consorts, is altogether *sui generis*, and can only stupefy those whom it is supposed to enlighten. The effect of their regulation is to make grammar an end instead of a means. Scholars learn the language and nothing else. Their studies are simply a series of linguistic exercises.

Pedagogues à la Katkoff do not deny this. They merely contend that there is nothing so well suited for the development of the intelligence as the study of the dead languages. According to an expression of theirs which has been much in vogue, it is a mental gymnastic exercise which no other study can equal. With this inscrutable word "gymnastic" they meet all the arguments of their adversaries. Thus for seven years past the youth of Russia have been doing nothing but gymnastics, whose uselessness is admitted by teachers and bitterly deplored by parents.

The effect of the system on pupils is nothing less than disastrous. Boys of ten and eleven years old, who are compelled to give sixteen hours a week to a language so different from their own as Latin, end by conceiving for it such a distaste and disgust that its study becomes painful and unproductive. The examinations for removes are moreover so difficult—by special order of the Minister—that an immense number of boys fail to pass them, and are summarily expelled. According to the report of the Department of Instruction for 1879, which gives the results for the seven years then ending, 6,511 pupils only had completed their course during that period, while no fewer than 51,406 had either been expelled for failure to satisfy the examiners or had abandoned the attempt in despair. The chances against a boy in the first (lowest) class going through all the upper classes, and so being able to enter a university, are nine to one; that is to say, eight-ninths are rejected. Of the second class three-fourths fail, of the third two-thirds, and of the select few who successfully run the gauntlet and reach the seventh class one-fourth break down in their final examination.

These figures tell their own tale. The system is not a test of fitness; it is a massacre of innocents. The plan invented by Count Tolstoi dooms thousands of children to ignorance, and deprives many of them of all chance of a useful career. And it cannot be urged on behalf of the Government that they are unaware of the evil which it works and the discontent which it causes. For years past the Press, fettered as it is, has never ceased to protest against the new system of education and the deplorable consequences which it entails. Despairing parents bewail the fate of their unfortunate children, and the growing frequency of suicides among boys under thirteen lends to their complaint a terrible significance. But the Government remains firm, and the massacre of innocents goes on.

But why, it may be asked, do parents continue to send their children to the shambles? Are there in Russia no other schools than these classical gymnasiums? There are. The new classicism is designed only for the well-to-do. The classical gymnasiums do not give a complete education. They are merely preparatory schools for the universities. To the numerous class who look to education for the means of ensuring their children a livelihood, the gymnasiums are of no use whatever. It is consequently necessary to throw them also a bone, and for their benefit have been founded the professional institutions known as "real" or "realist" schools. But there are very few of them—thirty-nine; while of gymnasiums and pro-gymnasiums there are a hundred and eighty.

At St. Petersburg, where practical instruction is so greatly needed, there are two "real" schools, as compared with sixteen classical gymnasiums and pro-gymnasiums, a state of things which proves that the Government has very little desire for the diffusion of instruction among the middle classes. But it is in the general organization of these schools that the ill-will of the Government is more particularly manifested. Their object, according to the original regulation, is (1) to afford young men an education susceptible of immediate practical application; and (2) to prepare them for the higher professional schools; and they profess to devote much more time and attention to the study of the mother tongue, mathematics, and natural sciences, than the classical schools. Yet these studies, useful though they are as the foundation of a sound technical education, are purely theoretical; they do not alone conduce to any practical results. To remedy this defect, a supplementary class (the seventh) has been organized, which, however, remedies nothing. This class is composed of two sections —one mechanico-technical, the other chemico-technical. In these two sections, though the course is five years, all the practical scientific instruction is comprised within two and ranges over many subjects—mechanics, chemistry, mines, engineering—everything, in fact, that it is hardly possible for a pupil to get even a smattering, much less an efficient knowledge of any one of them.

The confusion which this system must needs entail is self-evident. These are not courses, rather a *catalogue raisonné* of every sort of science, a harlequin performance, a kaleidoscope composed of fragments of everything. The result is, that when pupils have passed through this supplementary class, they are no more capable than before of applying practically any of the scientific knowledge they are supposed to have acquired. A manufacturer never thinks of employing in his establishment a "realist" graduate, for the latter's pretended science is inferior to that of an overlooker or workman who has been taught only by personal observation and experience.

Russian commerce requires only men of inferior education, but without diplomas none can become schoolmasters and instructors. Yet comparatively few either obtain diplomas or complete their studies in the superior technical schools, the reason being that there is not a sufficiency of these institutions to receive the pupils sent up by the "realist" gymnasiums. According to the report of the Minister of Public Instruction, published in 1879, the thirty "real" schools having the seven classes turned out 330 students fully qualified for admission to the superior schools. But as the latter had room for no more than 151, less than half could be received, and the greater part were consequently rejected. And these "real" school scholars are far from being the only candidates for admission to the four superior professional schools. In the year 1879 alone, for instance, there were no fewer than 380 applicants for admission to one technical school which could accommodate only 125. In No. 2638 of the *Novori Vremia* (*New Times*) a professor, in warning young men in the provinces not to count too confidently on being able to enter these institutions, mentions that out of one thousand candidates who in 1883 presented themselves for admission into the two schools of industry and mines, no more than two hundred could be received, the rest having to be rejected simply for lack of room. But despite the warnings and discouragements, so great is the eagerness of our youth for superior instruction that they still apply in crowds for admission to the schools, only to meet, time after time, with the same rebuffs and the same disappointments. The demand for professional instruction in Russia arises not only from a thirst for knowledge, but from a natural desire to develop the great natural riches of the country, for which a measure of technical education is absolutely necessary.

But the Government, so far from affording increased facilities for instruction, actually forbids the foundation of new colleges, as we have seen in the case of Kharkoff, and will not allow existing institutions to add to their accommodation. The motive of this dog-in-the-manger policy is the fear that, recruited as they are from classes comparatively poor, technical schools are more likely to become infected with subversive ideas than the classical gymnasiums of Count Tolstoi. The fate of the rejected among the "real" school men is very sad.

Unable to enter the universities, and debarred from the callings for which they were destined, the greater part of them "remain in the streets." Well may they call themselves the "Minister's bastards," for while youths from the classical schools, once they have matriculated, are received with open arms, the luckless "realists" are rejected everywhere; against them all doors are closed. Yet neither society nor the Press can either rest indifferent to the troubles of these unhappy waifs, or ignore the national loss entailed by the running to waste of so much intellectual energy. Their position has been the theme of hundreds of articles, written in the cautious and measured language which an imperious necessity imposes on Russian journalists. The best and natural solution of the difficulty would be the enlargement of existing technical colleges and the re-establishment of new ones; but this being evidently out of the question, no more is asked than that matriculated "realists" may be allowed to enter the universities and graduate in medicine, science, or mathematics, for which they are far better prepared than their *confrères* of the gymnasiums, whose acquisitions are limited to Latin and Greek. It will hardly be believed that even this modest request was refused. In 1881 the Zemstvo took action in the matter, and, following the example of the Zemstvo of Tchernigoff, made a general demand for the admission of "realists" to the scientific faculties of the universities. The Ministry, not deeming it politic to reject peremptorily this petition, appointed a commission to whom the question was to be referred, and a time (January 19, 1882) was actually named for the first meeting. But on the 18th the members of the commission received a notification from the Minister that the meeting was to be adjourned indefinitely, and it stands adjourned to this day.

It is thus evident that the Government accepts without reserve all the most reactionary ideas of Count Tolstoi, who, unfortunately for our country, exercises a predominant influence over its domestic policy, and the Minister of Public

Instruction has as evidently decided to deny, as far as he can, facilities for higher education to all whom lack of means compels to take to professional pursuits. It is this class, he thinks, which is most disaffected to the State, and he would make superior instruction the exclusive appanage of the rich and noble, whose position, either as landowners or servants of the Tzar—if urged by necessity, or prompted by ambition, they have entered the service of the State—constrains them to support the existing *régime*.

III.

Unsatisfactory as is the condition of our scholastic institutions—badgered by the Government, watched by the police, exposed to all sorts of demoralizing influences—yet so great is the need of instruction, so eager are our youth for knowledge, that schools of every degree are besieged by applicants willing to submit to all the conditions which the State may see fit to impose, but unable to obtain admission. That this is no overdrawn or partisan statement, the following extract from the *Nedielia* of August 26, 1883, will show:

"The end of the summer vacation and the beginning of the scholastic year are marked by the usual chorus of complaints about the lack of vacancies in the public schools, and parents are cruelly embarrassed in their efforts to procure suitable instruction for their children. As the facts set forth in country papers abundantly testify, this evil is by no means confined to one locality. None of the classical gymnasiums at Moscow have vacancies for first class pupils. In those of St. Petersburg vacancies are extremely rare. In the gymnasium of St. Petersburg no places whatever are to be had in the first class; in the pro-gymnasium there are only six disposable places; in the first class and in the real school there are no vacancies whatever, not even in the second class."

At the Cronstadt Technical School there were 156 applicants and only thirty places. A correspondent writing from Kieff to the same paper mentioned that for every vacancy there were five postulants, for some classes there were eight and ten. The natural consequences of this state of things are excessive crowding and inefficient teaching. Masters are at their wits' end to find room for those whom they actually receive; at every desk there are four boys instead of two. According to the *Saratoff Gazette* there were sixty-six applicants for thirty-seven places in that town, and the masters, shrinking from the invidious task of personal selection, made the candidates contend by competitive examination for the vacancies at their disposal.

These citations, which might easily be multiplied, will give a fair idea of the relation of supply to demand in the domain of Russian secondary education. The same story comes from every part of the empire, and this has been going on for years. It is a virtual denial of education to thousands of Russian youth, for, as I have already mentioned, there is no room for private effort in the dominions of the Tzar. The Government, which throws away scores of millions in Court festivals and distant wars, spares only a poor ten millions for purposes of education. And yet, in spite of its mania for repression and the resolute will of Count Tolstoi, the Government is forced from time to time to make concessions, often, however, more in appearance than reality. Every class is interested in the education of its youth. For the higher orders, without distinction of political opinion or social position, for Government *employés* as well as for ordinary citizens, the question is one of life and death. For if their children be not instructed, how can they live? And these classes combined, albeit they possess no recognized political influence, are able, up to a certain point, to force the hands of Government. But when the Government yields to pressure, it yields reluctantly and slowly, and with the worst possible grace. For instance, during the last ten years, notwithstanding increase of population and the ever-growing demand for greater educational facilities, the credit for the gymnasiums has been increased by only 1,400,000 roubles on an expenditure of six millions, a sum altogether and ridiculously inadequate for the needs which it is supposed to satisfy. Tired of pestering the Government with petitions and complaints, some of the municipalities and the Zemstvo lately took the extreme resolution of building new classical gymnasiums, burdening their modest budgets with an outlay which ought really to be borne by the State. The expenditure of the Zemstvo of eighteen provinces on secondary education amounts to from 25 to 30 per cent. of the total sum assigned by these bodies for public instruction in general. This proves to what point the Government has carried its policy of opposition to the extension of middle-class instruction.

The policy of the Minister of Public Instruction as touching secondary schools may be thus summarized :—(1) To oppose by every possible means the diffusion of secondary education, to render it as difficult as possible, and make no concession save at the last extremity, when all the means of resistance have been exhausted. (2) When resistance becomes impossible, to try to exclude from the benefits of secondary education the professional classes (to whom it is a matter of life and death), in order to confine it, as far as may be, to the higher nobility and richer citizens. (3) The privilege once granted to these classes, to make the instruction given to their children as sterile as possible, and so arrange matters that it may be imparted to the fewest number.

These conclusions read more like a bad joke than stern reality, yet are they not fully justified by the facts we have cited—facts, be it remembered, taken from official documents or from a censured and semi-official Press?

CHAPTER XXVII.

PRIMARY INSTRUCTION.

I.

PRIMARY instruction in Russia is of very recent growth, dating no further back than from the emancipation of 1861. It is true that great proprietors and serf-owners used to let a few of their thralls learn enough to become stewards and book-keepers. But, on the well-understood principle that educated slaves make dangerous servants, the mass of the rural population were deliberately left in the deepest ignorance. On the domains of the Crown alone were there a certain number of primary schools, but being placed under the supervision of the priests and the *tchinovnik*, who had neither the time nor the wish to look after them, they fell into a state of utter inefficiency. The few pupils they had learnt little or nothing, and more often than not the schools themselves were purely imaginary, "they existed only on paper," as we say in Russia—in other words, they were to be found only in the reports of the administration, in whose accounts always figured divers sums, supposed to have been paid for teachers' salaries and repairs of buildings, sums which, it is hardly necessary to say, went into the fathomless pockets of the *tchinovnik* and their accomplices. When the schools were afterwards made over to the Zemstvo, the frauds of this sort that came to light were absolutely appalling. At St. Petersburg, when the management of the popular schools was handed over to the municipality of the capital, in 1872, three, out of a nominal sixteen, were missing. They had never existed; the very names of them were fictitious. Of the remainder one alone was tolerably efficient, the remainder being badly organized and destitute of nearly every faculty for study. The first proceeding of the municipality was to provide fresh buildings, furnish the school with books, and appoint a new and competent staff of teachers, and organize everything afresh. Yet these schools were founded more than a hundred years ago by the Empress Catharine, and had been ever since under the supervision of the State.

If this was the condition of primary instruction in the capital, it is easy to understand what it must have been in the country. So far as it existed at all, it was due to private effort, either on the part of private individuals or of the Zemstvo. The Government, as I shall presently show, did little then, and it does little now, but thwart, openly or covertly, the noble endeavors of Russian society to impart some slight degree of instruction to the masses of the people. In 1859 the instructed classes, roused to enthusiasm by the approach of emancipation, were eager for all sorts of reform, and, above all, to do something for their poorer fellow-citizens, so soon to be free. The idea of education took as much hold of the imagination of the youth of that day as did later the idea of a Socialist propaganda. But the establishment of children's schools was not enough to satisfy these aspirations. The effects of their teaching would not be manifest for a whole generation. What could be done to fit fathers and mothers for the boon of freedom and make them more worthy members of the new society? The question was answered and the want supplied by the creation of Sunday-schools in every city, and in almost every town of the empire. The youth of both sexes threw themselves into the work with great ardor, and very soon excellent results were obtained. At Odessa alone six hundred persons offered themselves as teachers—of course without pay. But the Government viewed all this enthusiasm with dire alarm; there was no telling to what terrible consequences the mixing of the poor and the rich, the ignorant and the instructed, might not give rise, and in the autumn of 1862 the Sunday-schools were suppressed by order of the Tzar. And so ended a good work nobly begun. It was the first check imposed on the initiation of the public in this work. Popular instruction was again turned over to the priests and the *tchinovniks*, to the end that they might reduce it to a sham and a pretence.

In 1864, however, a step in the right direction was taken. The oversight of primary education was confided to the Zemstvo and other local bodies. In every district a School Board was constituted, of which three members were nominated by the Zemstvo and the municipality, and three elected by the commune. The Board was supervised by a provincial council composed of five members, of which two represented the Zemstvo and two the *tchinovnik*. The fifth member was the bishop, or his substitute, whose special duty it was to see that the character of the teaching in the popular schools was loyal and religious. The bishop received his information and gave his advice through the village priests, who were authorized to visit the schools and direct the masters, and if the latter did not conform to their counsel to make formal complaint against them. But as neither the bishop nor the *tchinovnik* gave much thought to the matter, rarely attending the meetings of the council, the management of the schools was left virtually to the Zemstvo. The new regulation was thus much more liberal and popular than its authors meant it to be, and offered great facilities for the establishment of primary schools. The greatest difficulty encountered by the Zemstvo was paucity of funds, their expenditure being limited to a twentieth of the national revenues. Yet stirred by a noble zeal for education the Zemstvo did wonders. In 1864 the number of primary schools was 17,678 with 598,121 pupils. We have now 25,000 schools with 1,000,000 scholars. But the progress achieved was even greater than these figures denote. The quality of the teaching was vastly improved. The old teachers were composed chiefly of sacristans, church singers, and old soldiers, most of whom could hardly read, much less write or cipher. To remedy this evil the Zemstvo started teachers' training schools, and raised the pay of the teachers from fifty to sixty roubles a year to an average of two hundred roubles, in exceptional cases to three hundred and to three hundred and fifty roubles. Courses in pedagogy were also organized by which teachers could profit during the holidays, and by these means the efficiency of the schools was improved beyond measure. Though no general statistics are obtainable as to the results of the new departure, some suggestive facts and figures are to be found in the reports of the Zemstvo of Novgorod, Moscow, Samara, and a few other districts.

Of the present teaching staff about one-third have received a superior education in the middle class schools and seminaries, another third holds certificates from the normal school, and the remainder are men of the old *régime*. From their modest revenues of 18,000,000 roubles the Zemstvo spare 4,000,000 for purposes of education; while from its revenue of 360,000,000 the Imperial Government spares for the same object only a million and a half, and of this sum 300,000 is taken by the inspection—that is to say, by the police of the schools. The country population—freed serfs and their children—whom many consider hopelessly ignorant and brutalized, and unfitted for any public function, show an almost pathetic eagerness to secure for their little ones the benefits of education. Notwithstanding their proverbial poverty, our rural communes voluntarily contributed as much towards the maintenance of the primary schools as the Zemstvo and the Government put together. Of the total amount (about 7¼ million roubles) required for these schools, the peasants pay 41, the Zemstvo 34, the Imperial Government 14, and private individuals, mostly landowners, 11 per cent. And it is a fact of much significance that the provinces which make the greatest sacrifices for the promotion of education are exactly those in whose Zemstvo the peasants have the greatest proportion of deputies. The towns too and, above all, St. Petersburg, have made strenuous efforts to popularize education. The thirteen wretched schools of

1864, with a few score pupils, had grown in 1882 to 158 excellent establishments with a staff of certificated teachers and 6,000 scholars of both sexes. The province of Tamboff, which, before the creation of the Zemstvo, had 174 primary schools with 7,700 pupils, possess now 500 schools with an average attendance of 27,000 children. In 1860 Nijni Novgorod had 28 schools and 1,500 scholars; twenty years later the Zemstvo of the province had organized 337 schools, in which nearly 12,-000 children were receiving the rudiments of education. The progress thus achieved would be remarkable in any circumstances; if account be taken of the hostility of the Government and the difficulties thrown in the way of the Zemstvo by the official class, it seems prodigious. The Government shows scant favor to the universities and superior schools; to the primary schools it shows even less; and its treatment of them has been so unworthy of the rulers of a great country that, if the facts I am about to set forth were not proven, that is to say, if they had not appeared in official reports and been stated in newspapers over which is always hanging the Damocles sword of censure and suspension—they would seem nothing less than incredible, and I should be accused of wilful exaggeration in repeating them.

II.

The Zemstvo hardly began the work of reorganization when they encountered the opposition of the Ministry. Their most pressing need was good teachers. They wanted to be allowed —they asked nothing more—to establish teachers' colleges. After two years of waiting and dozens of petitions, Mr. Golovnine, the then Minister of Education, seemed to be on the point of giving the required authorization, when (in 1866) the first attempt to assassinate the Emperor came to pass—an event which was followed by the accession of Count Tolstoi to the Ministry and his assumption of the portfolio of Public Instruction. His first proceeding was to impose a peremptory veto on the proposed organization of teachers' colleges, and in his report to the Tzar, published in 1867, he takes special credit to himself for having burked so pernicious and revolutionary a scheme. In his opinion, normal schools, besides becoming centres of democratic agitation, would be the means of contaminating the minds of Russian children with subversive ideas. For five long years the Minister remained deaf to the prayers and remonstrances of the Zemstvo, who were compelled to get teachers where they could and retain the services of many of the sacristans and old soldiers, who were hardly less ignorant than their own scholars. But the events of 1870 wrought a startling change, for it was said—and all believed—that the victories of Worth, of Gravelotte, and of Sedan were won, not in the cabinet of General von Moltke, but in the schools of the Fatherland. Then it dawned on the minds of some of the Emperor's advisers, notably on that of the Minister of War, that men make none the worse soldiers for knowing how to read and write, and the interdict on the establishment of normal schools was removed. There are now sixty of them; but Count Tolstoi, while yielding to necessity, yielded reluctantly, and some of the Zemstvo—though their petitions have been incessant—have not even yet received the needful concession. But from their very inception these excellent institutions have been the objects of official jealousy and incessant suspicion, and are continually exposed to the double fire of the police of the State and the police of the Ministry of Education.

And a regard for truth constrains us to say that in this strife the Minister of Instruction displayed far greater zeal than the Third Section. The fate of our best schools of this class, founded by the efforts of the Zemstvo and the enterprise of private citizens (by Mr. Moksimov at Tver, Mr. Dronginune at Torjok, the Zemstvo of Kiasan, and many others), destroyed for " admitting too much air," for " extending too largely the scholastic curriculum," for "reducing too much the charges for admission," and for other crimes of the same sort, are perfect illustrations of the spirit in which, for the last fifteen years, our so-called Minister of Instruction has conducted the business of his department and promoted the cause of education.

III.

The crusade against the universities is of long duration; that against the gymnasium and secondary education began in 1866. As for the primary schools, they remained for several years comparatively free from interference; but about 1874 it occurred to the Government that by preventing the seeds of disaffection from being sown in infant minds they might destroy Nihilism at its source. This idea was due to the discovery that several of the teachers were revolutionary emissaries. As a rule, these emissaries, in order the better to win over the working classes, assumed the character of common workmen, and actually worked as blacksmiths, masons, bricklayers, and laborers. A few, probably not more than a score, became teachers in village schools, their object being to carry on a propaganda among the peasants, certainly not to impart Nihilistic tenets to children struggling with the alphabet or deep in the mysteries of multiplication. This portentous discovery led to the placing of all the 25,000 schools of the empire under the ban of the police, and suggested to the Government the idea of the famous regulations of 1874. The character and consequences of these regulations were described by a St. Petersburg journal on November 2, 1880, shortly after the temporary disgrace of Count Tolstoi, when, during a brief space, it was possible for a paper to speak the truth without fear of prosecution or extinction, in the following terms:

"Alarmed by the spread of socialism in the provinces, Count Tolstoi, casting about in his mind for the cause of so portentous a phenomenon, came to the conclusion that the primary schools were the source of the mischief, and that the schoolmasters were the most formidable of revolutionary propagandists. So the Minister of Public Instruction, instead of favoring the creation of schools for the diffusion of exact knowledge and correct principles among the masses, began to put every obstacle in the way of this great work. He tried to protect the popular schools, as yet hardly established, from dangerous influences by measures much more likely to kill than to cure. In the eyes of Count Tolstoi our village schoolmasters, for the most part poor, ignorant, and inexperienced (it was only in 1871 that leave was given for the opening of teachers' training colleges), are enemies of the State and a danger to society, upon whom it is necessary to keep a perpetual watch with thirty-six eyes. Instead of being instructed in their duties, they are treated with contumely, and supervised like released malefactors. Instead of receiving the moral support of the authorities, they are cowed by threats; they know that the least display of spirit or of independence would bring them under suspicion of being politically heterodox: and their lives are made miserable by the knowledge that all their movements are watched, and that at any moment they may fall under the lash of the law for offences they wot not of.

"To keep in check enemies so redoubtable as these poor schoolmasters, it was clear that some agencies were needed even more powerful than the general police and the Third Section. So, under the form of provincial and district scholastic councils, Count Tolstoi created a police of his own, which it were no misnomer to call the political police of the primary schools. Nothing like it exists or ever did exist in any other country. Never were schools so watched, guarded, tutored, and controlled. Every children's school in the country is supervised, in the first line by the governor of the province and the bishop of the diocese; then come the two ordinary councils, with their fifteen members, making a total of eighteen persons, all of them possessing large powers, though two only, the director and the inspector, have any special knowledge of pedagogy. [In this the writer is wrong. According to Article 20 of the regulations of 1874 these two only are authorized to direct the details of instruction, but it by no means follows that they have special qualifications for this duty; they are often, indeed, less competent than their *confrères*.] The surveillance of the other fifteen persons must therefore needs be almost purely inquisitorial."

Nor is this all. The author of the "regulations," being apparently of opinion that fifteen inquisitors were not enough to safeguard the schools from political contamination (Art. 41) authorized the President of the Council to choose at his discretion from the nobility of the district several private persons for the purpose of keeping an eye on the character of the instruction imparted in the primary schools with special reference to its political tendencies. These persons, albeit no executive functions are conferred upon them, were invited to communicate their "observations and conjectures (*sic*)" to the President of the School Council—in other words, to play the spy. M. Kosheleff, one of the most respected members of our Zemstvo, said in an article printed in the *Zemstvo* (No. 2) that he doubted if there could be found in the whole of Russia a member of the nobility sufficiently servile to accept so ignoble a mission. But this renders the regulations in question neither less characteristic of the methods of our Government, nor the position of village schoolmasters more tolerable. The *rôle* refused by the gentlemen of the nobility is accepted by the *stanovoi* (constable) of the district, the *staroste* of the commune, or village innkeeper, any of whom may communicate his "observations and conjectures" to the school inspector, a proceeding that generally entails the poor schoolmaster's prompt dismissal.

"The position of our teachers," observes the priest Kultchinsky in the *Samara Zemstvo*, "is really insupportable. They are controlled not alone by their many superiors, but by all the busybodies of a neighborhood, in such a manner that it is quite impossible for them to satisfy demands so various and tastes so conflicting."

The following passage appears in the Report of the Commission of Inquiry of the Zemstvo of Rheinigoff (1880):

> "The political element which of late has disturbed our provincial life has caused a number of persons and institutions to meddle with school affairs, from whose interference has followed no good results. Teachers find themselves at the mercy, not alone of a crowd of superiors, from the Marshal of the Nobility to the village priest, but of policemen, rural guards, and communal *employés*. Worried by so many masters, the teacher becomes incapable of performing his duties; he loses his head, and in order to obtain a little repose is often compelled to abandon his post."

It is also unfortunately the fact that the best men are the worst treated. The more a master is intelligent, instructed, and devoted to his duty, the more is he likely to be suspected by his superiors and denounced by some agent of the police as a fomenter of sedition and a corrupter of youth. If, on the contrary, he be ignorant and incapable, a drunkard and an idler, it is never imputed to him that he is a wolf in sheep's clothing, a revolutionist in disguise. The effect of the existing regulations is thus to drive from the schools the most competent teachers—a fact which is well understood by all the Zemstvo. It has even been publicly acknowledged by the School Council of Novgorod, who in an official report express surprise that any properly qualified teachers can be found ready to accept the conditions imposed upon them, and that it has been possible to achieve the very modest results already set forth.

IV.

And all this vandalism, this reign of terror, because among 25,000 teachers there have been found twenty or thirty apostles of sedition! Can it really be that the Russian Government is so ludicrously nervous as to tremble at the thought of a score or two, or even of a hundred, Nihilist emissaries being scattered over the length and breadth of the empire? or is it only a pretext to hamper primary education? Pending an answer to this question I freely give the Government credit for all the stupidity which their conduct, on the hypothesis that they are sincere, inevitably implies.

But as we shall presently see, its policy in the matter of popular instruction possesses a remarkable peculiarity which cannot be ascribed to fear of socialism.

As I have already mentioned, the regulations of 1864 placed the direction of the primary schools virtually in the hands of the local authorities. It was the best and most natural arrangement; it worked to the satisfaction of all; and the Zemstvo by their zeal, and the peasants by their contributions, showed themselves fully worthy of the trust reposed in them. But from 1869 the Government began, little by little, to undo the good they had done ; by the regulations of 1874 the local authorities were completely ousted from the management of the schools, and the *tchinovnik* ruled in their stead. The Zemstvo may pay if they like, for the payment is optional, but they have no longer any right to control the expenditure or take part in the direction, which is vested altogether in the nominees of the Minister under the official designation of Inspector of Popular Schools. The power of these functionaries is little less than despotic. Without their authorization it is not permitted either to build a school-house, engage a teacher, begin a new course of instruction, or even purchase a primer. An inspector, by a mere stroke of the pen, can dismiss a master, close a school, or suppress a course of lessons. The so-called council may ask, but they cannot require, information touching the progress of the schools which they subsidize ; the inspectors even refuse to communicate to them the results of the periodical examinations, for this, as one of these functionaries lately explained to the Zemstvo of the province of Taurida, would be admitting their right to meddle in matters which concern the inspectors alone. Thus the sole sphere of activity left open to the two councils is that of police ; and it is a curious fact that albeit certain councillors may, if they discover anything politically suspicious, either dismiss a master, or shut up a school, they have no right either to recommend a manual or offer an opinion on the quality of the teaching or the progress of the scholars. And the inspectors, be it remembered, have no special qualifications for the positions which they occupy. "During the last few years," runs the report of the Zemstvo of Tchernigoff for 1881, "the inspection of our schools has become more stringent and less pedagogic. Among the new inspectors of primary schools is hardly to be found one who has received a superior education or obtained a certificate of proficiency as a teacher. Some of them are men of phenomenal ignorance. Of one, a certain Mr. Jaukovsky, the report of the Zemstvo of Berdiansk mentions that, during a public examination held in presence of the governor of the province, he showed utter inability to understand some of the simplest rules of arithmetic, such as are taught to children of tender age.

What, it may be asked, can be the cause of this reactionary policy of the Russian Government in regard to primary education? To push police supervision over the person of the schoolmaster to so absurd a length as that which I have described seems nothing less than a senseless freak of power. It is like burning down a house to rid it of mice. There is, nevertheless, a sufficiently obvious, yet utterly inadequate, reason for all these proceedings. The schoolmasters are generally young men, the mistresses young women, and the young being more receptive of new and strange ideas than the old, are therefore more likely to be contaminated with the pest of Nihilism. It is surely against them that the Government aim these measures of repression, even at the risk of destroying primary education altogether or rendering it inefficient to worthlessness. Yet this theory, though it may be good as far as it goes, does not explain why the management of the schools was taken out of the hands of the Zemstvo. For a proceeding so contrary to common sense no deep political motives can be assigned. It has never occurred even to the most suspicious of Ministers that the Zemstvo are capable of converting the schools into centres of a socialist agitation. The Zemstvo are composed of landowners, priests, merchants, and *starchina* (rural mayors), none of them in the heyday of youth, or men whom even the most keen-scented of police functionaries can suspect of socialist tendencies. It is true that they are not in favor of the present *régime*. Every member of a Zemstvo, if he be not a traitor to his cause, must needs desire self-government and the free initiative of society—therefore political freedom more or less extensive. On the other hand, there has never been an instance of the Zemstvo using the schools for the propagation of—let us say—constitutional ideas. During the twenty-one years' existence of the thirty-four Zemstvo, no such charge as this has been brought against them.

We are thus driven to the conclusion that the reactionary measures of the Government are dictated by an instinctive dislike of education for its own sake, and a desire to check what they deem a too rapid enlightenment of the masses of the people. At first sight this conclusion may seem as extravagant as some other conclusions concerning the motives of the Russian Government, which, nevertheless, there is no evading. For in this regard the Government has the merit of being frank to cynicism, as the facts I am about to adduce abundantly prove.

The regulation of 1874 strictly limits the instruction to be given in the primary schools. In other countries there is a *minimum* of education which all children must reach; in Russia there is a *maximum* beyond which none may go. It is strictly forbidden to our little peasant children to acquire more than (*a*) an elementary knowledge of the catechism and of sacred history, (*b*) of reading and writing, and (*c*) of the four first rules of arithmetic. Over and over again have the Zemstvo besought the Ministry to let them enlarge a little this meagre curriculum, and give the poor little ones—some of them very intelligent and eager to learn—an idea of geometry, of decimals, and of the geography of the land they live in. All in vain ; such requests are either treated with contemptuous silence or answered with a peremptory negative. The same obscurantism explains the refusal of the Government to permit the use of any other language than Russian in the folk-schools of Finland, the Ukraine, and Poland, albeit the peasants of those countries know no tongue but their own. The consequence is that the children for the most part learn neither Russian nor anything else, which is probably what the authorities want.

The management of the schools under the present system, as must always be the case when a bureaucracy meddles with local affairs requiring special knowledge, is radically bad. The money spent on the 112 inspectors, which would suffice to build annually 700 new schools, is simply wasted. Each of the 112 has the care of 122 schools, and, as the primary schools make only about 156 working days in the year, it follows that the inspector of a district can give little more than one day during that time to each school—or could if they were close together. But seeing that they are generally spread over an area half as large as Ireland, destitute of railways and ill provided with roads, it is evident that no inspector, let him be ever so zealous, can give much more than an hour a year to each of the schools within his jurisdiction—even if he were to spend every moment of his waking hours in galloping over the length and breadth of his district.

These hard-wrought officials, moreover, have a terrible amount of office work to get through. They are always writing and answering letters, making reports, and filling up returns. The inspector of Beloosero, when the Zemstvo complained that he never visited their schools, asked indignantly how they could expect him to do anything of the sort, seeing that he had to send off 2,000 departmental and other business papers in the course of the year. In 1879 the Zemstvo of Novgorod complained that the inspectors had not time to visit even the model schools of the district, or be present at the examinations, to the great inconvenience of all concerned, none save the inspectors having power either to give orders or present reports. Similar complaints are continually made by other Zemstvo (for instance by those of Saratoff, Tchernigoff, Ekaterinoslav, and many more), and, though the latter have repeatedly offered to appoint supplementary inspectors at their own expense, they have not yet succeeded in prevailing upon the Ministry to accept this reasonable solution of the difficulty.

V.

The schools are thus in effect left without any true scholastic (as distinguished from political) oversight or direction whatever. The inspectors neither act themselves, nor let others act, and the Zemstvo are placed between the alternatives—watching with folded hands the destruction of their favorite work, and engaging in perpetual conflict with the agents of the State. Hence arise retrogression on the one hand, and endless contests with the inspectors on the other. The miserable history of our primary schools is that of an interminable war between these irreconcilable elements, a war in which the inspectors, backed by the Minister, always prevail. In a country so habituated to despotism, moreover, it is inevitable that the contest should often assume a character of pure vandalism. Of this the affair of Berdiansk, among others, offers a remarkable instance. Berdiansk was remarkable for its zeal in the cause of education; the best-schooled district in the well-schooled province of Taurida, only one of its eighty-eight primary schools was subsidized by the Government; all the rest were supported by the locality. It had no special inspector. The functionary who was charged with the duty, having two other districts to look after, could naturally give very little attention to any of them. So the Zemstvo, having no hope of being allowed to appoint a qualified school inspector of their own, resolved, if possible, to secure the services of a *tchinovnik* inspector. A request to this effect was forwarded to the Minister in due form, the Zemstvo offering, if it were granted, to pay the man's salary out of their resources. For five years this modest request, though continually reiterated, remained unheeded and unanswered. But perseverance does wonders, and in the fifth year they were gratified by the appointment of a certain Mr. Garousoff, a favor for which they tendered the Minister their warmest thanks. But the Zemstvo were not long in finding out that they had made as great a mistake as the frogs who asked for a king and got a stork. The new inspector conducted himself like the master of a conquered country. "He annuled all the instructions and rules for the management of schools without substituting others, a proceeding which produced at first indescribable confusion;

and when (after some time) Mr. Garousoff's rules and prescriptions appeared, they were so contradictory that the teachers did not know what to do or whom to obey. He next, without any plausible pretext, dismissed and transferred from one place to another the best teachers. Alarmed by threats 'to throw them on the streets with a stroke of his pen,' which Mr. Garousoff continually repeated, the teachers began to leave the district. And when, to increase his power, the inspector brought against several of them political accusations—completely false, as was subsequently shown—the teachers were thrown into a veritable panic."

The Zemstvo complained to the director, as also to the Minister, and prayed to be relieved of the Vandal with whom the latter had presented them. But all in vain, and in the end the Zemstvo only got rid of their unloved inspector by a happy accident. He made a charge against a teacher of so outrageous a character that Todtleben was constrained to dismiss him, and in October, 1879, Garousoff was succeeded by Saukovsky. But the Minister evidently held the district in detestation. Its schools were altogether too popular and successful. Saukovsky was no improvement on his predecessor. He dismissed teachers without cause, and when the Zemstvo protested against the discharge of a governess whom he had accused of socialism, he threatened to accuse the entire Zemstvo of sympathizing with subversive ideas. He gave no heed to the wishes of the Zemstvo as to the management of the schools, saying that their only duty was the payment of his salary. He introduced so many changes into the scholastic course that the books did not arrive until the end of the year, when the course was over, and the schools were kept without teachers merely because the inspector did not take the trouble to confirm his appointment. This barbarous *régime* lasted two years and did not terminate until the papers were filled with letters on the subject, and the schools of Berdiansk became the question of the day and a public scandal.

Were incidents like these of rare occurrence, they might,

by no great stretch of charity, be ascribed to accident or official stupidity ; but they are too frequent to be unintentional, and must be held to express, in deed if not in word, the deliberate policy of the Ministry of Education. In the provinces of Tamboff, Ekaterinoslav, and many others, analogous facts have come to pass, and instances of conflicts between the Zemstvo and the inspectors, arising from similar causes, might be produced *ad infinitum*. In the session of 1879 the Zemstvo of Raizan presented an address of thanks to the five inspectors of the province for " having abstained from using the means at their disposal to thwart the Zemstvo in their efforts to promote primary education and increase the usefulness of the village schools." What irony could be more bitter, or better proof be adduced of the determination of the Government to hinder in every possible way, short of absolute suppression, the development of our popular schools ? True, they have increased in numbers ; but owing, on the one hand, to the absence of any real inspection, and, on the other, frequent changes of system and dismissals of teachers, their efficiency is impaired to an extent that renders them powerless for good. In some instances the Zemstvo, weary of petitioning and remonstrating, have withdrawn their subsidies and left the schools to take care of themselves. During Count Tolstoi's temporary disgrace there was a hope of better things, and his successor, M. Sabouroff, was literally bombarded with petitions from all parts of the country, beseeching him to restore to the Zemstvo their liberty of action in the matter of education. But when, three months later, Count Tolstoi returned to power as Premier and Minister of the Interior, all hope of amendment was at an end.

VI.

The Ministry of War has always shown more favor to education than the Ministry of Public Instruction, and, according to the law of conscription now in force, young men who have completed their course in a popular school are let off with four years' military service instead of six. . But owing to the indifference of the peasants, arising from the obvious inefficiency of the schools, this clause has become almost a dead letter. "The condition of our schools," says the *Russian Almanac* for 1880, "is shown by the great number of pupils who abandon their studies before completing their course. In 1877 certificates were granted to no more than 88,255, equal to about 8 per cent. of the total number of scholars." Figures like these are more eloquent than words. Only one scholar in twelve or thirteen succeeds in reaching the very low mark set by the examiners.

With this result the Government might surely have been satisfied, for they have virtually suppressed eleven schools out of twelve. But so far is this from being the case, that the Minister of Public Instruction contemplates a measure even more sweeping than the deposition of the Zemstvo—a measure which would be equivalent in the end to the entire suppression of primary instruction throughout the empire.* He proposes to take the schools out of the hands of the Zemstvo altogether, and to make the clergy the sole managers of primary education. He might as well propose to make the management over to the children; for the work would never be done, and the schools would perish of neglect. The clergy have neither time nor inclination for any other than their strictly clerical duties.

The Zemstvo of Kazan complained a little while ago that for two years the schools had not once been visited by a priest; formal complaints on the same score have been made by the Zemstvo of Moscow, Voronej, Tchernigoff, Tamboff, and St. Petersburg. In some provinces even the priests have met and passed resolutions to the effect that religious instruction can only be efficiently given by secular teachers, for even this duty it is quite out of the power of the clergy to perform. Nor when it is remembered that some of the parishes are so exten-

---

* This was written before June 12, 1884.

sive that to give one lesson a week in each school would take two or three days, is this result very surprising It is not given even to a priest to be in two places at one time. What would be the consequence of handing over the schools to a class of men already so heavily burdened (to say nothing of their utter lack of pedagogic qualifications) may easily be imagined.

All this is well known to Count Tolstoi, both as ex-Minister of Education and ex-President of the Holy Synod. For my own part, I do not think that a scheme so monstrous can be carried into effect. There are limits even to the blindness and wickedness of an autocracy based on ignorance and buttressed by lies. But it is characteristic of the spirit which animates the advisers of the Tzar that a scheme so inimical to the best interests of the country should be seriously entertained.

I wrote thus in the *Times* in the spring of 1884, and I reproduce the foregoing lines by way of penance for my want of foresight and the misplaced optimism which I then expressed. The substitution of the clergy for the Zemstvo in the management of the schools which less than a year ago I believed to be morally impossible was effected by the law of June 12, 1884, abolishing the School Councils and transferring all their powers to the bishops and their nominees among the clergy.

If the result of this measure be not to throw back the peasantry into their anti-emancipation condition when, as one of our writers has said, you might travel a week without meeting a *moujik* who could sign his name, it will be because the *moujiks* themselves have acquired a desire for knowledge.

As for the Minister of Justice, we must do him the justice to acknowledge that he has now done everything that man can do to realize the golden dream of despotism—complete ignorance.

CHAPTER XXVIII.

THE ZEMSTVO.

I.

THE principle of self-government is no novelty in Russia. "When the Muscovite depotism crushed every class under its leaden weight and deprived the people of their most sacred rights," says Kostomaroff, "men and citizens protected after their fashion. They indemnified themselves by putting their hands on everything confided to them by the State. To cheat Government, take its money, sell the justice which they dispensed in its name, and pillage the provinces they were charged to administer became among the public functionaries of ancient Muscovy an accepted, inveterate, and hereditary custom." From the highest to the lowest, everybody stole. They made no distinction between theft and remuneration, robbery and profit. The Central Government itself did not oppose these practices or principles; they only protected against peculation and exaction, when, as sometimes happened, the plunderers went to extravagant lengths. A poor boyard, on asking the Tzar for the post of *voevoda*, made no attempt to disguise his motives, generally putting his request in some such terms as these: "And I, thy faithful slave, am reduced to beggary and my servants perish under the sticks of tax-gatherers. Give me then this place that I may feed myself a little."

To "give food," or "receive food," was the accepted euphemism to designate nomination to the governorship of a province, a city, or a fortress. In course of time the phrase became obsolete, but until very lately the idea still survived. When the Grand Duke Michael Paolovitch (brother of Tzar Nicolas) was told that the colonel of a regiment of guards had handed over to the regimental fund a sum of 30,000 roubles, saved out of his allowance for supplies, his Highness exclaimed angrily, "It was not to pick up crumbs that a regiment was given him."

But the appetites of the locusts who were sent into the provinces to fatten, "growing by what they fed on," became so insatiable that the Central Government, even at a very early date, began to take alarm, the residue left for purposes of State was so little. The check exercised by the *privases*—chambers composed of Muscovite functionaries (*dyaki*), and themselves as great thieves as the *voevodas*—was quite illusory, and the Government were constrained to call into existence local institutions for protection against the depredations of their own agents.

The first attempt to organize a system of local self-government was made in the reign of Tzar John IV.

In the first part of the St. Petersburg period of the Russian Empire (the reign of Peter the Great), no further attempt to introduce self-government was possible, all the valid forces of the country being engaged in the service of the State. But when a century of progress had produced an educated class the attempt was renewed, taking shape in the so-called Franchise Charter of the Nobility, granted by Catharine II. By this instrument the Empress conferred on the provincial nobility, in meeting assembled, the right of nominating the agents of the local administration and the magistracy; the right of controlling all Government functionaries, including the governor-general of the province himself, who had to lay before a commission of the nobility the financial results of his administration.

In seeming, at least, nothing could well be more complete than the right of control, especially as touching the provincial budget. Yet this function could never be more than a formality; for seigneurs living amidst hordes of slaves it would have been the height of folly to quarrel about a few thousand roubles belonging to the "Crown mother" with the governor of the province and supreme commander of the military forces, which alone held in check the multitude of serfs who cultivated their estates. The new system of aristocratic self-government was really a lifeless institution from its very inception, and utterly incapable of defending the State from the colossal depredations of its *tchinovniks*. It was rightly said after the Crimean war that the enemies who had vanquished the armies of Russia were not the allied forces, but her own administrators, furnishers, and functionaries.

When at the conclusion of that contest a general reorganization of the national institutions was found needful, the one essential element for safeguarding the State to a certain extent from the immeasurable voracity of its *employés* could not be overlooked. To this end some sort of local representative government was clearly indispensable. Hence, next to the emancipation of the serfs, the most pressing reform was that of the Zemstvo, and of all the institutions reformed during the first years of the second Alexander's reign none has suffered relatively so little from the subsequent ferocious reaction as the new Zemstvo.

II.

The decision being taken to establish a system of local self-government as an absolute necessity, a measure to this effect was introduced in 1864. But care was taken not to administer it in too large a dose, the more especially as reactionary views were already beginning to prevail. The part assigned to the Zemstvo in local affairs was, in effect, very limited. They could only deal with twenty-two millions (roubles) of the provincial revenues, and out of this sum they had to support a variety of heavy extraneous charges—keep barracks in repair, feed soldiers, pay the cost of military conscriptions, subsidize the imperial ports, and meet other demands of the same sort. These requirements, which had nothing to do with local government, absorbed the lion's share of the local revenues, and left the Zemstvo only four millions for purposes within their own discretion, and in which they had any direct interest—schools, sanitation, economic enterprises, and so forth. It was not much, and if the Zemstvo were to do any good it could hardly have been less.

This restriction was a desire to hinder the Zemstvo from displaying too much activity in the domain of finance. To prevent them from trespassing on the domain of politics measures equally efficacious were taken.

Their sessions were very short, and held at long intervals. The deputies could meet only once a year—the district Zemstvo sitting for a fortnight, the provincial Zemstvo three weeks. This scarcely afforded them time to discuss general questions and give their instructions to the *onprak*, an executive commission appointed by each Zemstvo to look after matters in the intervals between their sessions.

In some particulars, indeed, the system of self-government organized in 1864 was inferior to the aristocratic charter of Catharine II. So far from controlling the governor-general, the governor-general controls them, and in the most absolute manner. He audits their accounts, and without his permission the proceedings and discussions of the Zemstvo cannot be made public. He can intervene at any moment and suspend by a word any measure which, in his opinion, is not in conformity with the general interests and utility of the State, that is to say, which does not precisely please him. True, this veto is merely suspension, and the Zemstvo may appeal against it to the senate; but as the local parliaments meet only once a year, a resolution tabooed by a governor cannot, in any event, be put in force for a twelvemonth—even if the senate should grant his decision at once, and not keep the matter in suspense two or three years. In questions of local administration, which do not admit of delay, the governor's veto is practically absolute.

To render the dependence of the Zemstvo on the Government still more complete they were deprived of a right formerly enjoyed by their predecessors of the nobility. They could not appoint the chiefs of the inferior administration—*ispravnik*—the right of appointment being vested in the governors. The Zemstvo, moreover, have no executive agents. Whatever they want done must be done by agents of the Government, who give them much trouble, particularly in anything which concerns finance. The collection of the taxes assigned to the Zemstvo, being for the agents of the Imperial Treasury only a secondary service, and, so to speak, a work of complaisance and supererogation, is badly done. The sums due from public properties as well as from great landowners remain outstanding, and arrears accumulate in all directions, to the great annoyance and inconvenience of the Zemstvo.

But to return to the subject more especially before us—the precautions taken to prevent the Zemstvo from meddling with politics. One of these precautions is the denial to them of the right—if so modest a privilege can be called a right—of petitioning the Tzar, a right fully enjoyed by the assemblies of nobles. They are not allowed, in fact, to take the initiative in any question of public utility whatever. They cannot make their voices heard anywhere but in waiting-rooms of the Minister, who is their master, and nine times out of ten does not deign to honor them with a reply.

But the new system of self-government, whatever may be its faults, had one incomparable advantage over the old system—it was not a fraud. The law of emancipation destroyed slavery. It made nobles and peasants fellow-citizens of the same country and equal before the law. It was impossible to limit self-government to a single class; that would have been to revive the old serfage in a new shape. All classes had thus their part, albeit the division was flagrantly unequal.

The deputies of the Zemstvo are chosen by the order which they represent. The peasants, the towns, and the nobility, elect their representatives separately in separate electoral meetings, which differ somewhat in their composition. The number of the deputies of each order is a fixed quantity, and nothing can be more unfair than the arrangement for the distribution of seats, which is all in favor of the nobility. The peasants, who count sixty millions and pay 83 per cent. of the taxes (90 per cent. according to the calculations of Prince Vassiltchekoff), are represented, in the mean, by 38·6 per cent. of the total number of deputies. The landowning class, numbering only a million individuals and contributing only 7 per cent. to the national revenue, elect 46·2 per cent. of the members of the Zemstvo, while the share of the third estate—the towns—is 15·2 per cent.

In many provinces—the eight central provinces, for instance—the anomaly is still greater ; 93,000 great landowners being represented by 1,817 deputies, while six million peasants are represented by only 1,597.

On the whole, therefore, the nobility hold nearly one-half of the seats in our local parliaments. But this proportion is far from being the measure of their influence, especially in the provincial Zemstvo, where the election is double. The village ancients, who for the most part represent the peasants, are administratively subordinate to the Marshal of the Nobility, who is both chief of the bureau which regulates rural affairs and president of the Zemstvo.

And, finally, in order to exclude from the body the more democratic element of the smaller landowners—the little nobility—the electoral qualification was made inordinately high : the possession of from eighty to one hundred and twenty acres in thickly populated districts, and eight hundred in localities more sparsely peopled. By this expedient the number of voters belonging to the more highly educated of the aristocratic class is kept very low ; they are rather a *coterie* of personal friends and acquaintances than a body of electors.

In point of fact, therefore, the self-governing scheme of 1864 placed the nation under the tutelage of the privileged class, or, more correctly, under the richer and more conservative of that class, to the exclusion of its more liberal and progressive element, the inferior nobility. It is difficult to imagine how Mr. Valouzev could have desired anything less liberal or more capable of converting self-government into an instrument of reaction and an obstacle to reform. But the Government, after all, was out in its calculations. The occasions on which the aristocratic members of the Zemstvo have tried to use their power for the profit of the privileged order to which they belong may be counted on the fingers of the two hands. One of the first proceedings of the Zemstvo was an earnest effort to give more seats to the peasants—an effort that the Government, which is always proclaiming its partiality for the peasantry, of course opposed. And when at a later date (1871) the Government asked the Zemstvo of the thirty-four provinces for their advice concerning certain changes in the incidence of taxation, all the thirty-four pronounced for the abolition of privilege, advocated a lightening of the heavy charges laid on the peasantry, and recommended the adoption of a scale of taxes proportioned to the means of those on whom they were imposed.

Our Zemstvo, on the other hand, are open to the reproach of an excessive deference to authority and a want of civic courage. The political theories of those of their leaders who have had the boldness to expound them in papers and pamphlets, printed abroad, are far from being models of political wisdom. Their projects of economic reform which have been allowed to see the light are the merest palliatives. I have no desire to sound the praises of our local parliaments. But nobody can deny that they have shown a praiseworthy activity, or that, at the beginning of their career, before the administration laid its hands on their throats, the Russian Zemstvo labored with all zeal and devotion for the good of the people, and not for the benefit of the class which the majority of them represented. In the modest sphere assigned to them, moreover, they displayed a thorough knowledge of the real needs of the country; and the measures they adopted proved them to be possessed of sound sense and practical views. This they showed by taking so much to heart, and at once, the question which is above all others and on which everything else depends—popular instruction, whereby alone the masses can be rendered capable of judging and acting for themselves. We have seen how energetically they wrought to organize primary schools, and how strenuously they defended their work against the attacks of the Minister of Instruction. But the Zemstvo did not limit themselves to the organization of primary education. They tried to create secondary and professional schools in order to bring within reach of the masses technical instruction and a knowledge of practical science. They desired to co-operate with private effort—of which instances are frequent in Russia—in the foundation and endowment of educational institutions of this class, and did space permit I could adduce many other proofs of the energy and enterprise of our local parliaments. They have done everything, in fact, that with their limited resources it was possible to do. The Zemstvo were the first to give to the peasantry some sort of medical care, with which, up to that time, they had been no better provided than African savages. They engaged doctors for country districts, giving the preference to women and competent dispensers. Where they could they built hospitals. They did all in their power, too, to aid economic enterprises which promised to better the wretched lot of the peasantry. The co-operative cheese factories of Vereshaghin, the co-operative enterprises of Shapiro, and many other similar undertakings, received from them generous encouragement and substantial support. Among other good works the Zemstvo founded rural banks, which, by making loans to the peasants at easy rates of interest, rendered them independent of blood-sucking usurers. They advanced money for the purchase by the peasantry of small allotments of land, and introduced the practice of fire assurance. They made every effort to protect the rural population from intimidation on the part of the inferior agents of the administration at election times; to safeguard their home-life from the meddlesomeness of the civil *ouriadnik,* an inferior order of policeman, yet with extensive powers; and their souls from the spiritual *ouriadnik,* the pope —the priest-chicaner and informer, who is continually appealing to the police for aid in restraining his flock from lapsing into heresy and schism.

In all this useful yet moderate activity the greatest obstacles encountered by the Zemstvo, were the indolence of office and the open ill-will of the administration. To secure passable dispensers, special schools were necessary, a project which at once roused the spectre of propagandism; and in October, 1866, a law was passed making nominations to the schools contingent on the approval of the governors-general. If it were a question of buying a large lot of seigniorial land, there was always some zealot of order to decry the proceeding as part of a confiscatory scheme for the benefit of the peasants and the subversion of the existing *régime.* If it were a question of making head against plagues of locusts and other insectivorous depredators, and engaging in the work the combined Zemstvo of an infected district, the matter would be allowed to drag on for months, for years even, before the necessary authorization could be obtained—so great is the dread of the Government that if once the Zemstvo of several provinces come together they will take to political discussion.

Despite obstacles, however, the Zemstvo made a beginning in all these things; and if they have not been able to do anything great, if they have not succeeded in providing the peasants with good schools and efficient doctors, nor in assisting the progressive impoverishment of the masses, the fault is certainly attributable neither to want of will nor lack of capacity and business aptitude, but to the narrowness of their field of action, and the severity of the restrictions imposed upon them by the State, restrictions which, from the very inception of local self-government, has been gradually intensified and increased.

III.

M. Leroy Beaulieu, in his chapter on the Zemstvo, graphically describes, from his own personal observation, the enthusiasm with which the decree of 1864, for the organization of local parliaments, was received by the Russian people. Next to the emancipation of the serfs, there was no reform that gave so much satisfaction and kindled so many hopes as the establishment of the Zemstvo. The sagacious French writer is, however, mistaken in saying that Russians, in the fervor of their excitement, overlooked the shortcomings of the new measure. A reference to the democratic papers of the time is sufficient to show that the more advanced party of society were fully alive to its serious and manifold defects. And if the bulk of the lettered public, little conversant with practical questions, overrated the merits of the measure, the men of the Zemstvo —the *Zemzy* themselves—were far from sharing in their illusion.

In and about the year 1860, the delegates of the nobility, who afterwards furnished the largest contingent to the Zemstvo—including those of St. Petersburg—expressed on several occasions, in their addresses and petitions, a desire for a measure of local self-government, much more extensive and efficient than that which, four years later, was granted. These men, it may be supposed, could not possibly be blind to the true character of the reform of 1864, yet they, of all other people, were the most deceived as to its true character and probable results.

The readiness of a certain class of Russians to be "thankful for small mercies," and welcome with joy concessions which a man of the west would simply despise, is a noteworthy feature of the national character, contrasting curiously with the reverse tendency of another party, towards absolute Utopianism—a party which desires to change everything radically and at once, as by the stroke of a wizard's wand, without granting the least indulgence to this decrepit old world, or considering its wants, weaknesses, and long-confirmed habits.

"One of the anomalies of Russian life," is the stereotyped explanation of this phenomenon. But do not these flagrant contrasts all arise from the same source—the ardent desire, now latent, now acute, to do something for the welfare of the people which is seething at the present time in the conscience of instructed Russia? And the lions that stand in the way may surely be vanquished by courage and devotion. There have been dreamers in Russia who hoped to metamorphose the country by means of schools, model farms, and mutual help societies, just as there have been socialist visionaries who hoped to bring back the age of gold by the magic of a revolutionary propaganda.

This faculty for dreaming, which renders people unfit to appreciate hard facts and deal with the things of this world, has greatly impeded social and political progress. Perhaps the time may come when it will prove a blessing. The future will show. In the meantime we have to note a striking example of its baneful results—the creation of a party which in absurdity and self-illusion does not yield even to the Slavophilism of Aksakoff and Khomiakoff—the party, once sufficiently numerous, of which the old Slavophile, Kosheleff, was the leading spirit, and whose fundamental idea was a combination of representative government below with autocracy above. As well try to unite fire and water, or keep iron hot in fresh-fallen snow.

The Zemstvo is not a rural commune. It cannot, like the *mir*, sequester itself in its microscopic world, happy if only left in peace. A Zemstvo represents a province, often half as large as Spain, and with a population equal to that of Wurtemberg or Denmark. A thousand interests concern it, a thousand ties unite it with neighboring provinces. At every step the Zemstvo come in contact with agents of the State. Having to deal with a twentieth part of the provincial revenues, they cannot regard with indifference the stupidity and ingrained incapacity of the *tchinovnik*, who dispose of the remaining nineteen-twentieths. The wish to restrain the bureaucracy, to deprive them more and more of the management of public affairs, is inherent in any system of representative government. The greater the zeal of the Zemstvo for the common weal, the greater must be their desire to lessen still further the power of officialism, beginning with provincial administration, going on to regional business, to finish by controlling and managing the State itself. Political reorganization, representative institutions on the European model, are the ends towards which self-government as inevitably tends as a round stone rolls down an inclined plane, and whatever may be the ideas of Mr. Kosheleff and the Slavophilized *Zemzy*, nothing can arrest its course.

This the Central Government, being a government of *tchinovniks*, are unable to comprehend. But the Zemstvo, as other Russian representative bodies have done, do not fail, on occasion, to make the administration acquainted with their views. In 1860, and again in 1862, the Assembly of Nobles openly expressed their desire for constitutional reform. The dispersion of the Assembly of St. Petersburg—one of the boldest in the land—and the exile of the principal leaders of the nobility of Tver, are further instances in point. But it is unfortunately a habit of Russian citizens to wait for favorable opportunities for expressing their opinions instead of making them. The nobility waited for the advent to power of Loris Melikoff to offer some protest, and the St. Petersburg Assembly alone had the hardihood to applaud the frankly liberal speech of Mr. Platinoff,* Marshal of the Nobility of Zarskoi Selo, when he demanded representative institutions and constitutional guarantees for the entire body of citizens. Yet, after all, they had not the courage to signify their approval of the speech by a formal resolution.

The Zemstvo showed more courage, though by no means too much. They have taken frequent occasion to express, under

---

* See on this point M. Leroy Beaulieu, vol. ii.

divers pretexts, their constitutional aspirations. Sometimes an appeal from the Government to society for help in the contest with terrorism has afforded the opportunity; sometimes it has been found on the presentation of an address to the Emperor after an attempt on his life; or perhaps in a request from the Government for information or advice touching some proposed local measure. Copies of these documents may be found either in the censured or the clandestine Press. According to the organ of the Zemstvo, edited by MM. Kosheleff and Skalon, there have been presented to the Government since the beginning of the revolutionary period fifteen addresses demanding constitutional reform—three in 1878-79, twelve in 1881. During the existence of the Commission of Experts the greater part of the Zemstvo expressed their desire for a Constituent Assembly, representative of the entire country. The majority of these declarations are expressed in obscure and indirect terms, bordering sometimes on servility. Too often these worthy gentlemen of the Zemstvo, intent on pleasing the police-ridden government, describe the liberty of the future as the faithful servant of the Third Section and hold before it the attractive perspective of a common crusade against sedition. But happily not all the Zemstvo hold the same language. Russia will always remember with respect the names of Noudatoff and Idanoff of Samara, Petrounkevitch of Tchernigoff, Netchaeff of Novgorod, Vouberg of Taurida, Gordienko of Kharkoff, and others who have had the courage of their opinions and, in some instances, paid for their temerity with long terms of exile.

I make no citations from these addresses and speeches· English readers would find them modest enough in all conscience. I will merely add that in Russia they have a more than ordinary significance. They display civic courage for which, unhappily, Russians in general are not distinguished. Everybody knows that for every speech, like that of M. Noudatoff, and for every address, like that of the Tchernigoff Zemstvo, there are ten which remain inarticulate—hidden *in petto*—and that if they are not proclaimed the reason is easily understood.

IV.

The Government understands and has always understood this. It is not deceived as to the real sentiments of the Zemstvo. The Zemstvo is its natural enemy. The bureaucracy hate it all the more that they are powerless to destroy it, and feel instinctively that sooner or later—if not to-day, then tomorrow—they will have to yield it precedence.

There is nothing surprising in the fact that, when the forces of reaction began to gain ground, the bureaucracy should desire measures for keeping the enemy in check, for preventing the possibility of the Zemstvo taking root in the sphere of its activity, or acquiring a moral influence over public opinion in general, or uniting together and making combined manifestations and protests against the Government.

But as the Zemstvo were established in 1864, and the reaction began in 1864, it is evident that our young representative institution has had a hard life. Let me enumerate some of the principal laws—all of them premeditated strokes—which, since that time, have been launched against the Zemstvo. The first affected the most vital principle of public finance. The regulation of 1864 conferred on the Zemstvo the right of levying taxes. But to impose additional burdens on the already overcharged peasants was extremely difficult and painful for an institution whose chief aim was to better the peasants' condition. It was an expedient, moreover, not likely to be very productive. The only means of ensuring financial prosperity was for the Zemstvo to find new sources of revenue. They thought they had found them in charges on industrial undertakings. Nothing could have been wiser or more just, and the Zemstvo prospered accordingly. Yet the taxes they imposed were very light compared with those imposed on agriculture. In some provinces industry paid on a scale equal to an income tax of two roubles per thousand, while agriculture paid eleven and a half times as much. But it was not long before Government came to the rescue of the privileged, and by the law of November 19, 1864, put an end to the equitable and successful system of finance which the Zemstvo had introduced.

The famous measure in question interdicted absolutely the levying of taxes on the capital or profits of industrial enterprises. As a set-off the Zemstvo were allowed to put an insignificant duty on trade certificates, and lay a trifling rate on factory buildings. This was to re-establish an unjust exemption and virtually ruin the Zemstvo. The law of November 19th was looked upon by the friends of the institution as indirectly involving the destruction of local parliaments, and deliberately designed to render them both powerless and unpopular. So heavy was the blow that over half the Zemstvo joined in a chorus of indignant protests. The Government retaliated by dissolving the Zemstvo of St. Petersburg, and all the others laid down their arms.

The year following—seven months later—came the law of June 13th, which sapped the Zemstvo on the side of their political importance. No longer content with controlling them through the provincial governors, the Government resolved to have an agent in the very heart of the citadel. The chairman of the Zemstvo ceased to be a mere director of debates. He became at once president and chief. The Minister nominated him, and only the Minister can depose him. He is a mere *tchinovnik* whom the new law empowers to interrupt any speech at discretion, or stop any motion, discussion, or resolution which in his opinion might give umbrage to the Government.

Between these two laws—one of the economic order, the other of the political order—the Zemstvo were held as in a vise. The other proscriptions concern only matters of secondary importance. By the regulations of 1864 the different Zemstvo could, in cases of emergency, enter into communications with each other, always provided, of course, that the Government did not object. But on May 4, 1867, there appeared an "instruction" which explained that this clause must be construed in a strictly Pickwickian sense—that the Zemstvo would not be allowed to communicate with each other in any case, let it be as urgent as it might. The stringency of the Government on this point was so excessive that, when a plague broke out in Astrakan and the local Zemstvo asked leave to confer with the Zemstvo of neighboring provinces as to the best means of meeting the emergency, the request was refused.

The "instruction" as to the printing of the Zemstvo's accounts and the reports of their proceedings may also be noted as a curiosity of Russian administration. It explained that these reports might indeed be printed, but only as many copies were to be issued as there were members of the Zemstvo—not one more.

It is evident that with a code of laws like these, to which must be added the right exercised by the Government of arresting and exiling any deputy whom it may dislike or mistrust, the utility of our local parliaments is attenuated almost to nothingness. In these circumstances it is not surprising that the public should have lost all interest in an institution which at the outset they so enthusiastically acclaimed. The best men have withdrawn altogether from the Zemstvo, and are too often succeeded by intriguers and self-seekers. Members are slack in their attendance, and it not unfrequently happens that a session cannot be held for want of a quorum. The discussions have degenerated into formalities. Nobody takes an interest in them, for all know that any proposal for the benefit of the people will be tabooed by the Government. The Zemstvo simply vegetate in sordid abandonment.

But they still exist in a fashion, and serve as a framework capable of being filled up at any moment with solid material; and, should a crisis come to pass, the Zemstvo may exercise a decisive influence. The Government fears them, and would gladly destroy them utterly. The celebrated commission under the presidency of General Kakhanoff, the little Lykurgus of the reaction, proposed so to raise the voting qualification that the suffrage be restricted to the largest landowners, who were among the most inveterate of the anti-abolitionists. This, as Russian papers have rightly said, would be to re-establish the bureaucratic *régime* in all its purity. It would not even be an oligarchy, for Russia possesses no aristocracy in the true sense of the word. Count Tolstoi's oligarchic dreams are no less absurd than the clerical dreams of his worthy colleague, Pohedinostzeo. Our great landowners, who spend their lives in the capital, occupying nearly always places in the administration, are an element altogether heterogeneous and strange in the localities to which they belong.

Not desiring to repeat the penance I have had to perform for my incredulity as to making the clergy the directors of primary education, I refrain from saying that the project in question is impossible. The reaction has become so reckless that it is ready to attempt even the impossible. I will say only that, in view of the general impoverishment of the country, the definitive abolition of the Zemstvo (or a measure equivalent to its abolition) would have the most disastrous effects, and might not improbably be the precursor of national bankruptcy.

"If anybody would know the incapacity of our bureaucracy to administer any public affairs whatever," wrote an old member of the Zemstvo, in a pamphlet printed not very long ago, "I would recommend him to study the papers published by the earlier Zemstvo on the state in which they found the interests confided to their charge. According to these reports, especially when read between the lines, the condition of the country could hardly have been worse if it had just been wasted by a foreign invasion. Instead of stores of grain the Zemstvo found in one place only empty barracks; in another they found no trace of a school whatever, although it was entered in the reports of the *tchinovniks* as possessing several schools, for the maintenance of which they had received yearly grants of money. In another, again, had disappeared a bridge, nobody knew exactly when, which for years past had required periodical repairs. In still another locality the same fate had befallen an hospital. The report of the commission of the Zemstvo of Perm thus describes the state of affairs when they first took them in hand : "We examined the public granaries. One was quite empty ; in the other we saw only a number of boxes gnawed by rats. On inquiry we were told that they contained the confiscated property of some sectaries. We opened them. Instead of property they contained only rat nests. Of the corn entered as being in store there was not a grain. The funds assigned for supplies existed only on paper ; those for agricultural subsidies the same. For medical purposes the same, and where hospitals existed they were in such a state that the people fled from them as if they were slaughter-houses" (pp. 3 and 4).

I leave the reader to judge for himself what state the finances of Russia are likely to be in when the provinces relapse into their former condition.

CHAPTER XXIX.

THE DESPOTISM AND THE PRESS.

I.

If anybody required a thermometer of great sensitiveness, showing at every period and every moment the variation in the intensity of Russian despotism, he would find it in the position of the Press. "The liberty of the Press is the chief guarantee of the liberty of a country," said Milton. With equal reason we may affirm the opposite—the existence of a despotism depends on the fettering of the Press. Despotic governments understand this. There is no department of human activity which despots regard with so much suspicion as the press. In Russia, as we have seen, the Government has not too much love for schools any more than for local parliaments; but the Press is in much worse case than either of them. Self-government and schools bring forth their fruits in a time more or less distant; the Press acts immediately. The domains of the schools and the Zemstvos are limited; the Press commands the whole extent of the empire. In every other field of action the adversary is always somebody; professors, members of the Zemstvo, and the rest, however disagreeable they may be, are at least people, men, known personalities. But a writer, what is he? Perhaps a monster without law and without faith, capable of anything. To what purpose may he not turn that mysterious power which by virtue of his venomous pen he wields over the weak and foolish?

On the other hand, no human institution is naturally so

defenceless as the Press. In all others thought and spirit are more or less intimately allied with matter. Self-government and instruction are necessary for the State itself, for its efficient working and its material well-being. But of the Press the State has no need. True it has recourse to the printer for the preparation of its official publications; but that is not the Press. The veritable Press, the brain of the nation, despotism can well spare and still live, just as certain animals can survive for a long time the loss of a cerebral lobe. The Press, so to speak, is sublimated thought, and incapable of self-defence. It is the duty of the other members of the social body to unite for the protection of this vital part of the system; if they are incapable of doing this the Press is at the mercy of Power. The Government holds it in its grasp, and can either crush the victim to death or let it live and breathe according to its good pleasure.

The position of the Press is thus an excellent thermometer for measuring at every moment the intensity of despotism. From this point of view the history of the relations of the Russian Press and the Russian Government is very interesting.

Russia has never known anything which remotely resembles the liberty of the Press or tolerance for political and religious ideas. Peter the Great, whose reign was the apogee of imperial liberalism, tortured and put to death the sectarian writers who wrote pamphlets against his reforms. But the Tzar was all in favor of European culture, and everything savoring thereof passed the frontier without inspection. It is told that when the translator of Puffendorf's "Universal History" proposed to omit some passages not too complimentary to Muscovy, Peter gave him a little paternal correction with his famous cane, for showing so little respect for the great historian, and ordered the scribe to print the passage just as it was. Peter's successors followed his example. They protected letters and science, made *mezenots,* founded academies, and established literary journals. Catharine II. posed as a literary character, wrote with her own hand moral tales and insipid novels " with a purpose," and deigned to plagiarize Shakespeare's " Merry Wives of Windsor." True the censorship existed at that time, but it was not the heterogenous body of *tchinovniks,* instinctively hostile to authors and letters, which it has since become. *Savants* and professors censured the works of other *savants* and professors, younger or less distinguished than themselves. And, curiously enough, the animosities and jealousies of the writers of that epoch were more inimical to the freedom of the Press than the despotism itself. Scabitchevsky, in his history of the censorship in Russia, relates that when the *Academic Journal* was published without being submitted to the censors, the writers of that day, like the lackeys that they were, mutually denounced each other, and lauded the censorship as an institution of the highest value. The Government, on their part, vainly tried to make these angry scribes listen to reason, exhorting them to be more tolerant, and showing them that the world would not come to an end even if people were allowed the free expression of their opinions.

It would be a mistake to attribute the patriarchal relations which prevailed between the Tzars and the tzarnas and the writers of this period, either to the liberalism of the former or the docility of the latter. The cause was much more simple.

The reforms of Peter the Great had brought Russia into temporary unison with the rest of Continental Europe, and at that time the autocracies of the Continent were bureaucratic autocracies like that of Russia. So long as this unison existed the science, laws, and histories of neighboring nations could present no danger. In what respect could they be dangerous? An occasional sarcastic reference to Muscovite barbarism, like that of Puffendorf, there might be; but nothing serious, nothing to imperil the basis of the *régime*. True, in the eighteenth century there was a vast philosophic movement in Europe, which contained the germs of a great political reform. But as yet these germs had not shown themselves. They were hidden under the mask of humanitarianism and philosophy. Princes associated themselves with the movement, thinking they would be able to dominate and direct it. And our Catharine II., like Frederick the Great, was a philosopher and paid court to Voltaire.

The revolution changed all this, then and forever. As touching its political institutions and its culture Europe made a great step in advance. Russia remained what Peter had made her. Then began the persecutions. Radiscoff and Novikoff were the two first martyrs of the Russian Press. The one was exiled to Siberia, the other imprisoned for the advocacy of ideas which Catharine, before the revolution, had herself professed. The mutual positions of the Government and the Press were then distinctly defined. Since that time the persecutions may have varied in intensity, but they have never been intermitted.

How Nicolas dealt with authors and journalists is known to all students of contemporary history. In the time of Alexander the Press was the first institution to feel the weight of his hand. The elder Kosheleff, in his posthumous memoirs, tells how in 1858, in the very honeymoon of Alexander's liberalism, when the Tzar, supported by the flower of the nation, was waging war against the obscurantism of the old nobility for the emancipation of the serfs, the persecution of the censorship reduced him to despair and ruined the paper edited by the Slavophile, Aksakoff, and himself. This although the journal in question was an ardent advocate of emancipation and its two editors were inveterate monarchists! Despotism will tolerate no criticism, even from its partisans. The condemnation of Mikailoff and

Schapoff and the moral ruin of Tchernychevsky, men of the greatest intelligence Russia ever possessed, were also the work of the first period of Alexander's reign.

Sometimes waxing, at others waning, according to changes of the wind in high quarters, the persecution of the Press went on without surcease the whole of the twenty-six years during which the late Tzar swayed the destinies of his country.

II.

But it is with the actual condition of the Press, not with the past persecutions of poets, novelists, historians, and journalists, that we have to deal. And here, at the outset, it is well to notice a significant and characteristic fact—that whenever the Government are constrained by financial requirements or political necessity to concede some measure of reform the Press is the last to profit by the change. When the emancipation of the serfs, the organization of the Zemstvo, and the establishment of the New Courts lent to the life of the country another aspect and gave promise of a better and a brighter future, the Press, whose duty it is to animate, to enlighten, and to encourage, was still left to the tender mercies of the ancient censorship. Not until 1865 was the new Press Law promulgated, and even then, few as were its concessions, it was granted grudgingly and ungraciously. The Russian Government never hesitates to retrace its steps, or take back with one hand what it gives with the other, and the new law was expressly termed "a provisional regulation." It was an experiment which could be discontinued at any moment that might be deemed expedient. Its application was, moreover, restricted in a manner altogether exceptional. New laws, if they make for more liberty, are rarely applicable to the whole of the empire. Thus the Zemstvo, the justices of the peace, and the new Courts were instituted gradually, as if the authorities were afraid of disgusting the country with too much freedom; and the process has been so cautiously conducted that there are still districts where the reforms in question have not even yet come into operation. But, as touching the new Press Law, the authorities surpassed themselves; not content with making the regulation provisional, they limited its application strictly to the two capitals. It is true that the Government officially undertook to extend the enactment to the provinces so soon as the new tribunals were completely organized; but the promise was never fulfilled, and the whole of Russia outside Moscow and St. Petersburg still remains under the domination of the old Press Law of Nicolas I.

Let us see what were the character and extent of the concessions which the Government so timidly and so reluctantly granted. The new law substituted the correctional for the preventive censure; but, as touching works with less than ten sheets of original matter, or twenty sheets of translation, the old system was retained. Periodical publications whose proprietors desired to enjoy the privilege of the correctional censure could only do so by obtaining a special authorization, not as a right, but by favor of the Minister.

Yet, although the preventive censure was abolished, measures were taken to hinder the privilege from being abused. It was ordered that after an edition had been printed, and before being sent out for sale, a copy of the book should be submitted to the committee of Censors, nominated by the Minister—a body which had power to forbid being delivered to the publishers any work which they might deem dangerous to loyalty, morality, or religion. As for newspapers and other similar publications, the law authorized the Minister, at his discretion, to warn officially any journal of the views or statements to which he might take exception. A third warning entailed, *ipso facto*, the offending paper's suspension and the prosecution of its conductors.

The Minister may, moreover, by administrative order, which means by the simple exercise of his will, suspend any journal whatever for from three to six months. He has further the right to stop the sale of any paper in the kiosques and by newsboys in the streets—that is to say, he may cut off half its sale at a stroke; he may also forbid it to publish advertisements. These two measures, when enforced against any journal so unfortunate as to incur the Minister's displeasure, are tantamount to the infliction of a heavy fine, which, if repeated, it is impossible for the victim to survive, there being practically no limit to the amount of the penalty he may inflict. This method of crushing an obnoxious journal has of late been frequently practised, for it makes less noise and seems less arbitrary than suspension by administrative order, or even after three warnings.

On the other hand, the law of 1865 possessed one great and positive advantage. The definitive suppression of a book or a newspaper could be pronounced only by the judgment of a court, and though provisional suspension by Goverment decree or administrative order, or deprivation of its advertisements, might ruin a journal utterly, the mere possibility of an appeal was a decided gain, tending as it did to make the Minister more cautious in the exercise of his powers, and more amenable to public opinion. The appeal could be made in the last resort to the Senate of the Empire —a body not likely to treat revolutionary theories or subversive ideas too leniently, as was sufficiently proved by its condemnation of the journal conducted by M. Aksakoff, the Muscovite Slavophile. Nevertheless, the Senate acted always judicially, and, as it showed in the matters of the translation of the first volume of Lecky's "History of Rationalism," and of Voundt's "The Soul of Man and Animals," did not hesitate to check flagrant injustice by reversing the decisions of the Committee of Censors. In cases of urgency, however, the authorities did not scruple to disregard the law which they themselves had made. In 1866, hardly a year after its enactment, Prince Gagarine and his friends resolved by hook or by crook to effect the suppression of the *Contemporary* of Nekrasoff and the *Russian Word* of Blagosvetloff, and they prevailed on the Tzar to act as their *Deus ex machinâ*. One evening at a ball His Majesty gave the order in two words for the extinction of the obnoxious journals, and they were suppressed accordingly without any formality whatsoever. But after a while it was deemed expedient to convert the exception into the rule. Trials, even when won by the prosecution, made a noise, excited public opinion, and helped to spread ideas which the administration desired to crush. Despotisms prefer darkness and shade to publicity and light, and in 1872 the law of 1865 was " amended " by a supplementary enactment, depriving the tribunals of the power of intervening in the affairs of the Press, and vesting the control of them in the Council of Ministers, who decide, in final resort, on the fate of any book or periodical which may be in question, after hearing the report of the Minister of the Interior. Thus the latter, being both accuser and judge—for his colleagues, in matters that concern his department, must necessarily adopt his views—became the supreme arbiter of the Press and purveyor of literature for the entire Russian nation. In 1882 another change was introduced, though, practically, it made no great difference. A committee of four was substituted for the full Ministerial Council, but, as before, no defence was admitted, the committee deliberating and deciding *in camerâ*. Another measure was the application to recalcitrant journals of the preventive censure. What the preventive censure is and how it works, I shall explain presently.

Since 1872 suspensions, suppressions, deprivations of the right to receive advertisements and sell single copies have rained on the unfortunate Russian Press as from a horn of abundance. Books banned by the censors are remorselessly burnt. Thus were condemned to the flames the second volume of Lecky's "History of European Morals" (the first volume was sanctioned), Hobbes's "Leviathan," Haeckel's "History of the Creation," Voltaire's "Essai sur les Mœurs," and many more. The same fate has also befallen divers Russian authors, who are treated with so little ceremony that Prougavine's book, entitled "Religious Sects" (albeit the articles composing it had appeared in the periodical form, and, therefore, been passed by the censors), was burnt by order of the Committee of Ministers.

III.

But to gauge rightly the real position of the Russian Press something more is required than mere knowledge of the law as it stands. We must go behind the scenes, because it is there, in the shade, that the despotism shows itself without disguise. When the Minister desires to impose his will on the Press he has recourse to secret *ordonnances*, which end always with the same formula—"In case of disobedience the articles of this or that regulation will be applied to the refractory journal," which means that contempt of the order will be visited either with suspension or suppression. This proceeding, re-establishing, as in effect it does, the preventive censure under another form, is of course flagrantly illegal, and contrary both to the letter and the spirit of the law. But the despotism of those above is so absolute, the submission of those below so complete, that the representatives of the Press have never been able to join in a protest against the tyranny by which they are so ruthlessly victimized, and the protest of a single journal would expose it to the implacable vengeance of the Government. To give an idea of the character of the *ordonnances* in question, I cite a few specimens which were given in the

Narodnaia Volia of August, 1883, a clandestine journal being the only medium through which facts of this sort can be made known.

On March 4, 1881, three days after the murder of Alexander II., the Minister sent to the Press a secret *ordonnance* thus conceived: "Several organs of the Press, under the pretext of extraordinary circumstances, have allowed themselves to print articles very indiscreetly suggesting the expediency of re-organizing our political system, and expressing doubts as to the existence of patriotism in the higher circles of our society, which are accused of indifference to the true interests of the nation. The appearance of articles of this character will entail the suppression of the journals in which they may be published."

On March 25th, the department, "considering the near approach of the trial for the abominable crime of March 1st, reminds conductors of journals of the order against printing, under pain of suspension, original accounts of political trials." (The papers were permitted to print only the carefully prepared account of the proceedings given in the Official *Gazette*.)

In April, 1881, there occurred some disorders among university students. On the 16th of the same month the following order was issued: "It is considered necessary to forbid the Press to discuss this matter, to give any news concerning it, or print any communications relating thereto. Disobedience of this *ordonnance*," etc.

The next order I shall cite is very curious and merits particular attention. It was issued on April 29th, "In view of the *coup d'état* which has come to pass in Bulgaria, and considering the necessity of supporting Prince Alexander, the Government is desirous that our Press should speak with circumspection (*sic*) of the events accomplished at Sofia." This order was supplemented by a circular dated May 9th, wherein it is explained that, although the papers are forbidden to censure, they are free to praise the *coup d'état* of General Ernrod. The *ordonnance* was, therefore, in effect, an invitation to the Press to defend an arbitrary and illegal act committed in a foreign country, the object being to make it appear that not alone the Russian Government but Russian society fully approved the proceeding. The explanatory circular was issued because the Press, either out of malice or timidity, construed the order too literally, and made no comment whatever on the incident in question.

The resignation of Loris Melikoff involved, as is well known, the downfall of the moderate Liberal party and the extinction of all hope of reform, a result that excited among all classes of the capital so general a feeling of disappointment and discontent as seriously to annoy the Government, and on May 18th a circular was sent to the papers instructing them to make no mention whatever of " to-day's proceedings in the Municipal Council, or to discuss the proposal to present General Loris Melikoff with the freedom of the city." It was equally forbidden to publish the debates of the Council on this question.

On August 17th of the same year the Press was requested, in the accepted form, to refrain from printing any articles whatever against General Baranoff, former Prefect of St. Petersburg. The General had a short time before distinguished himself by some very original measures for the preservation of order, and by his so-called " Parliament," an institution which excited general ridicule.

The Liberalism which prevailed in the higher circles of the administration during the Melikoff period produced a movement among the Zemstvo that continued after the Minister's dismissal, a fact that sufficiently accounts for a circular issued on May 28th, inviting the journals of the two capitals to abstain from all comment on the " decisions, motions, and addresses " of the Zemstvo and the municipalities.

When Count Ignatieff, the successor of Loris Melikoff, came into office, one of his first proceedings was to appoint numerous commissioners for the elaboration of projects of reform in various branches of the administration. Troubles in the south and outrages against Israelites in other parts of the empire had directed attention to the Jewish question, and a commission was nominated to prepare a report on the subject. It was a question which greatly interested both the public and the Press, and an open discussion of the matter could hardly have failed to facilitate the work of the commission and might have given rise to some valuable suggestions. But the Government, fearing criticism, and haunted as always by the dread of "exciting public opinion" and thereby producing all sorts of terrible consequences, sent out, on May 31, 1881, a circular, "forbidding the publication of articles likely to create discontent with the measures of the Government, which cannot be tolerated, above all at a time so difficult as the present." In other words, the sole alternative of silence was to praise all Government measures without distinction.

A few days later (June 3d) an *ordonnance* was issued directing the Press to "speak with the greatest circumspection (the reader will understand the meaning of this phrase, so frequently used) of the proceedings of the special commission for reducing the price of the lands acquired by the peasants." On September 19th it was considered necessary to forbid the "publication of any news whatever concerning the report of the special commission on the relations between the indigenous population and the Jews." On October 10, 1881, an interdict was laid on the publication "of any articles whatever on peasant migrations." On January 28, 1882, it was ordained in the usual manner that, "in view of the preparation of reforms in the organization of professional schools," no discussion of the subject shall take place, nor any news about it be published. On March

17th, "it is absolutely forbidden to publish in the papers any news whatever concerning the re-partition of properties, equalization of lots, etc., or any articles suggesting the justice of changes in the economical condition of the peasantry." On April 20th was issued another circular about the Jews forbidding "all reference to the deliberations of the Council of Ministers on the subject, or the publication of any articles whatever on the question in general."

On October 29, 1882, it was forbidden to speak of the expulsion of the gymnasium pupil, Fougalevitch (of Kamenez Padolsk, who insulted the inspector, but was acquitted by the tribunal). On November 1st a circular was issued inviting the Press to keep silence as to the troubles in the University of Kazan. On December 16th it was forbidden to say anything about the prosecution of the student Semenoff for insulting the Curator of the University. On February 4, 1882, it was forbidden to publish any news concerning the "domestic relations" of the family of Councillor Markus. On November 23d it was ordered that no mention should be made of the misunderstanding between the Curator Neuhart and Dr. Kwatz. On October 4th was issued the following order : "The foreign Press makes mention of the implication of Count P. A. Valueff in the trial relating to dilapidation of State property in the province of Orenburg. It is forbidden to reproduce this news." Here we have an illustration of the Russian proverb, "One dirty hand washes the other, and both become clean."

But the worst has yet to be told. On June 12th was issued a circular bluntly informing editors that the publication of articles on the relations of peasants to their landlords, or on "the Lutorique affair," would entail the suppression of the journal in which they might appear. On June 26, 1882, the Minister informed editors that "virulent articles having appeared on the affair of Prince Sherbatoff and his former serfs, and as such articles might have a bad influence on the relations of proprietors and peasants, it is expressly forbidden to speak of the Sherbatoff affair." The two affairs in question related to cruelties inflicted on peasants so horrible that in any other country the perpetrators would have been put upon their trial.

Still another fact. The catastrophe of Koukoueff was one of the most heartrending of our national calamities. A train ran off the line and went headlong into a morass. Many of the passengers were badly hurt and more than a hundred killed. The accident, as was fully proved, arose from the unsound condition of the permanent way and the rottenness of the piles, the engineers and managers having appropriated to their own purposes the moneys assigned for repairs. On this becoming known there was a cry of indignation from one end of Russia to the other. And the Government —what course did it take? Promise a searching inquiry and the exemplary punishment of the delinquents? Nothing of the sort. It issued this circular:—" August 19, 1882.—Since the disaster on the Koursk Railway, several papers have printed articles bringing grave charges against some of the *employés* of the Ministry of Roads. Articles of this sort having a disturbing character, their publication will bring on the offending journal the severest adminstrative penalties." Thus the State forbade parents and friends to protest against the authors of their misfortune, or to offer an opinion on the best method of preventing further similar disasters.

This terminates our record. The samples I have produced are eminently characteristic. They show the tendencies of the Russian Government, and reveal the crooked ways of bureaucratic despotism. The Press is regarded as a hostile and essentially pernicious force, to be partially tolerated only because it cannot be utterly destroyed. The policy of the Ministry towards the Press is dictated with the narrowest official spirit. The moment a question becomes prominent or interesting, its discussion is tabooed. Of publicity, talk, the free expression of thought, the Government stands in mortal dread. Even when it takes some hesitating step in advance, or resolves to attempt this or that reform, its first proceeding is to forbid all discussion of it by the Press. Everything must be done in silence and secresy and in the back rooms of Ministerial Cabinets. But human thought is not easily fettered. Harassed by proscription, indications, warnings and admonitions, threatened on the least show of disobedience with a whole arsenal of pains and penalties, opinion takes the weapon of the feeble and meets force with cunning. A secret understanding is established between writers and readers. An esoteric language, made up of allusions, hints, and conventional phrases, is created; and so the ideas which our rulers have banned still pass from mind to mind.

IV.

It is a patent fact that our Press is almost altogether Liberal and anti-Governmental. This Mr. Katkoff himself does not attempt to deny. The organs of reaction may be counted on the fingers of one hand. Most Russian papers are either frankly liberal or shrewdly artful, alternating between servility to escape the censure and opposition to please their readers. The opportunist tendencies of the Russian Press on the one hand, and bureaucratic obscurantism on the other, are leading rapidly to a collision which can hardly fail to be fatal to the weaker of the two forces. The history of the struggle between them—if that may be called a struggle in which one party can offer hardly a show of resistance—presents three distinct phases. The provincial Press was the first to suffer. Being under the preventive censure, the administration had only to draw the bonds a little tighter in order to crush it utterly. Less known, having less influence and fewer readers, country papers may be treated with less ceremony than their contemporaries of the two capitals. Altogether, it may be averred without exaggeration that, notwithstanding its lack of literary polish, the part of our Press the most sympathetic, the most devoted to the public weal and capable of promoting national well-being, were our country papers. But the *tchinovniks* of St. Petersburg were not at all disposed to allow free play to their usefulness. The spectre of separatism was summoned against them, and they became the victims of the reaction. The holocaust went on easily and quietly, without too much scandal, and was all but completed before the death of Alexander II. It required only a word to the censors, and the work was begun. One by one the best country papers, weary of the annoyance, the chicanery, and the oppression to which they were continually exposed, gave up the struggle. Suppression by decree was unnecessary; they were worried out of existence by Ministerial ordinances, each more impossible and absurd than the other. Purely political papers were ordered strictly to avoid domestic subjects. Journals founded for the express purpose of defending Jewish interests and promoting a fusion of the two races were forbidden to make any allusion to the Jewish question. The expedients of the department were sometimes marked by a grim humor all its own. One was to appoint as special censor of an obnoxious print an official living at the other extremity of the empire. This involved the sending to him of every proof, both of comment and news, before publication. Hence the paper upon which this practical joke was played could not appear until ten or fifteen days after its contemporaries of the same town or district. No journal giving news a fortnight out of date could possibly go on, and journals so treated rarely attempted to reappear. But as nobody could say that the Government had suppressed them, there was neither scandal nor "agitation of spirits;" one more unfortunate had died a natural death—that was all. Were dealt with in this way the *Novotcherkask Don*, the *Kama Gazette*, and the *Tiflis Obzor*. They were ordered to send their proofs, not as usual to the local censors, but to the censor of Moscow, which is distant in time (including the return journey) from Novotcherkask seven days, from Kama ten to twelve, and from Tiflis twenty. The two first made no attempt either to comply with the order or to continue their issues, but Mr. Nicoladze, proprietor of the *Obzor*, in order to preserve the right of publication (which lapses if not used during a year), brings out his paper every January. The *Obzor* is probably the only daily paper in the world which appears once a year.

It would, however, be a mistake to suppose that the department holds to the letter of the law, loose as that is. The expedients I have described, seem to be adopted out of a spirit of pure mischief, pretty much as a cat torments a mouse before giving it the *coup de grâce;* for when the humor takes them, the authorities do not hesitate to suppress by a stroke of the pen a paper which has been submitted to the preventive censure, and is therefore irresponsible to the administration. Thus were suppressed the Kieff *Telegraph*, the Odessa *Pravda*, and the Smolensk *Messenger*. The Tiflis *Phalanga* was suppressed *for presenting to the censor* a drawing which was deemed dangerous and unsuitable for publication ! I believe, too, that the Kieff *Troud* has lately shared the same fate. All these were under the preventive *régime*, which means, of course, that they were not allowed to publish a line unseen by the censor. In 1876, the Government, utterly regardless of the law, and without assigning a reason, suppressed an entire literature—that of the Ukraine. Except novels, it was forbidden to publish anything whatever in the language of that country—a proceeding absolutely without precedent even in Russia.

Nearly all these measures were taken in the time of Alexander II. By throwing every possible impediment in the way of starting new journals, by having censors only in a few of the principal towns (which rendered it well-nigh impossible to conduct papers in any other town), the Government found no difficulty in practically extinguishing the provincial press. Hence Alexander III. had only to do with the Press of the two capitals, and it must be admitted that in this contest Count Ignatieff and, above all, Count Tolstoi, showed more discernment than was displayed by our generals in the war against Turkey—they attacked the enemy where he was weakest.

CHAPTER XXX.

THE PRESS UNDER ALEXANDER II.

I.

RUSSIA, which differs from Western Europe in so many other things, differs also in the relative importance of its periodic publications. Daily papers, being essentially political, cannot, in a country without political life wield the same influence as in England, France, and the United States. Popular institutions we have none; public opinion is ignored. There are no questions which depend on the votes of a body of citizens to whom it is necessary to appeal day by day, and whose views may be influenced by argument and explanation. The struggle, so far as it goes, is with us limited to the domain of ideas. But for the discussion and development of ideas newspapers, even if they could always afford the necessary space, are not always the most suitable medium. On this point, moreover, the Russian public is exacting; they demand something more solid and serious than it is possible for daily journals to give. Vital questions, which in free countries are discussed in parliaments, meetings, and clubs, can be treated in Russia only in the Press—so far as the censor may permit. Hence the preponderance in our periodic literature of magazines and reviews, which, while not neglecting the events of the day, give a considerable portion of their space to the higher subjects of domestic and general interest, sometimes even to standard works of a class that in any other country would be published in separate editions. Works of fiction are confined to monthly publications. Novels of merit appear in the first instance nearly always in reviews as serials, never as *feuilletons* in newspapers. All this gives an exceptional importance to Russian reviews, and in its crusade against the Press the Department, guided and inspired by Ignatieff and Tolstoi, opened the attack, as has already been said, against the enemy's weakest part—the daily newspaper.

In order to form an idea of the damage sustained by Russian journals in this unequal warfare we have only to glance at the *Souvorine's Almanac,* where are recorded all the rigorous measures of which the Press has lately been the victim. Since the beginning of the present reign eight high-class St. Petersburg papers have been either summarily suppressed by administrative order or harassed to death by incessant persecutions. During this time they received forty-eight admonitions, were as often provisionally suspended (for from four weeks to eight months), and suffered incalculable money loss by interdicts to publish advertisements and sell by retail. The daily Press, in fact, has been virtually crushed, for among the defunct journals were some of the most important the country possessed, such as the *Poriadok*, the *Golos*, and others. Only two or three Liberal papers of any influence still survive the persecution, dragging on a miserable existence, threatened and badgered at every turn, and expecting that every day will be their last.

The war against the great reviews, which had been resolved upon from the first, albeit the resolution was allowed to remain some time in abeyance, began with the suppression of the *Slovo*. The editor having retired, the Department refused to sanction the appointment of a successor, and in a private interview with the publisher the chief cynically avowed that he would not accept even a declared monarchist. After eight months of resistance, remonstrance, and suspense, (during which time the review was not allowed to appear), the proprietor lost all hope, and the *Slovo* was numbered among the slain. Then, after an interval of admonitions which led to no particular result, the Government dropped the mask and suppressed the *Annals of the Country*. The *Annals* was beyond compare the best review we had. In circulation and in influence, as well as in the quality of its articles and the ability of its contributors, the *Annals* was far ahead of the best of its contemporaries. Its subscribers numbered nearly 10,000—a figure in Russia altogether phenomenal. The *Messenger of Europe*, its strongest competitor, could not boast of a circulation of more than 6,000. The tendency of the *Annals* being essentially Democratic, it naturally gave much attention to all questions touching on the condition of the people. In this regard it has rendered immense service to the nation; nobody can take a single step in the study of our domestic economy without referring for instruction and information to the back numbers of the *Annals*. Even the members of our unteachable Government, when it is a question of doing something for the toiling millions of the nation, preparing an important financial scheme, or introducing an economic reform, are compelled to go to the same source, as well for their facts as for their ideas. In an article which I contributed to the *Contemporary Review*, when speaking of the blindness of certain writers who contend that Russia is still unfitted to be her own mistress, I observed that the best proof to the contrary lay in the fact that the Russian Government has never adopted, or even submitted to the fruitless consideration of a commission of *tchinovniks*, a single progressive measure which had not been previously indicated, discussed, and put in much better form by the press and the Zemstvo. Of this the *Annals* afford ample illustration and abundant proof. Mr. Scalon pointed out, and thoroughly discussed in the pages of the review, the insuffiency of the allotments assigned to the peasants, at least ten years before the question was taken up by the Government. Mr. Chaslavsky and Mr. Trirogoff dwelt on the same thing, and called the attention of the authorities to the necessity of the measures. As is well known, when the socialist agitation and the gradual impoverishment of the peasants compelled the Government at length to act, they dealt, however inadequately, with the land question on the lines suggested by the review which they have since suppressed. Reform of the methods of taxation and of the law of settlement was exhaustively discussed in the review long before these questions were submitted for the consideration of Loris Melikoff's and Count Ignatieff's Commissions. The measures adopted to save from total ruin the so-called *chinsceviki*, a sort of perpetual farmer, were due to the articles of Mr. Koteliansky, who was the first to point out their wretched condition, and denounce the injustice to which they were exposed. A still more striking instance of the utility of discussion and the power of the pen is found in the fact that the abolition of the salt duty was brought about in great measure by the efforts of the *Annals*. At the time of Loris Melikoff's advent to power, there appeared in the review a series of articles by Mr. Leonidas Cherniaev, in which he sets forth with great force the impolicy of taxing salt, and the manifold hardships which the imposts entailed, and the new dictator, desiring to signalize his accession to office by an act of grace, abolished the obnoxious tax. Professor Janjiul in his articles on the English Factory Law urged the adoption of a measure for regulating the labor of women and children in the Russian factories. The Government followed his advice, and appointed him factory inspector for the district of Moscow.

In short there is no question of importance relating either to the land, to commerce, or to taxation, which has not been discussed by specialists in our great review. For the contributors to the *Annals* included men who were not alone theoretically acquainted with their subjects, but had seen with their own eyes the workings of the systems which they desired to reform and the evils which they wished to abolish. This lent to it an authority altogether exceptional, and the editor was enabled to enlist in the service of the periodical which he directed the most ardent and intellectual spirits of the time, every one of whom was animated with unbounded zeal to enlighten public opinion and promote the best interests of the country. And yet this great, this priceless publication has been struck down without warning, crushed by the stroke of a minister's pen, its useful career stopped, and its noble and enthusiastic band of writers silenced and dispersed. Why ? In the circular accompanying the decree of suppression the Government gives its reasons for this portentous proceeding. The *Annals*, it is alleged, was a subversive organ, a sort of *Narodnaia Volia* (a clandestine revolutionary print), published in defiance of the censorship. Several of the contributors were affiliated to revolutionary societies, and two members of the editorial staff were politically compromised. The futility of these pretexts is self-evident, especially when it is remembered that out of nearly a hundred contributors not one was punished for these pretended crimes.

We pass now to the accusation in chief, which suggests more important considerations than any of the others. The Ministerial circular charges the *Annals* and the Liberal Press generally with having caused all the sad events of recent years (that is to say, the assassinations and other acts of terrorism), with advocating doctrines absolutely identical with those of the clandestine revolutionary organs, with adopting a similar tone, borrowing their methods of exposition, and imitating their literary style.

Readers will remember that only a few years ago the Russian Government proclaimed everywhere that the revolutionary party was recruited solely among the ignorant and the young, among unsuccessful students and men of broken fortunes. Now it openly accuses the entire Liberal Press of having gone over to the enemy with arms and baggage. The importance of the fact, if it is a fact, cannot be over-estimated, albeit the prudence of the avowal may well be doubted, for in the Russia of to-day, as in France before the Revolution, all that the country possesses of worth, talent, intelligence, and instruction is found in the ranks of the Liberal Opposition. The reaction has but incapacities. The only true men of talent whom it has secured during the last ten years—from M. Dostoievsky, in *belles lettres*, down to Mr. Katkoff in journalism—are both renegades from the Liberal cause. The former was once a socialist, and suffered ten years' penal servitude for his connection with the Petrachevsky society; the latter, in his earlier and better years, distinguished himself by his warm advocacy of a constitution on the English model. Even the Souvourins and other minor lights of the reaction were once wanderers in the gardens of Liberalism. Yet, as I desire neither to falsify facts nor disguise the truth, even in the seeming interest of the party to which I belong, I am constrained to say that, strongly as the Russian press is opposed to the Government, it is not a revolutionary force, has not indeed as yet grasped the revolutionary idea.

II.

All who know our literature will agree that its most striking and characteristic tendency is not subversive, or, to speak more plainly, it does not use its influence to bring about a re-organization of our political *régime*. The censor stands effectually in the way of any advocacy in this direction being attempted, and our writers and publicists are too lacking in political instruction to make the attempt. True, they have high instincts and noble aspirations; but the instincts are ill-defined, the aspirations vague and unguided by a clear understanding and a resolute will. They are like a locomotive without rails, their course is erratic, and they are always encountering obstacles and being engulfed in quicksands. The most marked trait in our national literature, that which gives it a character all its own, is its deep-seated democratism, its generous and unselfish sympathy with the poor and lowly. The greater part of our publications are devoted to subjects connected with the well-being of the people and the amelioration of their lot. It is the same with all our leading periodicals. The peasant, his wants and his woes, are always their favorite theme. Nor is this merely a passing fashion. It has been thus for thirty years. If we pass from articles and reviews to *belles lettres*, we are struck by a peculiarity which distinguishes it from the light literature of all other countries. While fiction that deals with the lives of the lowly is elsewhere the exception and occupies an inferior position, in Russia the loves, the sufferings, and the virtues of the peasantry form the favorite and the frequent subjects of our younger and more popular authors. It would be difficult to find a more conclusive proof than this of the prevailing sentiments of our superior classes; for it is they, not the peasants themselves, who read these romances of humble life. This generous democratism of the instructed and well-placed, arises from the conditions and circumstances of our intellectual development; it is the best augury and the surest guarantee for the progress and eventual happiness of the people—once they are the masters of their own fortunes. The sympathy of the instructed classes for the common folk assumes among the leaders of the democratic movement a character peculiar to itself and essentially Russian, and is described by an untranslatable Russian word. The members of this party are called *narodnik*, or, to coin an English equivalent, "peasantists." The origin of this phase of opinion is sufficiently remarkable to merit a few words of explanation. How far it may be due to the deep sense of shame and disgust with which the institution of slavery inspired no inconsiderable portion of our nobility, and the desire thence arising to make some amends to the victims of a bad and degrading system; how far to the somewhat effusive enthusiasm of the Russian character and its proneness to raise every strong conviction to the dignity of a religious dogma, how far to our unfortunate historic past, which renders it easy for us to sacrifice our individuality on the altar of a cause which we deem high and noble, I will not attempt to determine.

These and several other factors have combined to produce the result in question, for ever since its inception Russian democratism has been marked by characteristics peculiar to itself. The old advocate, Spassovitch, in his speech during the Netchiaeff trial related that even in his earlier days it was not unusual for young aristocrats to dress as peasants and live among the people. In 1856, some young nobles of certain provinces, notably Tver, Kieff, and others, abandoned the privileges of their rank and inscribed their names in the registers of the rural communes as simple peasants, albeit they were thereby rendered liable to be flogged by a mere order of the police and exposed to other unpleasant possibilities. But the movement alarmed the Government, and was stopped by an ukase in the time of the Minister Lanskoy. It is now no more possible for a Russian noble to become a peasant than for a British peer to become a member of the House of Commons. The democratic party as a whole, although they did not go the length of offering to be flagellated out of love for the people, made enormous sacrifices in the people's cause; not alone material sacrifices, to which none could object, but sacrifices of principle. The instructed classes, nourished on the masterpieces of European literature, could hardly breathe in the stifling atmosphere of

Muscovite despotism. They thirsted for political freedom as travellers in an African desert thirst for a drop of cold water. An Englishman in such circumstances would have said, "I need, therefore I will try to have." Said the Russian *narodnik*, "I need, therefore will I resign myself not to have." And if asked for an explanation, he would have added that it was he and his like alone who had need of political freedom; the present—chief object of his solicitude—it would profit nothing. Flagrant error, for as touching natural rights, there can be no conflict of interests. But this the democrats of 1860 failed to understand, and they agreed to prostrate themselves before the autocracy on the sole condition that it should promise to promote the well-being of the masses. Revolutionists of the stamp of Herzen were unable to resist this tendency, and democrats like Nicolas Milutin (brother of the Minister) and Mouravieff (of the Amour) became humble servants of the Tzar. Than this it was impossible for men to push further the principle of abnegation, or more completely to efface their individuality. Their love was, indeed, like that of the fabled pelican, who fed her little ones with her own flesh. The stupid bird did not see that her death or disablement would of surety entail the destruction of her offspring. By voluntarily effacing itself the democratic party delivered the people, bound hand and foot, to the venal and cruel bureaucracy which is the true Russian despotism. It was this fatal error that wrecked the great Liberal movement of 1860, although it had the support of the Polish insurrection. The Government found no difficulty in forgetting its promises and preserving intact its prerogatives. When the reaction set in every concession which had been granted was little by little withdrawn, because, owing to the policy of the democratic party, no force existed whereby the bureaucracy could be withstood. Hence when, twenty years later, a new Liberal movement was initiated, everything had to be begun afresh.

The movement this time, born of the International and the Paris Commune, was purely socialistic. The leaders had no illusions about the autocracy. But as extreme socialists they are equally opposed to constitutionalism and to monarchy. Their ideal is the supremacy of the working classes. They would pass at one bound from barbarism and despotism to pure socialism. Here we have a new doctrine, revolutionary peasantism. The idealization of the people has reached its apogee. The people are omnipotent. True, they are ignorant and illiterate, but instead of culture they have a multitude of noble instincts, which will do quite as well. The favorite idea is to provoke an immediate social revolution; the idea of political revolution, of reorganizing the State on a Liberal and constitutional basis is clearly as little favored by the revolutionary *narodnik* as it was a generation ago by the monarchic *narodnik*. But as no step whatever in advance is possible without political liberty, it is evident that the *narodnik* of both categories are in contradiction with themselves, and their policy can result only in the maintenance of the existing *régime* just as it is, that is to say, of the reaction which now rules Russia with absolute sway. It is the union of these two influences, of the old *narodnik* and the new, that has given birth to the so-called *narodnicestvo*, or literary "peasantism," from which most of our extreme opposition organs draw their inspiration. In these circumstances, as may well be supposed, the political programme of the Democratic Press—not even excepting the *Annals*, which was also *narodnik*—is vague, inconsistent, and unreal. This being the case, and seeing, moreover, that there are journals such as the *Nedeilia*, which, while calling themselves Radical, adopt all the ideas of Souvourin (although they do not thereby avoid prosecution), and others that panegyrize the domestic policy of Prince Bismarck, it cannot seriously be contended that the democratic section of the Russian Press deserves to be called subversive. But there is another section of the same party, also represented in the Press, which claims to be "Liberal" *par excellence*. It professes to be neither *narodnik* nor Slavophile, and advocates, so far as its civic courage permits, the pure principles of European Liberalism. But in renouncing the errors of the oldest parties these Liberals have, at the same time, renounced the principle from which the former cause derives its strength— political Radicalism. Having made moderatism the basis of their political faith, refusing to admit even in theory the idea of any effective protest against tyranny, our so-called Liberals have doomed themselves to complete sterility. For in a country like Russia, where law violates justice, and justice disregards law, moderatism has no place. All that these Liberals can do is to implore the Government to be good enough to resign, and their shameful servility to the powers that be has alienated from them the best of our Russian youth, and all the most potent progressive forces of the nation. Few papers indeed have known how to reconcile in their programme true Liberalism with Radical Democratism—the only programme which has a future in our country. True, they did not advocate these ideas openly—the "censor" would not have allowed it—but they did so "between the lines," and never printed anything incompatible with its principles—which is all we have a right to expect from any Russian journal. Of these papers I will cite only one, the *Slovo* already mentioned. As it is irrevocably suppressed, I may speak well of it, without exposing it to unpleasant consequences.

We may thus safely affirm that our Press has done little for the political enlightenment of Russian society. The clandestine journals, printed abroad and circulated secretly at home, have done far more, notwithstanding lack of means and the difficulty of distribution.

III.

Yet we must give credit where credit is due, and there can be no question that the so-called Liberal and Radical Press, the *Annals* above all, have greatly helped in the development of revolutionary ideas, but in another fashion than by direct teaching. They have laid bare the evils of our social system and political order, proving their charges with undeniable testimony and irrefutable logic. For this sort of propaganda, none the less effective because indirect, it suffices to have a love for truth and to see things as they are; because in Russia of to-day only the blindest optimism or deliberate bad faith can defend the existing order, and impute, as do the Souvourins and Katkoffs, treason and wickedness to all who venture to cast a doubt on the wisdom or patriotism of the bureaucracy. This explains why the Press, almost without exception, is hostile to the Government. It is impossible in the nature of things that they should be otherwise. No censorship can effectually combat an opposition of this character. The only way to overcome the hostility of the Press is by suppressing all its existing organs and forbidding the establishment of new papers. A Government Press is all but impossible, for, to the honor of Russian journalism be it said, there are to be found in the country few, if any, journalists of the stamp of Mr. Zitovitch, and even if such editors were forthcoming readers would still be lacking.

In the year 1884, therefore, matters stood thus: Of old established reviews with some influence and a wide circle of readers there remained only one, *The European Messenger*. All the others had been harried out of existence by the censorship. Among the St. Petersburg reviews there was one, the *Dielo*, which, by an exceptional piece of spitefulness on the part of the Government, had always been censured before publication, thereby causing its conductors numberless embarrassments and continual annoyance. On occasions when the censors were more than usually censorious Mr. Blagosvetloff, the publisher, would be compelled to print five or six times as many sheets as were actually required— 150 or 180 instead of thirty. As many as five articles out of six were often rejected by the censorship. (The articles were presented in proof, not in manuscript.) The enormous useless expense incurred in this way may be imagined; but, as some set-off to all, the proprietors had at least a right to assume that the review would be guaranteed against complete suppression by the Government—if for no other reason because such a proceeding would be a palpable admission of the uselessness of censorship. And in effect the *Dielo* was not suppressed, technically. But all the same a very decided stop was put to its career. The Minister sent for Mr. Ostrogorsky, the nominal editor (who was also a tutor), and told him that he must choose between giving up that position and dismissal from the tutorship by which he made his living. The Minister evidently intended to play the *Dielo* the same trick he had played the *Slovo*. If Mr. Ostrogorsky yielded to the threat and gave up the editorship he would refuse to confirm the appointment of another editor in his place. But Mr. Ostrogorsky preferred to forfeit his means of livelihood rather than abandon the nominal editorship of the review. On this the Minister ordered the acting editor, M. Stanukovitch (M. Blagosvetloff's successor) to sell the review to Mr. Wolfman, a man whose opinions were altogether different from those advocated by the *Dielo*, threatening that, in the event of his refusal, the censorship should reject every article presented for approval. In this way the *Dielo* was worse than suppressed; it was transformed into an organ of the reaction.

As I have just observed, one review still survives in precarious solitude, the *Messenger* of Mr. Stassulevitch. People have been in daily expectation of its suppression. But as its editor (who has been taken to by several imperial grand dukes), and many of his contributors have "friends at court," Count Tolstoi has so far let it alone. How long he will hold his hand it is hard to say. In the meanwhile, however, he was preparing another stroke against his pet detestation—literature and thought. This time he surpassed himself, and his *Index librorum prohibitorum*—list of books excluded from libraries and reading-rooms—caused throughout Russia an astonishment mingled with laughter, which left no room for indignation.

CHAPTER XXXI.

A SAMPLE FROM THE BULK.

In December, 1884, at the Moscow assizes took place the trial of Rykov, once manager of the defunct bank of Skopine, who, by the enormity of his depredations, unmatched even in Russia, has obtained an almost European notoriety. For an entire fortnight the Russian press—albeit the Moscow papers had received more than one official caution—were simply full of the case. In society hardly any other subject was discussed. It was the burning question of the hour, and will not soon be forgotten. That malversations are often committed by functionaries charged with the care or administration of public funds is in Russia a matter of common knowledge. The public are so used to scandals of this sort that, as a rule, they attract little or no attention. They are regarded as being in the nature of things. To rouse people from their apathy the thieving must present some striking or dramatic feature, or the sums stolen be of startling amount. These features the Rykov case presented in abundance. The malversations of the ex-manager and his confederates are reckoned at 12,000,000 roubles—probably the biggest robbery of the sort ever perpetrated, even in the empire of the Tzar. This alone would have been enough to excite public attention. But when, after two years of waiting and suspense, the shameful secrets of this band of brigands were revealed in open court, the figures, portentous as they were, paled into insignificance as compared with the social and political questions raised by this extraordinary trial. It is from this point of view that the

Rykov case merits the attention of English readers. As a drop of water from a well defiled shows all its impurities, so from this trial may be inferred the unspeakable corruption with which, under the present *régime*, the official world of Russia is infected from top to bottom.

The Bank of Skopine was founded in 1863, at a time of considerable industrial activity, and was expected to prove eminently useful to the trade of the district. It was a communal, not a Government institution. On the other hand, the State had very much to do with the bank, for, like all other communal banks, it was placed under the control of the Ministries of the Interior and Finance, and had to render to the latter department a periodical and detailed account of its operations and its position. Rykov was appointed to the managership, although, as everybody knew, he had been guilty, while occupying a previous appointment, of malversation. But the offence was readily overlooked, perhaps for a reason suggested by the Russian proverb, "Only he who has not sinned against God has not robbed the Tzar." True, a few protests were made by the Skopine people. Yet Rykov was sustained by his superiors, and for a short time he seems to have justified their good opinion. But in 1868, as afterwards appeared, there was a deficit of 54,000 roubles. But, being reluctant to publish this unpleasant fact to the world or impart it to the Minister of Finance, he did what, as his advocate ingenuously put it, anybody in his place would have done—drew up a false balance-sheet, and of so satisfactory a character that it attracted deposits from all parts of the country. From this date the affairs of the bank went from bad to worse; but the more desperate became its condition the more brilliant grew its balance-sheets. Though he was doing no legitimate banking business whatever, Rykov, by the offer of $7\frac{1}{2}$ per cent. interest on deposits (while other banks were paying five), procured funds in abundance. To show how his exceptional profits were earned, Rykov entered in the bank's books divers ingeniously-contrived financial operations. There were fictitious discounts, fictitious loans, fictitious purchases, and fictitious sales. An old man in the pay of the bank, so illiterate that he could hardly write his own name, signed every December a contract for the purchase of several millions' worth of imaginary securities, and this transaction, and the resulting imaginary profit thereon, always figured on the bogus balance-sheet presented to the Minister and published in the *Gazette*.

Rykov not alone paid his depositors a high rate of interest, he gave away large sums to charitable institutions, supported schools, and subsidized churches, thereby securing the good-will of the clergy and acquiring a high reputation for piety and philanthropy, good works and right views. All these gifts, as well as Rykov's own personal expenditure, which was on a lavish scale, were taken from the bank's coffers and entered as payments to dummy customers. The remainder and greater part of the receipts and deposits were simply stolen, either for the manager's own purposes or to buy the silence of his confederates. Paper was made on an extensive scale, and with little attempt at disguise. Antieff, a man of straw, drew on Safoneff, equally a man of straw, for fifty or a hundred thousand roubles, discounted the bill, and got the money. Then the operation would be reversed, and Safoneff get the money. Purely fictitious bills with imaginary names were discounted, and the porters and messengers of the bank figure in the books as debtors for tens of thousands of roubles taken by their master. "Everything was done *en famille*," said one of the witnesses.

But to profit by all this profusion it was necessary to belong to the *clique*, to be either a protector, a kinsman, or an accomplice. Lists of suppliants (*sic*) were laid regularly before Rykov, who according to his caprice, wrote opposite each name "granted" or "refused." When a bill fell due the acceptor was courteously requested to accept another, including the discount, which, it is hardly necessary to say, nobody ever thought of paying in coin. But after a while even these formalities were dispensed with. When the favored few wanted money they simply asked for it—sometimes took it without asking. "They took money from the cash box without counting it," said one witness. "They came with a pocket-handkerchief, filled it with bank notes, and went home," testified another.

Such was the method of doing business in the famous bank of Skopine. And the swindle went on, not for a few weeks or months merely, but for something like fifteen long years, an astounding fact even for Russia, and elsewhere unimaginable. In a small provincial town, where everybody knows everybody else, Rykov's doings and the bank's position could not possibly be secret—were, in fact, so widely known that when the crash came, the entire province (Riasan) produced but nineteen unfortunates who had intrusted their savings to Mr. Rykov and his fellow robbers, and among the 6,000 customers of the bank not one dwelt in Skopine. How, then, was it possible for irregularities which were known throughout a whole province to escape for fifteen years the attention of the authorities, local and general? How, above all, did they escape the attention of the corporation, for the law places communal banks under the immediate supervision of mayors and municipalities. It is their duty each month to examine the books, count the cash, and overhaul the securities. How was it, then, that all this time, the municipality failed to remark the gross and palpable frauds perpetrated by their manager? The answer is simple. They were privy to the frauds and participators in the plunder. All robbed the bank. Mayor Ikonnikov robbed, Mayor Ovtschinnikov robbed, the Town Clerk robbed, every member of the municipality robbed. The monthly audit was a farce. The books were never looked at, the cash was never counted, the balance-sheet was signed without being examined.

And the authorities, the administration, the police, usually so vigilant, and, when it is a question of maintaining order or punishing political malcontents, so prompt to act, what were they doing? How could they be blind to facts known to all the world? The same explanation applies to them. They were in the ring; tarred with the same brush as the municipality, and they robbed with the rest. The *ispravnik*, chief of police, was in Rykov's pay. Aleksandroff, the local justice of the peace, called in derision Rykov's lackey, received from the bank a loan of 100,000 roubles and a stipend of 500 roubles a year. His successor, Likareff, was put on a similar footing. The connivance of the smaller official fry, such as the postmaster, the *pristavs* (inferior police), was secured in like fashion, as also the members of the force who acted as the manager's spies. Having thus bought the entire local administration, Rykov became as much the autocrat of Skopine, as the Tzar is of All the Russias. He could do whatever he liked, and conducted himself with all the insolence of an ignorant *parvenu*. There dwelt in the town a doctor of the name of Bitni, a man of good repute and highly esteemed for his integrity; but being so unfortunate as to offend Rykov, he was one day ordered by the police to betake himself to the town of Kassimvo and there abide. No reason for this arbitrary proceeding was assigned, and it was only when the day of reckoning came that Dr. Bitni learnt that his expulsion was due to Rykov, who had remarked to the *ispravnik* that the doctor was an "evil-intentioned man." On this hint the chief of police had acted. A young fellow named Sokoloff was so ill-advised as to whistle while passing the manager in the public garden of Skopine. Rykov chose to look on this as an insult, and, the *ispravnik* taking the same view of the matter, the youth was exiled by administrative order. With

Mr. Orloff, an engineer, it fared even worse. He was sent by a company to purchase some coal, the produce of a mine owned by the bank in the province of Riasan. But finding the article of indifferent quality, he refused, on behalf of his employers, to accept it, and, being presumably an honest man, he was not to be corrupted by the bribes which were no doubt offered to him. Be that as it may, Rykov charged Mr. Orloff with incendiarism, had him arrested, sentenced to a term of imprisonment, from which he was only saved by the intervention of the Imperial Procurator-General from undergoing. "The police of Skopine," said the witness Lanskoy, whose evidence was quoted in the indictment, "was ready at any moment to execute Rykov's least desire." The (two) brothers, Lanskoy, Sokoloff, and Tinogenoff, all *employés* of the bank, lodged in the house of a Mr. Brigneff, an arrangement which, for some inexplicable reason did not suit Rykov's purpose. So without more ado he ordered the police to remove them, and the order was duly carried into effect. They were one day waited on by the *ispravnik*, Kobelinzky, and three policemen, and compelled to leave their lodgings forthwith. Nor was this all. Rykov counted so confidently on the support of the local representatives of the Government that he lorded it over everybody, openly rated the fire brigade because they did not conduct themselves to his satisfaction at a fire, and, vexed by some show of independence on the part of the chief of police, told him that he had better take care what he was about. "You are nobody very particular," said Rykov, "and I have only to say a word to have sent down on your place a whole wagon-load of *ispravniks*." When, in order to ruin Mr. Diakonov, who, unfortunately for himself, owed the bank 10,000 roubles, he had this gentleman's house seized and offered for sale by auction, not a single bidder appeared on the scene, so great was the fear inspired by the all-powerful manager. This was exactly what Rykov desired. The house was worth 30,000 roubles; he made the complaisant police value it at 9,000, and he had the unfortunate Mr. Diakonov cast into prison, where he remained for eleven months. In this way an almost illiterate man—for the manager could only just read and write—became absolute master of Skopine. "God alone could contend against Rykov," said one of the witnesses.

But, it may be asked, were there not among this mass of cowardice, servility, and corruption a few just men, with sufficient public spirit to bring the doings of the Nabob of Skopine to the notice of the higher authorities, who could not possibly have yielded to his influence or accepted his bribes? Yes, certainly, there were several. One of them was the ill-fated Diakonov, and he had his reward. And then there was the ex-mayor, Leonoff, who gave evidence on the trial. While he was in office the affairs of the bank were kept in order, the books properly audited, the cash and securities regularly overhauled. But this did not suit Rykov's purpose; he bribed the electors and the municipality; Leonoff was turned out of office and a more complaisant mayor chosen in his place. Yet, though no longer a magistrate he did not cease his endeavors to protect the bank from the depredations of its managers. So far back as 1868 Leonoff and several other citizens addressed a petition to General Boldireff, governor of the province, in which they set forth the condition of the bank, and prayed him to order an inquiry. In 1874—six years afterwards—came the answer. It was to the effect that, the petition not being drawn up according to the prescribed form, no action could be taken thereupon. In 1878 another like attempt was made, the authority appealed to in this instance being the Minister of the Interior. The answer was as characteristic as before. As the document did not carry the proper stamp (20 kopecks, 10c.), the prayer of the petitioners could not be taken into consideration. On this the petitioners drew up another address correctly stamped, and sent that to the Minister, expecting that this time, at least, something would be done. "But," said one of them (Maslennikoff), when giving his evidence, "we have not received an answer to this day."

This indifference in high quarters is as easily explained as the voluntary blindness of the local administration. Boldireff, the governor of the province, was bribed like the rest. He received from Rykov 79,000 roubles. Volkov, the vice-governor, did better; he got 100,000 roubles. The Marshal of the Nobility sold himself for a paltry 12,000 roubles. When the inquiry was ordered in 1882 this gentleman found it convenient to be abroad. The Councillor of the Provincial Government, Koumiantzev, the members of the Tribune, Babine and Kirmilitzin, and the Procurator Pottavzki, were proved to have been all in the same boat.

The trial failed to furnish proofs equally convincing as to the parts played by the bureaucracy of St. Petersburg. Nobody cared to sift this side of the question—neither the President of the Court, the Crown Prosecutor, nor the prisoner's advocate. No functionary in the Ministry of the Interior was either summoned as a witness or required to explain his conduct. But Rykov hinted darkly that certain highly-placed personages deserved much more than he to stand in the prisoners' dock. The hints of a man like Rykov are very far from being trustworthy evidence, but several facts came to light which confirm in a measure the suspicions they suggest. For instance, a mysterious personage named Bernard, a civil general, acted as the manager's diplomatic agent at St. Petersburg, and arranged delicate matters for him in high quarters. As recompense for his services he received a million roubles—nominally as a loan. In the end they had a quarrel, and Bernard contrived to rid himself of his liability by an expedient as simple as it was significant. He applied to his particular friend, General Tcherevin, chief of the gendarmerie, who thereupon requested the manager of the bank at Skopine to return General Bernard his acceptances, amounting to 500,000 roubles. Rykov did as he was asked. It was hardly conceivable, however, that the chief's eloquence could alone have persuaded the manager to so great generosity. What, then, was the consideration that Rykov received, and the service which the other, a great man in the Third Section, rendered ? This mystery the trial left unsolved, but the names of some other personages of high position figured in the proceedings—not greatly to their advantage. The Emperor's Adjutant-General, Grabbe, owed the bank 242,000 roubles; Prince Obolinski owed it 60,000. and both debts were set down as "bad." How came it that these gentlemen, neither of whom were connected either with commerce or finance, were able to obtain from the bank these large sums ? When Rykov was pressed on the point, all he had to say was that he had lent them the money "under the guarantee of their high titles." But the explanation may be hazarded that he found it necessary to spend money at St. Petersburg promiscuously and without stint. In Russia you cannot move a step without paying. Rykov was well received everywhere, and made much of by great people. On the days of grand solemnity Ministers sent him congratulatory despatches. "How much did these despatches cost them ?" exclaimed the other day a Russian paper with seeming simplicity. And how much, we may ask, cost him the decorations and titles which were so lavishly conferred upon him ? A striking proof of the tenderness with which, even to the last, the arch rogue and his accomplices were treated by the authorities was mentioned by the *Russian Courier* of December 31, 1882. "Although," it wrote, "the Commission (of Inquiry) is working with zeal, the seizure of the property of Rykov's confederates proceeds very slowly. The accused, to the manifest detriment of the bank's creditors, have every opportunity of concealing and disposing of their assets. Ikonnikov (the mayor), notwithstanding the charges against him and his approaching trial, sends every night loads of merchandise out of the town. The seizure of the property of the other thirteen confederates did not take place until a month after their committal to trial.

The exposure of the frauds and the punishment of the criminals was due to the efforts of the three or four honest citizens already mentioned, Leonoff, Popoff, and Rausoff, and the courage of a single newspaper. If these men had not been ex-members of the municipality and well-to-do they would have learnt to their cost what it was to denounce a Councillor of Commerce and chevalier of several orders. Utterly unable to make any impression on the local administration, or to obtain a hearing from the higher authorities, they did that which in Russia is looked upon as a doubtful and desperate expedient, but which in any other country would have been done at the outset—they appealed to the Press. But even here the irrepressible manager barred the way. For two years the letters they despatched to various papers never reached their destination; they were stopped at the post office. According to the evidence of the witness Simonoff, evidence which was not gainsaid, Peroff, the postmaster, received from Rykov 50 roubles per mensem in consideration of which he intercepted and handed to his employer every letter addressed to a newspaper which came into the office, and any others that the manager wanted. Atlaroff, the telegraphist, rendered in his department analogous services on similar terms. It was only in 1882 that the gentlemen in question succeeded in getting printed in the *Russian Courier* several letters on the affairs of the bank of Skopine. The journal which did this good service for the community is one of the few liberal organs left, and it has been harried and persecuted by the Government to the verge of extinction. Other papers, either because they were paid to keep silence or hesitated to attack an institution so closely connected with the State, and enjoying the confidence of so many "supporters of order," refused to publish any letters whatever on the subject. Mr. Katkoff, the celebrated editor of the *Moscow Gazette*, had the questionable honor of being publicly praised by Rykov as one of his greatest and most esteemed benefactors!

The letters in the *Courier* were the death sentence of the Skopine bank. Creditors rushed from all parts of the country to withdraw their deposits; but the run ceased almost as soon as it began, for the strong room, instead of containing the twelve million roubles shown on the balance-sheet, was empty, and the bill-cases were filled with bogus paper. The bank fell, and great was the fall thereof. The scandal and the panic it caused spread far and wide, confidence was at an end, and there was a run on nearly every communal bank in Russia. A few stood the test, but a full dozen came to the ground, and when their affairs were looked into they were found to be pretty much in the same condition as those of the bank of Skopine.

Among others the bank of Kamychin (province of Saratoff) had to close its doors, and, when inquisition was made, serious irregularities were discovered; the mayor of the town and several of its richest merchants were arrested and put on their trial. They had depleted the bank of the whole of its paid-up capital and its reserve, for which there was nothing to show but worthless paper. It was the bank of Skopine over again, but on a less scale. At Krolevez (province of Tchernigoff) the entire *personnel* of the communal bank were placed under arrest, the charge against them being that, in collusion with several tradesmen of the place, they had committed extensive malversations. The manager and assistant manager of the bank of Roslavl (province of Smolensk), which also broke, were convicted of having embezzled 28,000 roubles of the bank's money. The accounts of this establishment had not been audited for eleven years. At Tamboff the inquisition brought to light quite a multitude of malversations.

When the manager wanted to oblige a friend and still keep up a show of regularity, he would discount his draft on his wife and provide for the bill at maturity by reversing the operation. Similar discoveries have been made and prosecutions instituted at Voronez, Kotelnich, Kozloff, and other places, and the papers announce that Airloff, ex-manager of the bank of Orel, and all his colleagues in the direction, are charged with misappropriating 4,000,000 roubles of the bank's money. As their defalcations were spread over twelve years, the case is not unlike that of Skopine.

So much for banks, but it is not bank managers and directors alone who rob their employers and betray their trust. Robbery is the rule, honesty the exception. Robbery goes on in every department of the State. In 1882 a Russian paper, the *Sovremenn Tzvestia* gave a list of the "great robberies" known to have been committed during the last few years by public functionaries. According to this account there were twenty-five thefts of from 20,000 to 60,000 roubles each; six ranging from 400,000 to 500,000; and six ranging from one million to twelve millions—in all, twenty-seven millions. This is exclusive of small affairs of less than 20,000 roubles, which are past counting. "Russia has in its service but two honest men, you and me," said the Emperor Nicholas to his eldest son, and whatever progress the country may have made since his time has certainly not extended to the character of its public servants.

One of the most significant facts brought out by recent revelations is the relatively modest part played by the representatives of the Central Government. In the matter of the banks, the agents of the local and superior administrations acted merely as accomplices and receivers of stolen goods. The active parts and the lion's share were taken by high-placed rogues, who were enabled to rob with impunity by subsidizing the venal army of *tchinovniks*, always ready to place at the disposal of the highest bidder the arbitrary powers with which they are intrusted. It may even be said that the inferior agents of authority have been more in fault than the higher representatives of the State. The latter intervene only in exceptional cases; smaller robberies are left to be dealt with by the local administrations.

During Rykov's trial he protested warmly and often against what he called the injustice of the public and the Press. "They say that I am a monster; that I have stolen six millions. It is a gross calumny. I swear before you, gentlemen of the jury, that I stole but one million; one million only," he protested with indignant gesture and unconscious humor. This was quite true, as his young advocate triumphantly proved. For his personal use Rykov had taken only a million. But he had been enabled to take that million, only by spending five millions more as hush-money. The Government by which Russia has the misfortune to be ruled is for the country pretty much what Rykov was for the bank. In order to obtain money for its own use it must connive at the depredations of its own agents. To maintain its prerogatives the central despotism must tolerate the despotism of thousands of local autocrats, governors, policemen, and *ispravniks*. To shield itself from criticism, the State must suppress freedom of speech, muzzle the Press, and, for fear lest the latter should expose the abuses of the system, forbid it to expose the malpractices of individuals.

To show fully what the *tchinovniks* of the White Tzar are I should have to rake up the scandalous trial of Boush, of the commissariat, tell the story of the Minister Makoff's suicide, make extracts from the bloodstained pages of the "Revision of Oufa and Siberia." There are things far more serious than the small pedantry of the Minister of the Interior in refusing to read a petition because it was insufficiently stamped, or the humor of the Minister of Finance in paternally recommending a forger to renounce his dangerous practices. But it is not within my present purpose to describe the Russian bureaucracy. I have exposed the case of the Skopine Bank only to give some idea of another peculiarity of the present Government—the facilities which it offers to the dishonest, so turning to account the prevailing system as to rob and ruin the country with impunity. It is easy to see from this episode what are the men who are filling the place left vacant by those whom the Government, by its laws and administrative measures, has excluded from all participation in public affairs on the ground of their suspected liberal tendencies. Whilst the most modest attempt to render the country honest service may endanger a man's liberty, thieves and scoundrels may count on the most ample protection. For dishonesty is the surest guarantee of a man's freedom from the taint of disaffection, and that he has approved himself a trustworthy supporter of the existing order.

CHAPTER XXXII.

RUSSIA AND EUROPE.

I.

Now we must stop. Our journey must end. It has been a very hurried one, and we could see only a small part of what is worth seeing. Thus far we have pointed out the principle and the spirit of the existing *régime;* we have exposed the conduct of the Government toward the superior—the instructed—classes, which, however numerically small, accomplish most important functions in the social life. It is over this limited field of governmental action that we must now take a retrospective glance.

Strange spectacle! Here are a State and a Government calling themselves national and patriotic, which systematically, from year to year, do things that the most barbarous conqueror could do only in some sudden access of wild rage and stupid fanaticism. For, without a shadow of exaggeration, the exploits of our rulers of to-day can be compared with those of the celebrated Kaliph of Egypt alone. Surely in no other country was such a government ever seen. If all we have exposed were not proved, and doubly proved, by heaps of official documents, we might be tempted to disbelieve it. But it is all unhappily only too true; and, what is still worse, will always be true so long as the autocracy rules in Russia.

Some optimist may be disposed to say that the policy of the Russian triumvirate is but a temporary aberration, caused by the overweening influence over the Emperor of

Potedonorzeff, Katkoff, and Tolstoi. Yes, the policy of the present government is surely an aberration; but only for its lack of policy, for its cynical frankness. If Potedonorzeff and Katkoff lose their influence and Tolstoi fall, his successor may prove less rash and more cautious. As to the main character of the interior policy, it cannot help but remain the same. The most elementary consideration of self-defence will render it imperative to preserve intact the main features of their domestic policy. At the end of the nineteenth century the sole safeguard of the autocracy consists in its utter ignorance of the people. It is not enough to confiscate books and suppress liberal papers; the only way to get rid of propagandism is to suppress readers. If peasants read nothing but the *Moscow Gazette*, they will find in the columns relating to "foreign affairs," reports of European politics, of parliaments and free meetings, and many other things that will equally "instigate" to disrespect of the existing Government. If they limit their reading to *Souvorin's Almanac*, they will find in it accounts of the incidence and distribution of taxation which, rightly understood, may prove as inflammatory as a revolutionary appeal. At the same time, the Government cannot help shutting out society from all part in the management of public affairs. On whom can the autocracy now rely but on the police and the bureaucracy? And even against the latter it must take precautions, as everybody knows.

Now being driven by and by to a flagrant contradiction with the culture, and to open war with the whole body of instructed classes, the autocracy is driven to be in contradiction with the State itself. It is prompting the very State to ruin by both hands. By opposing the instruction in every shape, it quenches the very sources of productivity of all the national labor. By leaving the management of all, or nearly all, the public affairs in the hands of a hired, uncontrollable bureaucracy, which is as unable as it is corrupted, the autocracy add to the original scarcity of resources the damages of their misemployment. The gradual impoverishment of the State, the growing embroiling of finances, the progressive misery of the masses tilling the soil, are but the natural and unavoidable consequences of such a *régime*. And it is no more a secret to anybody that it is just what we are witnessing in Russia.

II.

This most anomalous position of as great a country as Russia cannot last. In one way or another the catastrophe must come—that is what everybody says at present. Some very accurate observer finds many points of likeness between modern Russia and France before the Revolution. There is a good deal of analogy, indeed; the greatest stands, of course, in the diffusion throughout all the classes of the nation of anti-Governmental tendencies, and of those generous and creative ideas which are called "subversions," because they tend to subvert wrong and substitute it by right. The material condition and moral dispositions of the masses are not unlike, either. There is, however, a point of great difference also, on which we must dwell a moment, because it contributes greatly to quicken and intensify the decomposition of the Russian State, and to the approaching of the ultimate crisis. It is the political position of Russia.

The despotic France of the seventeenth century had around her neighboring States as despotic as herself. Russia has for neighbors constitutional States. Their constitution is very far from being the ideal of freedom. But in any case it prevents their Governments from being in open war with the whole country. Neither Prussia, nor Austria, nor any other Government in Europe prevent willingly the diffusion of education, or the more economical and reasonable management of public affairs, out of fear of giving dangerous arms to their enemies. All neighboring States are growing in strength and riches. All the Governments do their best to promote this general progress, which turns to their advantage. In Russia this progress is either stopped or extremely slow, from the check it encounters on every hand from the Government.

Now, being indissolubly united with the other European States by political ties—being obliged to sustain an economical, military, and political competition with those neighbor States, Russia is evidently obliged to ruin herself more and more. For it cannot without overstraining keep the front with them, notwithstanding the growing difference in the interior development of the respective countries. The longer this competition lasts, the more it becomes disastrous and difficult to sustain for the Russian State. The political crisis is, therefore, much nearer, forcible, and immediate than the social one. And the actual position of Russia in this point presents us a great analogy with the position of Russia itself in the period which preceded the reform of Peter the Great. The autocracy plays now just the same part as regards the culture as the Moscovite clericalism played in the sixteenth and seventeenth centuries. After being the instrument of the creation of Russian political power, it is now the cause of its gradual destruction. If the autocracy do not fall under the combined effects of interior causes, the first serious war will overthrow it, perhaps by shedding rivers of blood and by dismembering the State. The destruction of the autocracy is become a political as well as social and intellectual necessity. It is required for the safety of the State as well as for the welfare of the nation.

III.

Let us pass to the autocracy of central power itself. It is very edifying, and surely most consoling, to see how certain crimes against humanity generate out of themselves their own punishment. The Bible records the legend of a Babylonian Tzar of old—Nebuchadnezzar—who, in punishment for his excessive pride, was transformed by the Almighty into an ox, and for twelve years ate nothing but grass. I do not remember any more in what the pride of the Babylonian Tzar manifested itself to incur such a dire punishment. Surely it was not greater than the pride of his *confrère* of St. Petersburg, pretending to govern all, to decide for all, arbitrate for all what is doing and to be done in a nation of a hundred million, like the Russia of to-day is. It was quite just that the punishment inflicted on him may be something very (if not altogether) similar : he is condemned to masticate his life long nothing but paper.

In a bureaucratic State, where everything is to be done in writing, and nothing is left to personal freedom and initiative, the most trifling particulars ascend from the inferior agents of a bureaucratic system up to the topmost—the Tzar. What, for instance, will the reader think of the following, one out of thousands of quite similar "all highest orders," as they are called in official language, the Tzar's ukases. It refers to nothing more nor less than to students' blouses. I transcribe it in all its bureaucratical candor :—

"Having heard the all-humblest report (so the document ran) of the Minister of State Domain, his Majesty the Emperor—15th October of the current year (1884)—all highly deigned to order, in supplement to the model of dresses all highly approved by his Majesty, the 3d May, 1882, to the students of Moscow Agricultural Academy, is granted the permission during the lessons in the academy, and in practical work, to wear blouses ; the winter, of brown-gray woollen stuff, the summer, of light-yellow (unbleached) linen, with a brown leather strap adorned with metallic clasp, on which, interwoven with a crown of spikes, must be drawn the letters P. and A. in Old Slav character."

Can the time of the supreme ruler of one hundred millions be better employed than with the deep question of the color and material of students' blouse, their wearing blouses or jackets, the letters on the clasps being of Slav or Gothic character? This question is not very complicated it is true. If the Tzar have no particular taste for a tailor's trade, he may settle it at once. But this draft of order must be read to him before being signed, must be mentioned at least to him. He must give his yes or no; must lose a part of his time. And if every minister bring him a hundred of such trifles, how much of his work-time will the Tzar preserve for things that are not trifles? And it is easy to conceive that every minister can procure as many things of that and even of greater importance as required to fill up his master's leisure, and deprive him of any possibility of giving serious attention to matters of some importance. Thus the Tzar can only act by his ministers' advice. Even such a zealous absolutist as the defunct Moscow Professor Buslaeff, in a letter published in one of our antiquarian magazines, after computing the enormous quantity of this quite useless ukase signing, exclaims that to restore to the White Tzar his liberty of action a part of this futile, everyday, governmental drudgery must be put on a responsible minister; although the learned professor does not go so far as to make them responsible before a national representation. If we compare the position of the despots of various epochs, we may fairly affirm that the present mode of reducing to impotence the would-be all-powerful master is much more effective than the old one. A despot like the old Russian Tzars with an effort of will may have freed himself with remorse from one or another futility of the court observance. The chief of the modern bureaucratic despots may not, with the same calmness of mind, shun the duty of reading a dozen of voluminous suits on the decision of which are pending so many destinies, or a project of financial reform on which may depend the welfare or misery of a province.

And if it happened that, notwithstanding their material

obstacles, the Tzar being under some particular influence had enforced his own view on some subject, the would-be all-humblest executioners, the ministers, would have no difficulty to put the thing right. They have only to appeal to the marvellous slowness of bureaucratic proceedings, which allow to postpone every measure for as many years—I could say as many generations—as required. Nothing prevents them from effecting at the first opportunity a change in the Tzar's decision if they like. If they do not they may leave the thing to sleep in some office the sleep of the just. The history of our administration is but a long series of similar instances. If Alexander II. could do something in the beginning of his reign, it is only because he broke for a short time the bureaucratic routine, and appealed to society. From the moment when, prompted by fear, he threw himself into the arms of bureaucracy, he remained powerless, and went straight to his own ruin. Of all sorts of despots that history knows, the most helpless, most impotent, is surely the bureaucratic despots of our time.

We may go still further. As a rough rock of the mountain by long rolling in the bottom of a stream is reduced to a smooth, inoffensive pebble, which may be heavy but no longer cutting, so is the actual autocracy of Russia. The Tzars of old had for their political insignificance a consolation and compensation in their unlimited power of self-indulging mischief, if it may be called a consolation. This latter power in our modern Tzars is reduced to quite a platonic kind. There is the all-seeing, all-knowing reporter, with his shrieks and his laughter, his indignation and scandal, to limit their despotism in the inner circle where they move. Our forefathers said, to be near the Tzar is to be near to death. But a modern Tzar does not condemn to death anybody by the contraction of his brows as the Moscow Tzar did. And he does not exile to Siberia the courtiers who incur his displeasure, like the first emperor of the St. Petersburg period. All is done now by *tchinovniks*. Personally, a modern Tzar does no harm to anybody at all, and is just as quiet and inoffensive a person as any constitutional monarch. He has not given up his power; he is like a beast with strong teeth and murderous claws still, but he never uses them. He is now quite a tame, domesticated animal, who wears quite obediently the yoke of the courtier. With self-denial worthy of a better cause, he is serving as a screen to their misdeeds, exposing himself to all the just consequences of his assumed all-powerfulness which make his life miserable, his existence an eternal fear, his power a derision, his position a shame.

The evolution of autocracy is indeed complete. For it could hardly descend lower, it could hardly present a more exhilarating, pleasant, exalting spectacle to its enemies.

IV.

But how? Is it possible that a man without being a fool may act in so strange a mode? How can he remain in so disagreeable a position, causing the misery of a whole nation, who after all did him no wrong whatever? How could he refuse to redress public wrongs and better his own life by a stroke of the pen, if only he could? If he do not, it is evident that in reality he cannot. There must be, most likely, some hidden force and hidden party which hold a power over him. Such a doubt is very common, and to answer it there were created in various times different hypotheses of some extremely powerful court party, to which sometimes the name of old aristocratic, sometimes that of old Slavophile party is given, and so forth. They alone prevent the Tzar from doing that good to his country which personally he would be quite disposed to do.

It is strange how sometimes extremes meet. Just the same doubt—just in the same shape—rises in the minds of

Russian peasants, and is answered nearly in the same way. Only with the peasants the touch of their imagination gives these hypotheses quite a fantastical dress. Sometimes the legend assumes the character of dramatic performances, where the good principle embodied in the Tzar is overpowered by the opposite force embodied now in the Senate (usually confounded with the Synod, a permanent ecclesiastic council), now in the minister (always in a single person, for the peasant thinks there is only one minister as there is one Tzar). Sometimes these legends give the part of bad genius to some member of the imperial family. During the reign of Alexander II. this not too flattering part was usually conferred to the Tzarevitch (present Tzar); who fills his place now, when he becomes Tzar himself, I do not know. Somebody must be, and may depend on it. Many pages may be filled by recording the naïve and childish contrivances by which the peasants try to save the remainder of their belief in the Tzar against the rude evidence of everyday wrongs inflicted by his orders.

But only the peasantry indulge in Russia in such reveries. And even they will abandon it as soon as some glimpse of culture reach their minds. Instructed Russia has given it up long ago, knowing perfectly that nothing of the kind exists in Russia. The tales about old Slavophile, old aristocratic party, and such like, have quite the same value as the peasants' legends about the rascality of the Synod or the cunning of the Senate. Never in the course of our history was the upper classes able to acquire any political strength of their own. The reader remembers how our *soi-disant* aristocracy was created, and what it was of old. Such it remained for all time. In the first century after the transfer of the capital to St. Petersburg it seemed to be otherwise. Situated in a far remote, freshly conquered country, St. Petersburg was but a waste military camp. Its lower classes were composed of foreign Finish tribes; its upper classes of military and civil officers, most of whom were of foreign origin. Pretorian insurrection was extremely easy in such a town, and the ambitious foreigner and courtier were able some times to put their foot on the neck of their master. It was due not to the strength of the aristocracy, but the momentary dislocation of the State. These times, however, have passed away long ago. If there should be a Court revolution, it will be that which is directed against the autocracy as a principle, and is calculated on the immediate support of the progressive elements of the whole country. A violent change of government without changing principles is an utter impossibility. A *coup d'état*, in order to rise a step in court hierarchy, will hardly cross as yet the mind of a modern Field-Marshal Minich. At the Court there is no force whatever which could oppose effectually the will of the Tzar. There is no political body, no aristocracy, no statesmen even, in the European sense of the word. We have only courtiers—a type already forgotten in Europe, because only Russia is the unhappy country where the will of one makes the laws for millions. And what is a courtier? It is a man in whom training, from generation to generation, has developed to the highest degree and marvellous effectiveness one single capacity—that of enforcing his will on the sovereign, while making him believe he is obeyed. All other capacities, all feelings, all inclinations, as things useless and even hurtful, are depressed and gradually destroyed in this ignoble representation of the human race called courtiers. Now the thing which is the most dangerous and disagreeable impediment in the courtier's struggles is undoubtedly what is called political convictions—strong political opinions. Such things are not to be sought in the despotic court. A courtier may accept a political banner as he does a dress in the court's parades, when such give better chances to carry him on in the good graces of his master. I will not multiply proofs for things too self-evident. As a matter of curiosity rather than illustration, let us consider for a moment Mr. Tolstoi. There is no man, of course, whose reactionary convictions seem to be more intransigent, more deeply rooted. And yet this very pillar of reaction, in 1859, only a few years before his appearance as minister of white terror and obscurantism, published at Brussels a very interesting pamphlet entitled *A Voice from Germany*.* Treating of the European politic of the epoch, the author exposes his view and political convictions in general. He is all for liberalism, for constitutional guarantee, for respect to the will of the nation. He pities the Hanover Government, which has on its side only the officers of the Government, whilst all the country is against it (p. 7) (just the case in Russia now). Still less satisfied is the Liberal Count with the conduct of the Government of Bavaria, where the king maintained in power, for full nine years, a minister quite odious to the country (pp. 6, 7) (just the case of Mr. Tolstoi in Russia). He expresses the hope that the rulers of the various German States will not follow the pernicious example of Hanover, and will not crush by police reprisals the lawful aspirations of their subjects" (p. 61). "Because," he says, "to put obstacles to the progressive reforms, when they become urgent, is as dangerous as to make appeal to insurrection : it is setting fire to the edifice from another corner" (p. 61). He is a strong adversary of clericalism, and stigmatizes the Italian patriots of 1848 for having made "this monstrous alliance of liberalism with the papism" (p. 12). He is very severe on Napoleon III., in whom he cannot put confidence, because " he fights for the freedom of foreigners, whilst suppressing the freedom at home" (p. 14). And he is full of noble indignation against despotic governments, which, "having little sympathy with the aspiration of their countries, shouted, 'Let us have war!'

* *Une Voix d'Allemagne*, par le Comte Dmitry Tolstoy, Bruxelles : Muguardt, editeur, 1859.

15*

wanting war in order that people may forget what they are, and let them live at this price" (p. 10) (just what he is urging the Tzar to do now).

All this is taken from a copy of the brochure in my possession. All this the Count Dmitry Tolstoi, this very same present minister, wrote with his own hands in the year 1859. He had hardly the time to return from his journey abroad when his liberalism vanished away. In the year 1859 the influence of Grand Duke Constantine (brother of Alexander II.) was predominant. It was the epoch of constitutional aspirations. From 1863 Prince Gagarin and the anti-abolitionist party take the foremost. Count Dmitry Tolstoi, at a moment's notice, changes the inmost of his soul's convictions, and becomes the right hand of most sordid reaction.

With people of this sort a sovereign has no reason to fear opposition. If the Tzar resolved to change his politics, he would have only a sign to make; half of his court would become, in no time, of the color required, from deep red to the most tender blue, provided by this they could secure for themselves the best places.

V.

But, as sure as there is no material obstacle which could prevent the Tzar from changing policy, so sure is the fact that such a change will never be initiated by the will of the Tzar.

There are moral, intellectual impossibilities no less insurmountable than the material one. Despots are trained as well as the courtiers, still more carefully than the courtiers. If the despotism exercised by one transform the whole court into a school of servility, on the other hand those hundred courtiers react on their master, whom they surround and educate from their very childhood. One thing generates the other. The courtier is the counterpart of the despot; the despot is the counterpart of the courtier. And both are equally spoiling each other. If the courtiers have an insurmountable aversion to free institutions because they will render it impossible for them to make best use of the cunning craft they only possess, the despot is as fond of this eternal show of flunkeyism and obsequiousness, of this possibility to make a man rise and fall by a single word, of all this show of omnipotence, however void it may be. If the continual concentration of thoughts on the sole object to please the caprice of one man, narrow the minds of courtiers, depriving them of the capacity for any comprehensive view, the artificial life of the court, with nothing but its base desires, produces around the despot a sort of intellectual vacuum which renders him still narrower-minded than his courtiers.

Having the power to transform into act every thought, every whim of his, he is preserved from all that may suggest him such thoughts or whims. It is a fact that there is not a single man in the hundred and one millions of the Tzar's subjects who is more watched or observed in his personal intercourse, whose intellectual food is submitted to stricter censorship, or more carefully selected, than that of the Tzar. He reads only extracts of what is thought good for him to know; he does not meet with anybody whom his courtiers would like him to shun. There are hundreds of ways to obtain this effect without seeming to impose on the sovereign's pleasure. And that is done, and has been done, for years and generations; and not only with the Tzar himself, but with every member of his family.

What is more hopeless than the very depravation of despotism is the utter, hardly realizable ignorance prevailing in the court on the commonest questions, most elementary conditions of the country they are ruling. We must read the memoir of Senator Tolovieff, and other men connected with the former reign ; we must hear the professors of universities allowed to deliver private lectures to small grand dukes, and to speak to them occasionally; we must give a glance at the leaders of Mr. Katkoff's gazette, which may be said to be destined for the personal edification of the Emperor and his family—to form a feeble idea of this strange, sophisticated, intellectual world, in which our masters live. There is no absurdity about Russian condition that may not be believed there, and the commonest truisms will seem as strange as if they have told of Satan. It will not be at all surprising if the Tzar believe that Mr. Tolstoi's policy as to public instruction is the very embodiment of progress. Did not Mr. Katkoff say it in his leaders, affirming, for instance, that in this point Russia is far more advanced than England ? When Count Tolstoi fell into temporary disgrace and was removed from the post of Minister of Public Instruction there was joy in all Russia, as if the country had been freed from a public calamity. Eye-witnesses say that fathers joined in thanksgiving for the blessing of being, on behalf of their children, liberated from the fear of having their careers ruined and their hopes destroyed. It will be not at all surprising, however, if the present Emperor thinks that he has done the greatest satisfaction to the country by recalling Count Tolstoi to power, and fears that if he dismiss him all Russia would be inundated with tears. No absurdity, however gross, will be surprising, and we have many evidences of blunders no less enormous. We must transport ourselves many centuries back, and substitute the effect of time for the effect of social distance to realize something of the intellectual bewilderment of our rulers and masters. A scholar of Averroes' times resuscitated would have presented in our times no much greater confusion in his ideas on the science than our rulers on the interior politics.

And what must be said about the voluntary misrepresentations, about phantom and imaginary dangers, invented by the courtiers in order to impress, to puzzle, and frighten their master, who being on such a superior height is so easily alarmed ? The Senator Tolovieff's memoir shows evidence that Tzar Alexander II. was seriously afraid of such an absurdity as a murderous attempt on the part of anti-abolitionists ! I was told by a competent person that for some time Count Loris Melikoff was held up to the present Emperor as a threatening bogie of a Court revolutionist ! It will be not at all surprising if he is replaced now by some military general, of M. Komaroff's or Skobeleff's type.

Only a man with exceptional firmness of character, with extraordinary courage and, first of all, with quite superior intellectual capacity, may have contrived to break these invisible intellectual and moral ties and catch now and then a glimpse of truth. A man who is not favored by nature, a man who, although born in the purple, is rather of unsatisfactory intellectual power, such a man must be inevitably overcome by the incessant efforts of a crowd of eager, unscrupulous people, who with all their incapacity to real business had made a whole science of the art of leading their master by the nose, of playing on him as on a fiddle, and of putting everything to their profit, his caprices and his aspirations, his good and his bad humor, his foibles and stubbornness, his vices and his virtues, if he has any.* No, the

---

* The reader will allow me to give a little amusing anecdote of very little significance but quite authentic and characteristic, how the most simple contrivance serves to make a fool of the Tzar. It happened in the first years of Alexander III.'s reign, to a Samara nobleman of the name of K——. He wanted a Governmental allowance of 200,000 roubles to start his leather manufactory. Many big Russian manufacturers had got considerable sums of State money "as an encouragement of national industry." All was arranged well. Everybody who had to be bribed was bribed. Mr. K—— was quite sure of success, so far that, returning to Samara, he did not choose to wait the few weeks that remained before the Emperor's definitive confirmation, and borrowed from a Tartar merchant the sum promised him, and set to

crowned heads of our time can no longer take any effective part in the management of State affairs. They are organically incapable of doing it. They cannot govern, let them reign then, as long as people cannot do without them. If they attempt to do more they can but receive the punishment due to themselves, which is a curse for the nation: they become

---

work at once. Great was his disappointment and despair when he received a telegram stating bluntly that the Emperor did not comfirm the allowance. He rushes to St. Petersburg to his protectors. How? What is it? Nobody knew. All was done right, as promised. But the Emperor refused. A whim took him. "It is quite incomprehensible. We cannot help it." Mr. K—— deemed himself a ruined man. But one fine morning, when he left the Minister of the Interior he was followed by Holonatchalink, head clerk of one of the numerous offices. The man asked him plainly if he consented to give him the sum of 10,000 roubles if the thing was put right. Mr. K—— exclaimed he would be happy to give even 20,000. The clerk refused to give any explanation and they parted. The next month Mr. K—— received a telegram stating: the allowance is granted by the Emperor. Full of exultation, he rushed once more to St. Petersburg, received his 200,000, found the clerk his benefactor and presented him the 20,000 roubles promised. Touched by such an act of honesty and faithfulness to a promise escaped in a momentary excitement, the clerk said that he wanted to tranquillize the conscience of Mr. K—— by explaining to him that in obtaining for him the allowance no underhand means were employed, and all was done with complete honesty and fairness. He then told him the small device which was used to make the Emperor change his mind. "We have," he said, "always a great number of things to present for the Emperor's examination. And we know beforehand what he will be pleased to read and what will be unpleasant. Now all depends on the order in which a petition such as yours is placed. If before it we put four or five things which will be unpleasant to the Emperor, arriving at your petition he will be in bad humor and will refuse it. If, on the contrary, we put before it one after another five things that will be agreeable to him to read, on reaching your petition he will be put in good humor and will grant it at once."

Nothing more simple indeed. The fact is perfectly authentic, and would be difficult to invent.

marionettes, whose wires are pulled by unseen courtiers, as unscrupulous as they are irresponsible. To put hope in a Tzar's sudden change of mind is to put hope in the courtiers' turning suddenly honest, and willing to sacrifice their ambitions and interests to the weal of the country.

No; it is sheer madness to hope that the political reorganization of Russia will be due to the initiative of the Tzar himself. If some optimistical hope of this kind were pardonable in the beginning of the former reign, now, after thirty years of experience, we may doubt the very sincerity of such a tardy hopefulness. It is far more likely to be a mere device to conceal pusillanimity of heart; and there is before us the necessity of appealing to other things than the licking of despots' hands. The autocracy will be destroyed there may be no doubt of it, but it will be done by some force. No country had ever to sustain so hard a struggle for its political liberty as Russia of to-day. I do not speak of the unhappy social conditions and the enormous concentration of power in the hands of the Central Government. The worst is, that in other countries the struggle for liberty was over some time ago, when civilization had not yet put at the disposition of Government those material advantages of perfected weapons and surprisingly quick communications—advantages which are all in favor of the Government and which would have rendered utterly impossible or fruitless many a brilliant insurrection, many a splendid campaign of the heroes of liberty.

But there is no obstacle which cannot be overcome by energy, spirit of sacrifice, and courage. The Russian despotism must and will be destroyed; for it is not permitted to the stupid obstinacy of one, nor to the infamous egoism of a few, to arrest the progress and light of a nation of a hundred million souls. We can only wish that the mode of execution of the unavoidable may be the least disastrous, least sanguinary, and most humane. And there is a force which can strongly contribute to this—it is the public opinion of European countries.

It is strange, but quite true; Russian governmental circles are much more impressed by what is said about them in Europe, than by the wailing of all Russia from the White Sea down to the Euxine. There are many instances of this. All Russia heard of the horrors of our political prisons and shuddered. Year after year passed, yet the Government never thought of taking any steps to ameliorate them, nor gave a sign of having it in mind to do it. But some French papers began the agitation in favor of the unfortunate Jessy Helfman, saying that the Government, after having commuted her sentence of death, killed her by slow torture in the fortress; and the Government of the Tzar takes an unheard-of measure: it allows foreign reporters to visit the prisoner in her provisory cell to show that she is alive, and justify itself from the accusations. Thousands of complaints and remonstrances of the most respectable bodies of citizens are not honored by an answer, and do not produce on the wooden ears of the governing class more effect than the humming of an importunate gnat. But some leaders appear in the *Times*, and a correspondent telegraphs to this paper (Dec. 24, 1884), "An extremely sore feeling has lately shown itself here in the highest circles, in which the English Press is accused of having lately taken to basing its opinion about Russia upon the prejudiced writings of disguised and long-expatriated Nihilists."

And to give vent to the soreness of the higher circle's feelings, their writers spread some absurd libels about Nihilists.

Such instances are easy to be multiplied. What is the cause of this surprising and rather incomprehensible sensitiveness? It may be urged that European public opinion has a great influence on the very material condition of the Russian Government, which depends so much on foreign money markets. Yes, it is quite true; but it is not enough. The conduct of the Government in its interior policy is far more ruinous than any loss that may ever be inflicted on Russia from this part. It does not frighten it, however.

The sensitiveness of our *camarille* to the sense of blame from the European press must have some moral cause. There must be something of the very nature of the slave in the cruel master of to-day. His cruelty is prompted by cowardice. Being merciless toward the feeble, he is mean and timorous before the strong he is bound to recognize.

However it may be, the fact is a fact: the Russian governmental caste is extremely zealous to conceal from the public opinion of Europe their misdeeds, and very sensitive to what is said about them abroad.

But if the influence of European public opinion was limited only to the vexing of the governing caste, it would have been of little value indeed to have appealed to it. Its influence may be exercised in a much more effective way.

It is a mistake, even nonsense, I dare say, to affirm that the Russian Government is supported by the mere physical force of its soldiers or the ignorance of its peasants. If all those who are against the existing *régime* in their heart had resolved to show it openly, the autocracy could not stand a single day. However small in numbers, the instructed classes are the moving spirits and the nervous centres of every social body. These classes are in immense majority against the existing *régime*. There is a great deal of difference in the parties that divide it. But, besides those who do not care about anything at all, and a lot of scoundrels who profit out of the existing anarchy in the administration to fill their own pockets, all these classes are against the existing *régime*. And the reader who remembers what we have just exposed will surely find they have sufficient reason to be so. If these classes had resolved to act boldly and energetically, without being afraid of the temporary repression the Government may inflict on them, the autocracy, decrepit and timorous as it is, odious to a great part of its own functionaries, could not stand against their common effort. If the Press—when Russia had still a Press—would have profited by the many moments of governmental panic after the Terrorists' successful attempt, had had the courage to ask energetically as one man for freedom and reform, the Government would have hesitated perhaps before suspending it. If now all the Zemstvos made a general demand for a free constitution, the Government could not disperse them all. Such an act would produce a more disastrous and permanent effect on the Government's funds and finances than a permanent war.

It is on these elements of Russian society that the public opinion of free countries has—as every Russian will tell—a most decisive and beneficial influence. Every energetic manifestation of sympathy for our liberative movement from the part of the people of the leading countries is an event for Russia, and has no less a moral effect on our people than a manifestation of opposition in Russia itself. That is the mode in which European countries can contribute to strengthening the liberal movement of our country.

And no moment is more opportune for this kind of moral intervention than the present one. For the Russian liberative and revolutionary movement is passing now through an important phase of its development. Having begun by terrorism, it is entering in the period which may be called insurrectional. The attempts against the functionary and the Emperor are no longer its means of struggle. Having acquired great adherence in the army, and among the working classes of the capital and other principal towns, it has enlarged its aim and its prospects. It has written on its banner open, though unexpected attack, against the autocracy itself. Insurrections of the kind of that of the Decembrists of

1825, only more exclusively military, are now the chief object of Russian revolutionists. This is not an easy task, nor to be prepared from one fortnight to another, as is an attempt against the person of an Emperor. It is a long and hard work, and many a noble victim may fall; many unsuccessful attempts may precede the definitive victory of Russian liberty. The quickness of their success depends entirely on the degree of preparation of the bulk of Russian society, of the grade of its energy in the moment of the starting of such bold attempts.

Whether the initiative of the attack on the autocracy will belong to the revolutionists, or the more moderate part of Russian society will outstrip them by pacific but energetic demonstrations, which we revolutionists will be the first to applaud—in both cases the public opinion of European countries is of great, inestimable value. And that is the reason why we appeal to it.

Addressing ourselves now to the English people, we have not the slightest doubt that such an appeal will find echo in many thousands of English hearts. There was never a striving of any country for its liberty which found not the warmest support in England: from those of the small tribes of Candiots, to those of Hungarian, Polish, and Italian patriots. Our cause appeals no less to every generous being. Our sufferings are something unheard-of in the bloody annals of despotism. It is not a political party, I repeat, it is a whole nation of a hundred millions that is stifled, a nation, which by the intelligence, aptness to instruction, and kind-heartedness of its masses; by the good and unselfish disposition of its upper classes and generous ardor of the young generations, presents the best guarantees of a lasting progress and happy future.

Humanity is the chief, the main claim of our cause for sympathy and support. But it is not the sole one.

It was a question of pure humanity when the Bulgarian

horrors were spoken of. It was a question of humanity when Mr. Gladstone interrupted diplomatic communication with the King of Naples, nicknamed Re Bomba, for the atrocity committed against the Carbonari. With Russia it is no longer a question of humanity only, but of general safety and common interest. However badly administered, however ruined, it is too enormous a body not to endanger by its presence other political bodies which surround. It has an army of a million soldiers, who although dying from hunger and half clad, by its courage on the field, is not inferior to any other in the world. Such an enormous force left to the uncontrolled caprice of a despot or a courtier is surely a great inconvenience for human intercourse. To have such a State for a neighbor is nearly as unpleasant as to sit by an unfettered madman at an evening party. Nobody can answer for what he will do the very next moment. Now, when I am writing, an absurd, useless, bloody Afghan war is perhaps at hand. No Russian parliament would have answered the proposition otherwise than with laughter. It is a well-known device of despots to get rid of a burning internal question. If it pass over now who may answer for to-morrow, when the need of such a diversion may be more stringent, or the ambition of some bloodthirsty soldier more prevailing?

Only the destruction of Russian autocracy will keep Russia in certainty of peace, and yet rid Europe from the external danger. That is a consideration on which it is superfluous to insist.

I allow myself to point out another consideration which has not so great an interest for Englishmen, but which they will allow me to mention in a few words:

In 1547 the Tzar, John IV., sent to Germania, a Saxonian of the name Shlitte, ordering him to obtain for the Moscow service artisans and scholars of every kind. Shlitte did as bidden, and after some time he had more than a hundred people with whom he proposed to return to Moscovia. But the magister of the Livonian order, which then occupied the Baltic province, remonstrated with the Emperor, Charles V., of the danger that might come to Livonia and neighboring German states if the Moscovite Empire passed from barbarity to culture. The German Emperor listened to the remonstrance, and the Livonian magister was allowed to stop Shlitte's hundred men at Lubeck, and never to allow a single scholar or artisan to cross the Moscow frontier.

What in the sixteenth century the Livonian did, the German Chancellor is doing now. Russia would be too strong for him, once free. And the Iron Prince is doing his best to prevent the freedom to cross the Russian frontier. He does not want to appeal to any foreign power; to prevent such an annoyance, he has found the best ally in Count Tolstoi and his consorts. These work for their own as well as for his interest. What the triumvirs would fail perhaps to maintain by their own exertion, they do with the great personal influence and authority of the German Chancellor over the Tzar. The service is mutual. Tolstoi and company are masters of the State's cash-box. Bismarck is the master in Europe. Russia of to-day is nothing more than a Caliban, a savage and deformed slave, whom the Prussian Prospero with the three hairs on his head may use for every base work he likes. And with such a slave on his chain, what may this Prospero not venture? As long as Russia remains what it is he will be the dictator and arbiter of Europe, and so long Prussian militarism, which is the scourge of all civilized Europe, will remain unchecked.

All who are for progress, for peace and humanity, may unite in a moral crusade against Russian despotism.

The Twelfth Thousand now ready.

THE RUSSIANS
AT THE
GATES OF HERAT.

By CHARLES MARVIN,
Principal authority of the English press on the Central Asia Dispute.

Paper, 50 Cents. - - Cloth, $1.00.

ILLUSTRATED WITH PORTRAITS AND MAPS.

"A perfect mine of information."—*N. Y. Times.*

"The most important contribution to a complete understanding of the present quarrel between England and Russia."—*N. Y. Tribune.*

"Precisely meets the public want. The sale ought to reach 100,000 at least."—*N. Y. Journal of Commerce.*

"It is an admirable summary; as an introduction and key to the daily despatches it is invaluable."—*N. Y. Evening Post.*

"Mr. Marvin is the best informed man in England on the subject. . . . We commend his book."—*Washington Army and Navy Register.*

"The book abounds in vivid descriptions and is invaluable at this time."—*Philadelphia Bulletin.*

"Well written, highly impartial, and the best summary of the questions now in issue. It is heartily recommended to everybody who cares to understand the Herat trouble."—*Boston Beacon.*

"Absolutely necessary to an intelligent comprehension of the impending struggle, no work has been put forth containing so much accurate and trustworthy information as this."—*Newark Advertiser.*

For sale by all booksellers, or sent, post-paid, by the publishers.

CHARLES SCRIBNER'S SONS,
743 and 745 Broadway, New York.

An Inner History of Russian Nihilism.

UNDERGROUND RUSSIA

REVOLUTIONARY PROFILES AND SKETCHES FROM LIFE.
By STEPNIAK, formerly Editor of *Zemlia i Voila*
(Land and Liberty). With a Preface by
PETER LAVROFF.

1 *Volume, 12mo,* - - *$1.25.*

The very great importance of this remarkable book has now come to be generally recognized. Throughout all Western Europe it has created a most profound impression, and in Russia it marks an epoch in the history of Nihilism. How serious and significant is its influence, may be gathered from an extract taken from a long letter devoted to an account of the book, written by the St. Petersburg correspondent of the New York *Sun:*

"At this moment the Russian educated classes have forgotten all about their newly crowned autocrat and his manifesto. Their attention is so much concentrated on underground Russia for the time being, it seems as though there were no overground Russia. This has been brought about by a wonderful book, UNDERGROUND RUSSIA, by a well-known Nihilist journalist, Stepniak (son of the Steppes). The book first appeared in Italian, and on that account the Czar's ministers were greatly incensed against the Italian government. We hear that an English edition of the work has appeared in London and New York, and that the book is about to be put into French and German. The number of Russians who know Italian or English is limited, so the Italian book of the Russian author has been translated into Russian. Thousands of manuscript copies of UNDERGROUND RUSSIA are now circulated here from hand to hand, far and wide, and by its attempts to seize the book the government has made the forbidden fruit all the sweeter. In short, UNDERGROUND RUSSIA is the all-absorbing topic of the day."

For sale by all book-sellers, or sent, post-paid, by the publishers,

CHARLES SCRIBNER'S SONS,
743 & 745 Broadway, New-York.

TURKISH LIFE IN WAR TIME.

By HENRY O. DWIGHT.

One Volume, 12mo, ... $1.50.

Mr. Dwight's familiarity with the languages and manners of the capital, and his numerous sources of information from almost all parts of Turkey, have enabled him to give a most faithful account of the transactions of the war as seen from a Turkish point of view, and also incidentally to put his reader in possession of much information respecting the motley races under Turkish rule.

"The work can be especially commended as a graphic, and clear, and never-wearying story."—*N. Y. Commercial Advertiser.*

"The book fills a place in the literature relating to its subject which, so far as we can judge, would be empty without it."—*Boston Congregationalist.*

"It is even more charming than a good book of travel; for the author pictures scenes with which he is familiar, and knows the full value of every incident he records."—*Cincinnati Christian Standard.*

"It abounds in stirring incident of most exciting times, graphic descriptions of thrilling scenes, and information of importance to statesmen and of great interest to the general reader."—*N. Y. Observer.*

"A better idea of the Turkish character may be gained through the many anecdotes and descriptions of scenes given by the writer, than by the study of any previous history with which we are acquainted."—*Baptist Weekly.*

"No book yet published covers precisely the same ground, or handles the subject in precisely the same way. We find ourselves, in its perusal, lending very much the sort of attention to it that we should to the narrative of a friend who had passed through the scenes which Mr. Dwight's letters portray."—*Syracuse Herald.*

"This book is the most vivid and faithful sketch of Turkish character that we have ever seen. . . . It is mainly a series of interesting notes and sketches, giving those little details of life and thought from day to day, in a time of great excitement, which are so essential in order to gain an accurate knowledge of any people."—*The Nation.*

"The book has more than a transient value. It is a contribution to history. The author has not only descriptive talent, but a gift for discerning the meaning of the political and military manœuvres, which encompassed Constantinople. While sufficiently interesting to the general reader, the book is full of information for the student of manners and of political affairs."—*N. Y. Christian Advocate.*

"It is to us admirable in every sense. It is judicious, discriminating, comprehensive, impartial, free from animosity in its thorough and candid criticisms; eminently clear, vigorous, and animated in expression; tells us just what we wish to know, and wastes no time in doing it. . . . The book is one to which the reader can surrender himself and simply enjoy."—*N. Y. Christian Intelligencer.*

"'Turkish Life in War Time,' does not pretend to be a history of the Russian war, but it is a more valuable work than any so-called history we have seen. It is a record, the almost daily record, of a very keen observer, who set down the events that he saw, and who, from acquaintance with the Orient, understood the bearing of those events. It has all the interest of a personal narrative, and all the weight that we accord to an honest and well-informed observer. It is to such records of eye-witnesses as these that future historians must resort."—*Hartford Courant.*

*** *For sale by all booksellers, or sent, post-paid, upon receipt of price, by*

CHARLES SCRIBNER'S SONS, PUBLISHERS,

743 AND 745 BROADWAY, NEW YORK

Now in process of publication, uniform with EPOCHS OF MODERN HISTORY, *each volume in 12mo size, and complete in itself.*

Epochs of Ancient History.

A series of Books narrating the HISTORY OF GREECE AND ROME, and of their relations to other Countries at Successive Epochs. Edited by the Rev. G. W. COX, M. A., Author of the "Aryan Mythology," "A History of Greece," etc., and jointly by CHARLES SANKEY, M. A., late Scholar of Queen's College, Oxford.

Volumes already issued in the "Epochs of Ancient History." Each one volume 12mo, cloth, $1.00.

The GREEKS and the PERSIANS. By the Rev. G. W. Cox, M. A., late Scholar of Trinity College, Oxford: Joint Editor of the Series. With four colored Maps.

The EARLY ROMAN EMPIRE. From the Assassination of Julius Cæsar to the Assassination of Domitian. By the Rev. W. WOLFE CAPES, M.A., Reader of Ancient History in the University of Oxford. With two colored maps.

The ATHENIAN EMPIRE from the FLIGHT of XERXES to the FALL of ATHENS. By the Rev. G. W. Cox, M. A., late Scholar of Trinity College, Oxford: Joint Editor of the Series. With five Maps.

The ROMAN TRIUMVIRATES. By the Very Rev. CHARLES MERIVALE, D. D., Dean of Ely.

EARLY ROME, to its Capture by the Gauls. By WILHELM IHNE, Author of "History of Rome." With Map.

THE AGE OF THE ANTONINES. By the Rev. W. WOLFE CAPES, M. A., Reader of Ancient History in the University at Oxford.

The GRACCHI, MARIUS, and SULLA. By A. H. BEESLY. With Maps.

THE RISE OF THE MACEDONIAN EMPIRE. By A. M. CURTEIS, M. A. 1 vol., 16mo, with maps and plans.

TROY—Its Legend, History, and Literature, with a sketch of the Topography of the Troad. By S. G. W. BENJAMIN, 1 vol. 16mo. With a map.

ROME AND CARTHAGE. By R. BOSWORTH SMITH, M.A.

The above 10 volumes in Roxburg Style. Sold only in sets. Price, per set, $10.00.

₊ *The above books for sale by all booksellers, or will be sent, post or express charges paid, upon receipt of the price by the Publishers,*

CHARLES SCRIBNER'S SONS,
743 AND 745 BROADWAY, NEW YORK.

"These volumes contain the ripe results of the studies of men who are authorities in their respective fields."—THE NATION.

Epochs of Modern History.

Each 1 vol. 16mo., with Outline Maps. Price per volume, in cloth, $1.00.
EACH VOLUME COMPLETE IN ITSELF AND SOLD SEPARATELY.

EDITED BY EDWARD E. MORRIS, M.A.

The ERA of the PROTESTANT REVOLUTION. By F. SEEBOHM, Author of "The Oxford Reformers—Colet, Erasmus, More."

The CRUSADES. By the Rev. G.W.Cox, M.A., Author of the "History of Greece."

The THIRTY YEARS' WAR, 1618—1648. By SAMUEL RAWSON GARDINER.

The HOUSES of LANCASTER and YORK; with the CONQUEST and LOSS of FRANCE. By JAMES GAIRDNER, of the Public Record Office.

The FRENCH REVOLUTION and FIRST EMPIRE; an Historical Sketch. By WM. O'CONNOR MORRIS, with an Appendix by Hon. ANDREW D. WHITE.

The AGE OF ELIZABETH. By the Rev. M. Creighton, M.A.

The PURITAN REVOLUTION. By J. LANGTON SANFORD.

The FALL of the STUARTS; and WESTERN EUROPE from 1678 to 1697. By the Rev. EDWARD HALE, M.A., Assist. Master at Eton.

The EARLY PLANTAGENETS and their relation to the HISTORY of EUROPE; the foundation and growth of CONSTITUTIONAL GOVERNMENT. By the Rev. WM. STUBBS, M.A., etc., Professor of Modern History in the University of Oxford.

The BEGINNING of the MIDDLE AGES; CHARLES the GREAT and ALFRED; the HISTORY of ENGLAND in its connection with that of EUROPE in the NINTH CENTURY. By the Very Rev. R. W. CHURCH, M.A.

The AGE of ANNE. By EDWARD E. MORRIS, M.A., Editor of the Series.

The NORMANS IN EUROPE. By the Rev. A. H. JOHNSON, M.A.

EDWARD III. By the Rev. W. WARBURTON, M.A.

FREDERICK the GREAT and the SEVEN YEARS' WAR. By F. W. LONGMAN, of Ballic College, Oxford.

The EPOCH of REFORM, 1830 to 1850. By JUSTIN McCARTHY.

The above 15 volumes in Roxburg Style, Leather Labels and Gilt Top. Put up in a handsome Box. Sold only in Sets. Price, per set, $15.00.

*** *The above books for sale by all booksellers, or will be sent, post or express charges paid, upon receipt of the price by the publishers,*

CHARLES SCRIBNER'S SONS,
743 AND 745 BROADWAY, NEW YORK.

A New Edition, Library Style.

The History of Rome,

FROM THE EARLIEST TIME TO THE PERIOD OF ITS DECLINE.

By Dr. THEODOR MOMMSEN.

Translated, with the author's sanction and additions, by the Rev. W. P. DICKSON, Regius Professor of Biblical Criticism in the University of Glasgow, late Classical Examiner of the University of St. Andrews. With an introduction by Dr. LEONHARD SCHMITZ, and a copious Index of the whole four volumes, prepared especially for this edition.

REPRINTED FROM THE REVISED LONDON EDITION.

Four Volumes, crown 8vo, gilt top.   Price per Set, $8.00.

DR. MOMMSEN has long been known and appreciated through his researches into the languages, laws, and institutions of Ancient Rome and Italy, as the most thoroughly versed scholar now living in these departments of historical investigation. To a wonderfully exact and exhaustive knowledge of these subjects, he unites great powers of generalization, a vigorous, spirited, and exceedingly graphic style and keen analytical powers, which give this history a degree of interest and a permanent value possessed by no other record of the decline and fall of the Roman Commonwealth. "Dr. Mommsen's work," as Dr. Schmitz remarks in the introduction, "though the production of a man of most profound and extensive learning and knowledge of the world, is not as much designed for the professional scholar as for intelligent readers of all classes who take an interest in the history of by-gone ages, and are inclined there to seek information that may guide them safely through the perplexing mazes of modern history."

CRITICAL NOTICES.

"A work of the very highest merit; its learning is exact and profound; its narrative full of genius and skill; its descriptions of men are admirably vivid. We wish to place on record our opinion that Dr. Mommsen's is by far the best history of the Decline and Fall of the Roman Commonwealth." — *London Times.*

"This is the best history of the Roman Republic, taking the work on the whole — the author's complete mastery of his subject, the variety of his gifts and acquirements, his graphic power in the delineation of national and individual character, and the vivid interest which he inspires in every portion of his book. He is without an equal in his own sphere." — *Edinburgh Review.*

CHARLES SCRIBNER'S SONS, PUBLISHERS,

743 AND 745 BROADWAY, NEW YORK.

A New Edition, Library Style.

The History of Greece.

By Prof. Dr. ERNST CURTIUS.

Translated by ADOLPHUS WILLIAM WARD, M. A., Fellow of St. Peter's College, Cambridge, Prof. of History in Owen's College, Manchester.

UNIFORM WITH MOMMSEN'S HISTORY OF ROME.

Five volumes, crown 8vo, gilt top.　　　　　　　Price per set, $10.00.

Curtius's *History of Greece* is similar in plan and purpose to Mommsen's *History of Rome*, with which it deserves to rank in every respect as one of the great masterpieces of historical literature. Avoiding the minute details which overburden other similar works, it groups together in a very picturesque manner all the important events in the history of this kingdom, which has exercised such a wonderful influence upon the world's civilization. The narrative of Prof. Curtius's work is flowing and animated, and the generalizations, although bold, are philosophical and sound.

CRITICAL NOTICES.

"Professor Curtius's eminent scholarship is a sufficient guarantee for the trustworthiness of his history, while the skill with which he groups his facts, and his effective mode of narrating them, combine to render it no less readable than sound. Prof. Curtius everywhere maintains the true dignity and impartiality of history, and it is evident his sympathies are on the side of justice, humanity, and progress." — *London Athenæum.*

"We cannot express our opinion of Dr. Curtius's book better than by saying that it may be fitly ranked with Theodor Mommsen's great work." — *London Spectator.*

"As an introduction to the study of Grecian history, no previous work is comparable to the present for vivacity and picturesque beauty, while in sound learning and accuracy of statement it is not inferior to the elaborate productions which enrich the literature of the age." — *N. Y. Daily Tribune.*

"The History of Greece is treated by Dr. Curtius so broadly and freely in the spirit of the nineteenth century, that it becomes in his hands one of the worthiest and most instructive branches of study for all who desire something more than a knowledge of isolated facts for their education. This translation ought to become a regular part of the accepted course of reading for young men at college, and for all who are in training for the free political life of our country." — *N. Y. Evening Post.*

CHARLES SCRIBNER'S SONS, PUBLISHERS,

743 AND 745 BROADWAY, NEW YORK.

"A work of strange power and poetry."—N. Y. WORLD

THE COSSACKS.

TRANSLATED BY
EUGENE SCHUYLER, Ph.D.,
From the Russian of Count Tolstoy.

1 vol., small 12mo, cloth, ... $1.25

CRITICAL NOTICES.

"The translation is excellent, although the Russian flavor still remains. Yet this rather heightens than mars the fascination of the book."
—*Baltimore Gazette.*

"A story of high merit and well-sustained interest."—*Phila. Bulletin.*

"The Cossacks is a novel likely to please a much wider circle of readers in this country than anything that the more famous novelist (Turguénief) has done, than any other Russian novel which has been translated, indeed, including even the stories of Pushkin."
—*N. Y. Evening Post.*

"The characters are all sketched by a master hand, and the story, without being artistically woven, is full of living interest and warmth, and we thank Mr. Schuyler for breaking up this new ground, and hope he will follow up the lead, for he has whet our appetites for more of this brilliant writer's work."—*New York Herald.*

"Its interest, besides the interest of the qualities we have mentioned, resides in its broad and firm, yet delicate and subtle portraiture; and apart from its novel characteristics, it should be welcome for the acquaintance it enables one to make of the different personages it so admirably sketches."
—*New York World.*

"The story is one that American readers will enjoy, not only because it is in many respects a masterpiece of literary work, but also because it takes them into scenes entirely new to them, and among characters as strange as the scenes in which they are placed."—*New Haven Palladium.*

*** *The above book for sale by all booksellers, or will be sent, post or express charges paid, upon receipt of the price by the publishers,*

CHARLES SCRIBNER'S SONS,
743 AND 745 BROADWAY, NEW YORK.

Messrs. CHARLES SCRIBNER'S SONS
publish, under the general title of

THE CAMPAIGNS OF THE CIVIL WAR,

A Series of volumes, contributed by a number of leading actors in and students of the great conflict of 1861-'65, with a view to bringing together, for the first time, a full and authoritative military history of the suppression of the Rebellion.

The final and exhaustive form of this great narrative, in which every doubt shall be settled and every detail covered, may be a possibility only of the future. But it is a matter for surprise that twenty years after the beginning of the Rebellion, and when a whole generation has grown up needing such knowledge, there is no authority which is at the same time of the highest rank, intelligible and trustworthy, and to which a reader can turn for any general view of the field.

The many reports, regimental histories, memoirs, and other materials of value for special passages, require, for their intelligent reading, an ability to combine and proportion them which the ordinary reader does not possess. There have been no attempts at general histories which have supplied this satisfactorily to any large part of the public. Undoubtedly there has been no such narrative as would be especially welcome to men of the new generation, and would be valued by a very great class of readers;—and there has seemed to be great danger that the time would be allowed to pass when it would be possible to give to such a work the vividness and accuracy that come from personal recollection. These facts led to the conception of the present work.

From every department of the Government, from the officers of the army, and from a great number of custodians of records and special information everywhere, both authors and publishers have received every aid that could be asked in this undertaking; and in announcing the issue of the work the publishers take this occasion to convey the thanks which the authors have had individual opportunities to express elsewhere.

The volumes are duodecimos of about 250 pages each, illustrated by maps and plans prepared under the direction of the authors.

The price of each volume is $1.00.

The following volumes are now ready:

I.—The Outbreak of Rebellion. By JOHN G. NICOLAY, Esq., Private Secretary to President Lincoln; late Consul-General to France, etc.

A preliminary volume, describing the opening of the war, and covering the period from the election of Lincoln to the end of the first battle of Bull Run.

II.—*From Fort Henry to Corinth.* By the Hon. M. F. FORCE, Justice of the Superior Court, Cincinnati; late Brigadier-General and Bvt. Maj. Gen'l, U.S.V., commanding First Division, 17th Corps: in 1862, Lieut. Colonel of the 20th Ohio, commanding the regiment at Shiloh; Treasurer of the Society of the Army of the Tennessee.

The narrative of events in the West from the Summer of 1861 to May, 1862; covering the capture of Fts. Henry and Donelson, the Battle of Shiloh, etc., etc.

III.—*The Peninsula.* By ALEXANDER S. WEBB, LL.D., President of the College of the City of New York; Assistant Chief of Artillery, Army of the Potomac, 1861-'62; Inspector General Fifth Army Corps; General commanding 2d Div., 2d Corps; Major General Assigned, and Chief of Staff, Army of the Potomac.

The history of McClellan's Peninsula Campaign, from his appointment to the end of the Seven Days' Fight.

IV.—*The Army under Pope.* By JOHN C. ROPES, Esq., of the Military Historical Society of Massachusetts, the Massachusetts Historical Society, etc.

From the appointment of Pope to command the Army of Virginia, to the appointment of McClellan to the general command in September, 1862

V.—*The Antietam and Fredericksburg.* By FRANCIS WINTHROP PALFREY, Bvt. Brigadier Gen'l, U.S.V., and formerly Colonel 20th Mass. Infantry; Lieut. Col of the 20th Massachusetts at the Battle of the Antietam; Member of the Military Historical Society of Massachusetts, of the Massachusetts Historical Society, etc.

From the appointment of McClellan to the general command, September, 1862, to the end of the battle of Fredericksburg.

VI.—*Chancellorsville and Gettysburg.* By ABNER DOUBLEDAY, Bvt. Maj. Gen'l, U.S.A., and Maj. Gen'l, U.S.V.; commanding the First Corps at Gettysburg, etc.

From the appointment of Hooker, through the campaigns of Chancellorsville and Gettysburg, to the retreat of Lee after the latter battle.

VII.—*The Army of the Cumberland.* By HENRY M. CIST, Brevet Brig. Gen'l U.S.V.; A.A.G. on the staff of Major Gen'l Rosecrans, and afterwards on that of Major Gen'l Thomas; Corresponding Secretary of the Society of the Army of the Cumberland.

From the formation of the Army of the Cumberland to the end of the battles at Chattanooga, November, 1863.

VIII.—The Mississippi. By Francis Vinton Greene, Lieut. of Engineers, U. S. Army; late Military Attaché to the U. S. Legation in St. Petersburg; Author of "The Russian Army and its Campaigns in Turkey in 1877-78," and of "Army Life in Russia."

An account of the operations—especially at Vicksburg and Port Hudson—by which the Mississippi River and its shores were restored to the control of the Union.

IX.—Atlanta. By the Hon. Jacob D. Cox, Ex-Governor of Ohio; late Secretary of the Interior of the United States; Major General U. S. V., commanding Twenty-third Corps during the campaigns of Atlanta and the Carolinas, etc., etc.

From Sherman's first advance into Georgia in May, 1864, to the beginning of the March to the Sea.

X.—The March to the Sea—Franklin and Nashville. By the Hon. Jacob D. Cox.

From the beginning of the March to the Sea to the surrender of Johnston—including also the operations of Thomas in Tennessee.

XI.—The Shenandoah Valley in 1864. The Campaign of Sheridan. By George E. Pond, Esq., Associate Editor of the *Army and Navy Journal*.

XII.—The Virginia Campaign of '64 and '65. The Army of the Potomac and the Army of the James. By Andrew A. Humphreys, Brigadier General and Bvt. Major General, U. S. A.; late Chief of Engineers; Chief of Staff, Army of the Potomac, 1863-64; commanding Second Corps, 1864-'65, etc., etc.

Statistical Record of the Armies of the United States. By Frederick Phisterer, late Captain U. S. A.

This Record includes the figures of the quotas and men actually furnished by all States; a list of all organizations mustered into the U. S. service; the strength of the army at various periods; its organization in armies, corps, etc.; the divisions of the country into departments, etc.; chronological list of all engagements, with the losses in each; tabulated statements of all losses in the war, with the causes of death, etc.; full lists of all general officers, and an immense amount of other valuable statistical matter relating to the War.

The complete Set, thirteen volumes, in a box. Price, $12.50
Single volumes, ... 1.00

*** *The above books for sale by all booksellers, or will be sent, post-paid, upon receipt of price, by*

CHARLES SCRIBNER'S SONS, Publishers,

743 and 745 Broadway, New York.

NOW COMPLETE.

In three volumes, 12mo, with Maps and Plans.

THE
Navy in the Civil War

THE WORK OF THE NAVY in the suppression of the Rebellion was certainly not less remarkable than that of the Army. The same forces which developed from our volunteers some of the finest bodies of soldiers in military history, were shown quite as wonderfully in the creation of a Navy, which was to cope for the first time with the problems of modern warfare.

The facts that the Civil War was the first great conflict in which steam was the motive power of ships; that it was marked by the introduction of the ironclad; and that it saw, for the first time, the attempt to blockade such a vast length of hostile coast—will make it an epoch for the techinal student everywhere.

But while the Army has been fortunate in the number and character of those who have contributed to its written history, the Navy has been comparatively without annalists. During a recent course of publications on the military operations of the war, the publishers were in constant receipt of letters pointing out this fact, and expressing the wish that a complete naval history of the four years might be written by competent hands. An effort made in this direction resulted in the cordial adoption and carrying out of plans by which Messrs. CHARLES SCRIBNER'S SONS are enabled to announce the completion of a work of the highest authority and interest, giving the whole narrative of Naval Operations from 1861 to 1865.

I. THE BLOCKADE AND THE CRUISERS.—By Professor J. RUSSELL SOLEY, U. S. Navy.

II. THE ATLANTIC COAST.—By Rear-Admiral DANIEL AMMEN, U. S. Navy.

III. THE GULF AND INLAND WATERS.—By Commander A. T. MAHAN, U. S. Navy.

Uniform with "The Campaigns of the Civil War," with maps and diagrams prepared under the direction of the Authors.

Price per Volume, $1.00.

CHARLES SCRIBNER'S SONS, Publishers,
743 & 745 Broadway, New York.

THE
Navy in the Civil War

I.—THE BLOCKADE AND THE CRUISERS.
By Professor J. RUSSELL SOLEY, U. S. Navy.

"The book is well arranged, written clearly, without technical terms, and shows great familiarity with the subject. It is marked by thoroughness of preparation, sound judgment, and admirable impartiality. It is a promising beginning of the projected series; and if the other volumes prove worthy of this, they will make a valuable addition to the Army series, which has proved so useful and popular."—*The Nation*.

II.—THE ATLANTIC COAST.
By Real-Admiral DANIEL AMMEN, U. S. Navy.

Admiral Ammen's history of the naval operations on the Atlantic coast, from 1861 to the close of the war, describes the active work of the navy in attacking the defensive strongholds of the Confederacy from Hampton Roads to Florida Keys. It includes a full account of the long siege of Charleston, and the scarcely less arduous operations against Fort Fisher, the capture of Hatteras Inlet, Roanoke Island and Newbern, and other minor movements along the coast.

III.—THE GULF AND INLAND WATERS.
By Commander A. T. MAHAN, U. S. Navy.

The achievements of the Naval force on the Mississippi and its tributaries, and on the Gulf and the Red River, either independently or in co-operation with the Army, form one of the most thrilling chapters in the history of the Civil War. The exploits of Farragut, Foote and Porter, with their gallant crews and improvised vessels, teem with acts of daring, marvelous escapes, and terrific encounters. Commander Mahan has done full justice to this side of his narrative, but he has given at the same time a record of this part of the war that has greater claims to historic value than any which have preceded it.

Each One Volume, 12mo, with Maps and Plans.

Price per Volume, $1.00.

CHARLES SCRIBNER'S SONS, Publishers,
743 & 745 Broadway, New York.

AUTHORIZED AMERICAN EDITIONS.

Froude's Historical Works.

THE HISTORY OF ENGLAND,

From the Fall of Woolsey to the Death of Elizabeth.

THE COMPLETE WORK IN TWELVE VOLUMES.

By JAMES ANTHONY FROUDE, M. A.

MR. FROUDE is a pictorial historian, and his skill in description and fullness of knowledge make his work abound in scenes and passages that are almost new to the general reader. We close his pages with unfeigned regret, and we bid him good speed on his noble mission of exploring the sources of English history in one of its most remarkable periods. — *British Quarterly Review.*

THE NEW LIBRARY EDITION.

Extra cloth, gilt top, and uniform in general style with the re-issue of Mommsen's Rome and Curtius's Greece. *Complete* in 12 vols. 12mo, in a box. Sold only in sets. Price per set, $18.00.

NOTE. *The old Library, Chelsea, and Popular Editions will be discontinued. A few sets and single volumes can still be supplied.*

SHORT STUDIES ON GREAT SUBJECTS.

THE NEW LIBRARY EDITION. Three vols. 12mo. Uniform in General Style with the New Library Edition of the History of England. Per vol............ $1.50

THE ENGLISH IN IRELAND

During the Eighteenth Century.

Three vols. 12mo. New Library Edition. Per vol....... $1.50

*** *The above books for sale by all booksellers, or will be sent, post or express charges paid, upon receipt of the price by the Publishers,*

CHARLES SCRIBNER'S SONS,
743 AND 745 BROADWAY, NEW YORK.

STERLING BIOGRAPHIES.

Peter the Great, Emperor of Russia. A study of Historical Biography. By EUGENE SCHUYLER, Ph.D., LL.D. 2 vols., 8vo. With more than 200 Superb Illustrations. $10.00.

"A work which reflects upon the author very great credit as a painstaking and conscientious student, one who has toiled for the benefit of English readers in dark places to them inaccessible, and has supplied information which they may fairly consider trustworthy, even if they are, to a certain extent, prejudiced against some of the sources from which it is derived."—*London Athenæum.*

Life of Lord Lawrence. By R. BOSWORTH SMITH, M.A., Late Fellow of Trinity College, Assistant Master at Harrow School. With Maps and Portraits. 2 vols., 8vo, $5.00.

"We know of no work on India to which the reader can refer with so great certainty for full and dispassionate information relative to the government of the country, the characteristics of its people, and the faithful events of the forty eventful years of Lord Lawrence's Indian career."—*Harper's Magazine.*

Memoirs of Prince Metternich. Edited by Prince Richard Metternich, with portrait and fac-similes. 8vo. Vols. I and II (1773-1815), $5.00. Vols. III and IV (1815-1829), $5.00. Vol. V (1830-1835), $2.50.

The Correspondence and Diaries of John Wilson Croker, Secretary to the Admiralty from 1809-1830, etc., etc. Edited by LOUIS J. JENNINGS. With portrait. 2 vols., 8vo, $5.00.

"Since the Grenville Memoirs saw the light no documents have been published so rich in the material for the political history of England during the first half of the century."—*N. Y. Sun.*

"Altogether these volumes must be regarded as among the most valuable and readable contributions which have yet been made towards an elucidation of the political history of this country during the first fifty years of the present century."—*Saturday Review.*

Our Chancellor: Sketches for a Historical Picture. By MORITZ BUSCH. 1 vol., crown 8vo, $2.50.

In uniform style.

Bismarck in the Franco-German War, 1870-71. 1 vol., crown 8vo., $2.50.

Fifty Years' Observation of Men and Events, Civil and Military. By E. D. KEYES, Brevet Brig.-Gen. U.S.A., and late Major-Gen. U.S.V. 1 vol., 12mo, $1.50.

"Among the very best of the memories of America's public men."—*Philadelphia Bulletin.*

Cæsar. A Sketch. By JAMES ANTHONY FROUDE, M.A. 1 vol., 12mo, gilt top, $1.50.

For sale by all book-sellers, or sent, post-paid, by the publishers,

CHARLES SCRIBNER'S SONS,

743 & 745 Broadway, New-York.

ARMY LIFE IN RUSSIA.

By F. V. GREENE,
LIEUTENANT OF ENGINEERS, UNITED STATES ARMY,
Late Military Attaché to the U. S. Legation in St. Petersburg, and author of "The Russian Army and its Campaigns in Turkey in 1877–78."

One Volume, 12mo, ... $1.50.

Lieutenant Greene's opportunities for general as well as technical observation while with the Russian army in Turkey were such as have perhaps never fallen to any other student of the war. The story of this personal experience is embodied in this volume, which contains most vigorous and vivid descriptions of battle scenes, in the chapters on the Shipka Pass, Plevna, and in the very strong and excellent chapter on the winter campaign across the Balkans with Gourko. The chapters on the Tsar and the Russian generals, and the sections devoted to the Russian soldier, to St. Petersburg, and the army life of the Russian at home, are of absorbing interest.

"His sketches are excellently well done, graphic, evidently not exaggerated, and very readable. It is a book that will be read with pleasure, and one that contains a great deal of information."—*Hartford Courant.*

"This volume is in every way an admirable picture of army life in Russia. It is clear, concise, discriminating, and often very picturesque. The author, besides possessing an excellent style, is extremely modest, and there are very few books of travel in which the first person is kept so absolutely in the background."—*International Review.*

"Lieutenant Greene writes in a soldierly way, unaffected, straightforward, and graphic, and, though he has a keen eye for the picturesque, never sacrifices to rhetoric the absolute truthfulness so eminently to be desired in a narrative of this sort.—*New York World.*

"He was with the Russian army throughout the campaign, enjoying perfect freedom of movement, having every opportunity to visit the points of greatest activity, and to see the operations of greatest moment, in company with the officers who conducted them. His book is, therefore, for all the purposes of ordinary readers, a complete and satisfactory history of the war, founded upon intimate personal knowledge of its events, and of its spirit. It is a work of the rarest interest and of unusual merit."—*New York Evening Post.*

"It is most fortunate for the reputation of our country and our army that we had such an officer to send to the far-away land of Turkey in Europe, and most creditable to our War Department that it sent such a man. His book deseves to be universally read, and we are sure that no person whom these lines may lead to purchase it will fail to rejoice that they have been written."—*The Nation.*

⁎⁎⁎ For sale by all booksellers, or sent, post-paid, upon receipt of price, by

CHARLES SCRIBNER'S SONS, PUBLISHERS,
743 AND 745 BROADWAY, NEW YORK.

"A GREAT SUCCESS."—Pall Mall Gazette.

A NEW AND CHEAPER EDITION.
MR. EUGENE SCHUYLER'S
TURKISTAN:

Notes of a Journey in 1873, in the Russian Province of
Turkistan, the Khanates of Khokan and Bukhara,
and Provinces of Kuldja.

By EUGENE SCHUYLER, Ph.D.,
Formerly Secretary of the American Legation at St. Petersburg, now Consul-General
at Constantinople.

OPINIONS OF THE PRESS.
From the London Times.

"Mr. Schuyler will be ranked among the most accomplished of living travelers. Many parts of his book will be found of interest, even by the most exacting of general readers; and, as a whole, it is incomparably the most valuable record of Central Asia which has been published in this country."

From the N. Y. Evening Post.

"The author's chief aim appears to have been to do all that he says he tried to do, and to do greatly more beside—namely, to study everything there was to study in the countries which he visited, and to tell the world all about it in a most interesting way. He is, indeed, a model traveler, and he has written a model book of travels, in which every line is interesting, and from which nothing that any reader can want to hear about has been excluded."

Mr. Gladstone in the "Contemporary Review."

"One of the most solid and painstaking works which have been published among us in recent years."

From the New York Times.

"Its descriptions of the country and of the people living in it are always interesting and frequently amusing; but it is easy to see that they have been written by one who is not only so thoroughly cosmopolitan as to know intuitively what is worth telling and what had better be omitted, but who is, also, so practiced a writer as to understand precisely how to set forth what he has to say in the most effective manner."

From the Atlantic Monthly.

"Undoubtedly the most thoroughly brilliant and entertaining work on Turkistan which has yet been given to the English-speaking world."

From the Independent.

"It is fortunate that a record of the sort appears at this time, and doubly fortunate that it comes from the hand of so wise, well-informed, and industrious a traveler and diplomat."

From the New York World.

"Its author has the eye and pen of a journalist, and sees at once what is worth seeing, and recites his impressions in the most graphic manner."

Two vols. 8vo. With three Maps, and numerous Illustrations,
attractively bound in cloth, price reduced from $7.50 to $5.

⁎ *The above book for sale by all booksellers, or will be sent, post or express charges paid, upon receipt of the price by the publishers.*

CHARLES SCRIBNER'S SONS,
743 AND 745 BROADWAY, NEW YORK.

LIFE OF
Lord Lawrence

BY

R. BOSWORTH SMITH, M.A.,
LATE FELLOW OF TRINITY COLLEGE; ASSISTANT MASTER AT HARROW SCHOOL.

With Maps and Portraits, 2 vols., 8vo, $5.00.

"As a biography, the work is an inthralling one, rich in anecdotes and incidents of Lord Lawrence's tempestuous nature and beneficent career that bring into bold relief his strongly-marked and almost colossal individuality, and rich also in instances of his courage, his fortitude, his perseverance, his self-control, his magnanimity, and in the details of the splendid results of his masterful and masterly policy. . . . We know of no work on India to which the reader can refer with so great certainty for full and dispassionate information relative to the government of the country, the characteristics of its people, and the fateful events of the forty eventful years of Lord Lawrence's Indian career."—*Harper's Magazine.*

"John Lawrence, the name by which the late Viceroy of India will always be best known, has been fortunate in his biographer, Mr. Bosworth Smith, who is an accomplished writer and a faithful, unflinching admirer of his hero. He has produced an entertaining as well as a valuable book; the general reader will certainly find it attractive; the student of recent history will discover in its pages matters of deep interest to him."—*London Daily Telegraph.*

_{*} *For sale by all booksellers, or sent, post-paid, upon receipt of price, by*

CHARLES SCRIBNER'S SONS, PUBLISHERS,

743 AND 745 BROADWAY, NEW YORK.

www.ingramcontent.com/pod-product-compliance
Lightning Source LLC
Chambersburg PA
CBHW051744300426
44115CB00007B/687